MW00792065

FALSE FLAGS
DISGUISED GERMAN
RAIDERS OF WORLD WAR II

STEPHEN ROBINSON

EXISLE
PUBLISHING

First published 2016
This edition published 2019

Exisle Publishing Pty Ltd
PO Box 864, Chatswood, NSW 2057, Australia
226 High Street, Dunedin, 9016, New Zealand
www.exislepublishing.com

Copyright © 2016 & 2019 in text: Stephen Robinson

Stephen Robinson asserts the moral right to be identified as the author of this work.

All rights reserved. Except for short extracts for the purpose of review, no part of this
book may be reproduced, stored in a retrieval system or transmitted in any form or by any
means, whether electronic, mechanical, photocopying, recording or otherwise, without
prior written permission from the publisher.

A CiP record for this book is available from the National Library of Australia.

ISBN 978 1 925335 80 4

Designed by Nick Turzynski of redinc. book design
Maps by Nick Turzynski of redinc. book design
Typeset in Baskerville 11/15
Printed in China

This book uses paper sourced under ISO 14001 guidelines from well-managed forests and
other controlled sources.

10 9 8 7 6 5 4 3 2 1

Disclaimer
While this book is intended as a general information resource and all care has been taken
in compiling the contents, neither the author nor the publisher and their distributors
can be held responsible for any loss, claim or action that may arise from reliance on the
information contained in this book.

To my parents David and Alison

Stephen Robinson studied Asian history and politics at university, graduating with First Class Honours. He has worked at the Australian Department of Veterans' Affairs researching British atomic weapons tests and as a policy officer in the Department of Defence. Stephen is also a Major in the Australian Army Reserve and has served as an instructor at the Royal Military College of Australia.

While researching *False Flags*, Stephen conducted extensive archival research of German, British, Australian and New Zealand naval records, uncovering never-before-accessed eyewitness accounts and declassified intelligence reports. As a result, the complete and dramatic story of this naval campaign has finally been told for the first time.

CONTENTS

INTRODUCTION

The German auxiliary cruisers *Orion, Komet, Pinguin* and *Kormoran* terrorized the high seas in a forgotten naval campaign during the early years of World War II. After departing Germany, these raiders voyaged across the Atlantic, Pacific and Indian oceans, as well as the Arctic and Antarctic, sinking Allied merchant ships in Australian and New Zealand waters, and near exotic locations, such as Madagascar and the Galápagos Islands. Their extraordinary voyages are maritime sagas in the finest tradition of seafaring, and they fought a successful 'pirate war' in the middle of the twentieth century, sinking or capturing sixty-two ships.

The *Orion* and *Komet* raided the South Pacific before the Japanese attack on Pearl Harbor, when the war was supposed to be far away, and in this seemingly quiet backwater they mined New Zealand waters and destroyed the Allied phosphate ships at Nauru. The *Pinguin* operated extensively in the Indian Ocean before audaciously mining the approaches to five Australian ports and capturing the Norwegian whaling fleet in Antarctic waters. Ultimately she became Germany's most successful raider, accounting for three times more tonnage than the famous pocket battleship *Admiral Graf Spee*. The *Kormoran* successfully hunted merchantmen in the Atlantic before entering the Indian Ocean where she encountered the Australian cruiser HMAS *Sydney*. In one of the strangest naval engagements in history, the *Kormoran* sank the Australian warship but the crew scuttled their raider after she sustained irreversible damage. Most German sailors survived but all 645 men on board the *Sydney* perished in tragic circumstances.[1]

The Allied sailors who encountered these raiders often fought suicidal battles against a vastly superior foe, and their courage often saved other ships. Many unfortunate sailors and passengers, including women and children, endured captivity on the raiders, where unlikely relationships formed. Most prisoners expected sadistic treatment at the hands of the 'Hun' but the genuinely humane conduct of the raider crews, in most cases, transformed their fear into admiration.

The naval planners in Berlin co-ordinated the raider war while their opposite numbers in Britain, Australia and New Zealand desperately tried to stop the onslaught. The British Admiralty selected Sub-Lieutenant Patrick Beesly, an energetic young officer in the Naval Intelligence Division, to analyze raider operations and he fought a war in the shadows alongside his colleague Ian Fleming, who later based his James Bond novels on his wartime experiences.

As the Soviet Union and Japan provided clandestine support to the raiders, much intrigue, espionage and diplomacy surrounding their voyages unfolded in Moscow and Tokyo. The German naval attaché in Russia, *Kapitän* Norbert von Baumbach, exploited the Nazi–Soviet Pact to secure assistance for the raiders from a strangely willing Soviet Navy. *Konteradmiral* Paul Wenneker, the naval attaché in Japan, meanwhile obtained support from the technically neutral Japanese Navy while Allied diplomats plotted to sabotage his efforts.

Vic Marks, an Australian sailor, became a prisoner on the *Orion* in the South Pacific. After being transported to occupied France on the blockade runner *Ermland*, he experienced four years of captivity in Germany before returning home in 1945. Decades later, feeling forgotten, he wrote to a newspaper in 2001:

> Most people know of the sinking of HMAS *Sydney* by the raider *Kormoran* but few know about the sinking of 10 ships by the *Orion* and *Komet* in [and] near Australian and NZ waters in the Pacific with a heavy loss of seamen's lives.[2]

The story of this forgotten raider war has finally been told and does justice to men like Vic Marks, who will be remembered.[3]

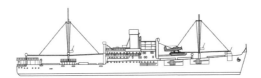

CHAPTER 1
THE RAIDERS PREPARE

Apart from the auxiliary-cruiser commanders and their crews, credit for
their successes is shared by the commanders and crews of the supply
ships, oil tankers and mother ships, by the engineers who converted
them for their tasks, and by all the numerous experts and others in the
naval department and the shipyards who took part in the preparation
and maintenance of the ships.[1]

Grossadmiral Erich Raeder
Commander-in-Chief of the *Kriegsmarine*

AN UNEXPECTED CONFLICT

To *Grossadmiral* Erich Raeder, Commander-in-Chief of the *Kriegsmarine*
(German Navy), war with Great Britain was unthinkable because Germany
could never hope to challenge the Royal Navy's might.[2] When Hitler came
to power in 1933, Raeder established an understanding with him that
peace with Britain had to be maintained through recognition of her naval
superiority. After Germany and Britain signed the Anglo–German Naval
Agreement in 1935, Raeder believed war between the two countries would
be impossible, but Hitler's ambitions would eventually spark war.[3]

After Hitler ordered the invasion of Poland, Raeder ordered the pocket battleships *Deutschland* and *Graf Spee* to the Atlantic, but he believed there would be no war with Britain as Hitler had produced a political miracle with the announcement of the Nazi–Soviet Pact to a stunned world.[4] On 1 September 1939 German forces invaded Poland and two days later Britain declared war on Germany. To Raeder, this unexpected conflict was a strategic nightmare given the Royal Navy's tenfold numerical superiority.[5] The unprepared *Kriegsmarine* could only wage a trade war against Britain's maritime commerce by attacking merchant ships.[6]

The *Graf Spee* claimed nine ships in the South Atlantic and Indian Ocean before being intercepted by the Royal Navy at the River Plate on 13 December 1939. The damaged pocket battleship retreated to Montevideo and *Kapitän* Hans Langsdorff later scuttled her. Meanwhile the *Deutschland* claimed three victims in the North Atlantic, but damage sustained during storms compelled *Kapitän* Paul Wenneker to return home. These raiders disrupted British maritime trade but operated for less than three months. The *Kriegsmarine* would be unable for some time to deploy conventional warships to the Atlantic, as Raeder required the entire fleet to support the upcoming invasion of Norway, but he had a secret weapon capable of waging raider warfare on a global scale. The *Kriegsmarine* was covertly building a fleet of auxiliary cruisers.

GERMAN AUXILIARY CRUISERS

Auxiliary cruisers are commandeered civilian vessels that have been converted into warships. They have normally been viewed as stopgap measures and given patrol missions but they have also served as commerce raiders. The Hague Conference of 1907 agreed that auxiliary cruisers had to fly naval ensigns, their crews had to operate under service discipline and they could not be armed in neutral ports.

German interest in *hilfskreuzers* (auxiliary cruisers) began in the late nineteenth century when the government asked the *Norddeutscher Lloyd* and *Hamburg-Amerika* lines to consider the requirements for arming ships in future designs. After the Spanish–American War, the government began subsidising shipping lines in return for co-operation with auxiliary cruiser planning.[7] By 1911 the *Kaiserliche Marine* (Imperial German Navy) had well-developed plans to convert liners into auxiliary cruisers for use as raiders in future conflict.[8]

After Britain declared war on Germany on 4 August 1914, cruisers operating from colonies, such as the *Emden* and *Karlsruhe*, initiated a campaign of commerce raiding — the *Kreuzerkrieg* (Cruiser War) — and auxiliary cruisers quickly saw action. The armed liner *Kaiser Wilhelm der Grosse* sank three freighters before being intercepted by HMS *Highflyer* off Spanish West Africa.[9] The liner *Cap Trafalgar*, after being armed by the gunboat *Eber*, headed towards Brazil only to be sunk by HMS *Carmania*.[10] After the *Karlsruhe* armed the liner *Kronprinz Wilhelm* near Cuba, she captured fifteen vessels in the South Atlantic before a lack of coal forced her internment in America.[11] The *Cormoran* and *Prinz Eitel Friedrich* departed Tsingtao, the German naval base in China, intending to raid Australian waters, but a lack of coal made this impossible.[12] The *Cormoran* eventually became interned in Guam and the *Prinz Eitel Friedrich* sank eleven vessels before being interned in America.[13]

The *Kreuzerkrieg* ended in 1915 due to the *Kaiserliche Marine*'s inability to despatch more raiders, and the capture of German colonies made it impossible to support operations far from home. The armed liners had high coal consumption, greatly reducing their range.[14] Before the war the Germans believed liners would make ideal raiders given their high speed, but limited endurance restricted operations and their large size made them easily recognizable.

The raider campaign appeared over until *Oberleutnant* Theodor Wolff had an original idea that revolutionized the war at sea. In August 1915 he wrote a memorandum arguing against using liners as raiders in favour of freighters, as they had far greater range and looked ordinary enough to evade detection. He recommended arming 4000-ton freighters, which could voyage for 140 days before being resupplied, and his memorandum reached *Admiral* Hugo von Pohl, who declared that 'such steamers can create great damage'.[15] Wolff never knew how much damage since he drowned after falling overboard from the submarine *U-73*.

Wolff's proposal met strong opposition. Critics argued that the slow speed of merchant raiders would doom the concept since any warship could outrun them, but Wolff's defenders responded that all would hinge on the clever use of disguise to avoid suspicion. Ultimately, the *Kaiserliche Marine* decided to test the concept and ordered *Korvettenkapitän* Nikolaus Dohna-Schlodien to find a suitable freighter.

Dohna-Schlodien selected the small freighter *Pungo* and, after her metamorphosis into a raider, he renamed her *Möwe*. All her weapons had been ingeniously hidden behind false compartments and the crew could change her appearance by altering the superstructure and masts, allowing her to adopt a variety of disguises.[16] The *Kaiserliche Marine* now possessed a radical new type of raider.

On 26 December 1915 the *Möwe* left Kiel disguised as the Swedish freighter *Segoland*. She laid minefields off Scotland, Ireland and France, sinking the battleship HMS *King Edward VII* and three freighters. The raider next claimed fifteen victims in the Atlantic before returning to Germany in triumph. Dohna-Schlodien also commanded the *Möwe*'s second voyage, which claimed twenty-five victims.

The *Grief*, the second merchant raider, departed Germany disguised as a Norwegian freighter on 27 February 1916.[17] However, HMS *Alcantara* intercepted her in the North Sea. The *Grief* sank the *Alcantara* but HMS *Andes* appeared and opened fire. A shell detonated the raider's mines, causing a massive explosion, killing ninety-seven German sailors but the British rescued 219 survivors.

The merchant raider *Wolf*, commanded by *Fregattenkapitän* Karl Nerger, carried a seaplane appropriately named *Wölfchen* (Wolf Cub). After departing Kiel on 30 November 1916, she laid minefields off Cape Town and Cape Agulhas in South Africa, and off Bombay and Colombo, sinking ten ships. Nerger next captured four vessels in the Indian Ocean before entering the Pacific. The seaplane *Wölfchen* proved her worth near New Zealand by stopping the vessels *Wairuna* and *Winslow*, which the *Wolf* subsequently captured.[18] The raider next mined New Zealand and Australian waters, sinking three ships, before returning to Kiel.

The *Seeadler*, a motor ship with three sailing masts commanded by Count Felix von Luckner, left Germany on 21 December 1916 disguised as the Norwegian vessel *Hero*. While attempting to break through the North Sea, the armed merchant cruiser HMS *Patia* boarded the raider but Luckner and his crew, all specially selected Norwegian speakers, bluffed their way through the inspection. The *Seeadler* claimed twelve ships in the Atlantic before entering the Pacific in April 1917. After sinking three American ships on the America–Sydney routes, the Allies became alerted to Luckner's presence and every spare warship in the Pacific hunted him. However, his career ended on 2 August 1917, after the raider was wrecked on a coral reef on Mopelia in the Society Islands.

Luckner intended to restart his raiding career by salvaging the *Seeadler*'s guns and capturing another ship. He sailed with five crewmen in a small motorboat via the Cook Islands to the Fijian island of Wakaya, pretending to be shipwrecked Norwegians. However, the Fijian Police arrested Luckner's group. Luckner resided in a New Zealand prisoner of war camp on Motuihe Island but escaped with eight other prisoners on 13 December 1917. The fugitives captured a motorboat and reached Red Mercury Island, where they seized the scow *Moa*. Luckner set a course for the Kermadec Islands, but the gunboat *Iris* captured him on 21 December and he remained a prisoner until the end of the war. Meanwhile, the remaining Germans on Mopelia captured the French schooner *Lutece* and sailed her to Easter Island, but they were interned by the Chileans after being shipwrecked. Luckner had become a legendary figure known as the 'Sea Devil' and is remembered as a raider captain with a strong reputation for honour and chivalry.

The *Leopard*, the last merchant raider, departed Germany on 10 March 1917 disguised as the Norwegian freighter *Rena* only to be intercepted by HMS *Achilles* and *Dundee* off the Faroe Islands. A torpedo from the *Achilles* sunk the raider and her entire crew of 319 sailors perished.

The high endurance and low profiles of disguised merchant raiders made them ideal weapons for sustained commerce raiding on the high seas. The *Wolf* could voyage for 194 days without being resupplied, compared with the *Prinz Eitel Friedrich*'s thirty days.[19] The *Möwe* sank the most tonnage but the *Wolf* achieved greater strategic success, as Nerger's patient and selective raiding, striking suddenly to sink a few ships before disappearing only to repeat the process later in unexpected waters, created chaos over the widest possible area. However, given rapid developments in aerial reconnaissance, many naval thinkers believed the golden age of auxiliary cruisers ended in 1918.

AUXILIARY CRUISER PLANNING

During the 1920s the *Reichsmarine* (Imperial Navy) secretly developed fast freighters designed to become raiders.[20] One decade later the *Kriegsmarine* planned to use auxiliary cruisers in the event of war to attack maritime trade between France and her colonies. In 1936 Nerger authored an official report explaining how auxiliary cruisers could operate alone, emphasizing the importance of minelaying and seaplane reconnaissance.[21] However, critics viewed auxiliary cruisers as obsolete and successfully advocated that they should only patrol home waters. Nevertheless, in 1937 the government signed an agreement with the *Hansa* and *Fels* shipping lines to provide subsidies in exchange for constructing vessels with strengthened decks for guns.

The German Auxiliary Cruiser (1937), an official history of World War I raiders, concluded that merchant raiders could be employed in future conflicts, although technological advances would make successful operations difficult.[22] Many unofficial histories also appeared, such as Luckner's *Sea Devil*. Hein Fehler, the future mining officer on the raider *Atlantis*, recalled how World War I raiders inspired his generation:

> Every kid in Germany had read of the deeds of ships such as *Moewe* [*Möwe*], *Seeadler*, and *Woolf* [*Wolf*]. . . . Their captains were equally famous: the Drakes, Cochranes and Paul Joneses as it were of the German Navy. Everyone knew how many miles the raiders had covered in their oceanic marauding, the extent of their heroic deeds and the endurance of their crews.[23]

By 1938 this romanticization helped those advocating that auxiliary cruisers should be used as raiders. The *Kriegsmarine* decided that most officers would come from the elite sail training ships, and during the Munich Crisis naval planners designated the six ships that would become raiders in the event of conflict.[24]

After the outbreak of war, the *Kriegsmarine* requisitioned the six freighters but detailed plans and blueprints for converting auxiliary cruisers did not exist, as Ulrich Mohr, the future adjutant of the *Atlantis*, explained:

Our crews had been forced to spend weeks of idleness before the ships were even brought to the dockside and, although, pre-war, a secret Government subsidy had been paid to the Fels line, it had covered only minor items such as the strengthening of the deck for gun mounts.[25]

The auxiliary cruiser programme adopted an improvised approach and the *Kriegsmarine* converted each raider individually through ad hoc measures.[26] Decisions had to be made on where to mount guns and how they would be disguised and swiftly brought into action. Space had to be allocated for crew quarters, ammunition, supplies and water, with a careful balance to assign the right amount of space for all these competing requirements.

Raeder carefully hand-picked highly suitable captains with unconventional thinking:

The choosing of commanders for these ships was no easy matter. They would have to operate at extreme distances from their home bases, they needed all-round knowledge in every aspect of seamanship, they had to be men of intelligence and initiative as well as exceptional fighting spirit.[27]

The raider captains directed much of the planning work and their sheer determination kept the troubled programme alive.[28] They faced opposition from a *Kriegsmarine* faction that believed aerial reconnaissance would detect raiders before they reached the high seas and bureaucratic indifference plagued the enterprise. The Personnel Office deliberately allocated undesirable sailors to the raiders, believing them to be suicide ships and an opportunity to get rid of discipline problems.[29] When Mohr requested modern guns, headquarters refused by stating that his ship would be sunk before it would have a chance to use them.[30] Nevertheless, the persistence of the raider captains paid off, and one by one each raider became operational.

THE *ORION*

On 5 September 1939 the *Blohm & Voss* shipyard in Hamburg began converting the 7021-ton *Hamburg-Amerika* Line vessel *Kurmark*, officially depot vessel 'Ship 36', into an auxiliary cruiser. The freighter, built in 1930, had previously served on *Hamburg-Amerika*'s Far East routes.[31] She had a straight bow and counter stern and her engines, salvaged from the liner *New York*, consisted of four steam turbines powered by oil-fired boilers. As the *Kurmark* had limited endurance, a top speed of only 14.5 knots and engines plagued by frequent mechanical trouble, she never should have become a raider.[32]

Korvettenkapitän Kurt Weyher took command of 'Ship 36'. Born on 30 August 1901, he joined the *Kaiserliche*

Korvettenkapitän Kurt Weyher, commander of the auxiliary cruiser 'Ship 36', renamed *Orion* after the constellation of the hunter. (AUTHOR'S COLLECTION)

The German auxiliary cruiser *Orion*, originally the 7021–ton *Hamburg-Amerika* Line vessel *Kurmark*. (AUTHOR'S COLLECTION)

Marine in April 1918 only to become the youngest naval cadet when World War I ended. He joined a right-wing *Freikorps* militia but returned to the Navy in 1922. After commanding a torpedo boat and a U-boat, he served on the cruiser *Königsberg* and the sail training ships *Gorch Fock* and *Horst Wessel* before becoming the Inspector of Training Establishments. Weyher's expertise in leadership made him ideally suited to command a raider.

Weyher became disillusioned with 'Ship 36' because of her inadequate conversion plans and because the *Kriegsmarine* had denied his requested alterations.[33] Nevertheless, he energetically made preparations, replacing two-thirds of his crew as they did not measure up to his standards. After 'Ship 36' arrived in Kiel, Weyher renamed her *Orion* after the constellation of the hunter and she conducted trials in the Baltic.

THE *PINGUIN*

In September 1939 the *Hansa* Line freighter *Kandelfels*, renamed 'Ship 33', proceeded to Bremen to be converted into a raider in the *Weser* shipyard. The 7766-ton modern vessel, built in 1936, had a two-deck cruiser stern and her high-endurance diesel turbines, which generated an impressive top speed of 17 knots, made her an ideal merchant raider.[34]

The executive officer, *Kapitänleutnant* Max Schwinne, took possession

The German auxiliary cruiser *Pinguin*, officially 'Ship 33' and formerly the *Hansa* Line freighter *Kandelfels*, a modern 7766-ton vessel, built in 1936. (AUTHOR'S COLLECTION)

Kapitän Ernst-Felix Krüder took command of 'Ship 33' on 11 November 1939. He renamed her *Pinguin* (Penguin) as he planned to raid Antarctic waters.
(AUTHOR'S COLLECTION)

of 'Ship 33', officially a depot vessel. More officers arrived, including the navigation officer *Kapitänleutnant* Wilhelm Michaelson, the former captain of the liner *Steuben*, and *Oberleutnant* Wolfgang Küster, a training officer from the *Gorch Fock*. Küster began training the crew, who endured insults from sailors stationed on warships but they kept their mouths shut and took the slander with good humour, secure in the belief that they would soon be hunting prey on the high seas.

Kapitän Ernst-Felix Krüder took command of 'Ship 33' on 11 November. Born on 6 December 1897, he joined the *Kaiserliche Marine* in 1915 and saw action at Jutland on the *Koenig* before being commissioned in 1917. He later served on the cruiser *Breslau*, taking part in numerous minelaying operations in the Black Sea.[35] After the war Krüder served on the cruisers *Karlsruhe* and *Konigsberg* before commanding the First Minesweeper Flotilla and working in the Inspectorate of Officers' Training and Education. An expert in mine warfare with strong leadership qualities, Krüder had ideal traits to become a raider captain.

After the *Kriegsmarine* commissioned 'Ship 33', Krüder renamed her *Pinguin* (Penguin) as he planned to raid Antarctic waters. He used his training connections to select competent officers, expecting them to be omnipresent with a good understanding of the crew. As a former sailor Krüder knew that officers had to earn the respect of their men.

After the *Pinguin* conducted trials on the river Weser, she stopped in Kiel to load ammunition and supplies before proceeding to the Baltic to conduct gunnery, torpedo and minelaying training. After the trials, the raider returned to Kiel to repair faults and load the last supplies. On 11 June 1940 she arrived at Gotenhafen and the men made final preparations for their upcoming voyage.

The *Norddeutscher Lloyd* ship *Ems*, a small 3287-ton freighter renamed 'Ship 45', was converted into an auxiliary cruiser and renamed *Komet*.

THE *KOMET*

On 1 November 1939 work commenced on converting the *Norddeutscher Lloyd* ship *Ems*, a small 3287-ton freighter renamed 'Ship 45', into an auxiliary cruiser at the *Howaldt Werke* shipyard in Hamburg. After being launched in 1937, she had served on the Bremen–Canary Islands route.[36]

Kapitän Robert Eyssen took command of 'Ship 45'. Born on 2 April 1893, he had joined the *Kaiserliche Marine* in 1911. During World War I he served on the *Karlsruhe*, which raided South American waters, and later commanded torpedo boats. After the war, Eyssen commanded a minesweeper flotilla and the survey ship *Meteor*. He volunteered to serve as a raider captain and approached this role with confidence, given his experience from the *Karlsruhe*. After the *Kriegsmarine* commissioned 'Ship 45', Eyssen renamed her *Komet* and the vessel conducted trials in the Baltic.

Kapitän Robert Eyssen, who took command of 'Ship 45' and renamed her *Komet*.
(AUTHOR'S COLLECTION)

RAEDER'S VISION

The *Kriegsmarine*'s Commander-in-Chief Erich Raeder, an expert on cruiser warfare, understood that weaker navies could use long-range raiders to create diversions and force the stronger enemy to disperse its strength.[37] As such, auxiliary cruiser operations in remote waters would weaken the Royal Navy by forcing it to divert warships from the North Sea and North Atlantic to conduct anti-raider operations.

Raeder's auxiliary cruisers would operate primarily in the South Atlantic, Indian Ocean and the Pacific, waters crucial to the British war effort as massive quantities of raw materials from Asia, Africa and Australia traversed through them. Only auxiliary cruisers had the range and endurance to achieve such a goal, as Mohr explained: 'The U-boats of 1939 might strike at the well-guarded heart of the enemy, but we alone could reach far enough to attack the less protected arteries.'[38]

In distant oceans, auxiliary cruisers could expect easy victories because most enemy merchant vessels proceeded alone but, to Raeder, success would not be judged by the amount of tonnage sunk. The auxiliary cruisers' primary purpose was the strategic disruption of British maritime trade by attacking shipping in remote waters to force the Allies to create more convoys. The Royal Navy routinely operated convoys only in the North Atlantic, where shipping was most at risk, and it did not establish them everywhere because they greatly reduced efficiency. Convoys proceeded only as fast as the slowest ship and over time this reduced the volume of trade. If the auxiliary cruisers could force the Allies to create more convoys, it would create much indirect economic damage. They could also delay merchant ship departures and force them to take longer routes, creating further inefficiencies, as Mohr explained:

> An action fought in the Indian Ocean may affect events in the North
> Sea or the Arctic. . . . For every ship, sunk by a single raider in the
> course of hours, scores of others may be re-routed or harbour bound
> for weeks, and the decisions of armies battling from Libya to the Volga
> can be governed by the fortunes of humble merchantmen.[39]

Raeder wanted his raider captains to sink a small number of victims in one area before disappearing, only to repeat this process in a new area, as a 'long term restriction and harassing of the enemy is more important to the success of the operation than a high record of sinkings accompanied by a rapid destruction of the auxiliary cruiser'.[40] By frequently altering operational areas, the raiders would spread disruption across greater expanses of sea as the *Wolf* had done. Mohr well understood these sentiments:

> To *Atlantis* the destruction of enemy shipping was only a subsidiary. Her main purpose was to launch sporadic and widely separated attacks, designed to cause diversions and delays, and force the hard pressed British Fleet to spread itself further afield in hunt and escort work.[41]

The *Seekriegsleitung* (Naval War Staff) based in Berlin would oversee auxiliary cruiser operations by assigning their operational areas. Each auxiliary cruiser would come under its control after entering the Atlantic, but while in the North Sea and Baltic, they would respectively be controlled by Group West and Group East. However, due to difficulties with maintaining communications, the raider captains would exercise much initiative.

The raiders would be disguised as Allied or neutral vessels and change identities by switching flags, but the key to deception was the application of fake superstructure. By raising or lowering false funnels, masts and other structures, the crews could completely change the appearance of their raiders to match pictures found in international shipping registers. Such practices were legal under the Hague Convention, but the *Kriegsmarine* flag had to be raised and all false insignia removed before opening fire.[42]

Auxiliary cruisers could be resupplied at sea through the *Kriegsmarine*'s secret global supply network, the *Etappen*, which managed shipping agents in neutral ports.[43] After a raider captain signalled the *Seekriegsleitung* requesting supplies, the *Etappen* would arrange a supply ship and the *Seekriegsleitung* would co-ordinate the rendezvous.

The *Kriegsmarine* also operated a fleet of six *Dithmarschen* fleet supply tankers, the largest and fastest naval tankers in the world.[44] They could supply raiders with fuel, food, spare parts and ammunition. The most famous *Dithmarschen* tanker, the *Altmark*, had supported the *Graf Spee*, but while returning home carrying prisoners, HMS *Cossack* intercepted her in Norwegian waters.[45] The British rescued the prisoners and turned the *Altmark* into a 'hell ship' in their propaganda war.[46]

Signals between the *Seekriegsleitung* and auxiliary cruisers had to be minimal. Although the Germans believed their codes were unbreakable, Allied direction-finding stations could still locate raiders. The signallers on the raiders were often former merchant sailors who were forbidden to learn proper naval signalling, as their individualistic styles would be less likely to attract the attention of enemy listening stations.

The raider captains would be sent intelligence reports from the *B-Dienst* (B Service), the *Kriegsmarine*'s signals intelligence unit. By April 1940 the *B-Dienst* had broken the Royal Navy's primary operational codes and the Merchant Navy code.[47] Information from the *B-Dienst* would allow the raider captains to avoid enemy warships, giving them an enormous advantage.

THE 'FIRST WAVE'

Raeder initially wanted the 'first wave' — the merchant raiders *Orion*, *Pinguin*, *Komet*, *Atlantis*, *Widder* and *Thor* — to begin leaving Germany during the winter of 1939–40, with a 'second wave' of another six raiders following in the summer.[48] However, this assessment was too optimistic, and Raeder changed the departure date to February 1940; this revised estimate also proved unrealistic.[49] The *Seekriegsleitung* nevertheless assigned operational areas to the raiders; the *Orion*, *Atlantis* and *Pinguin* would operate in the Indian Ocean while the *Thor* would operate in the South Atlantic and the *Widder* in the North Atlantic.

The *Atlantis*, *Orion* and *Widder* proceeded through the Kiel Canal on 11 March 1940 with the help of the ancient battleship *Hessen*, a veteran of Jutland but now a training ship, which broke a path through the ice. Their crews spent the rest of the month training and making final preparations.

The *Atlantis*, commanded by *Fregattenkapitän* Bernhard Rogge, left her hiding place in the Schleswig-Holstein bay disguised as the Soviet freighter *Kim* on 31 March. With a U-boat escort she evaded the British blockade and successfully entered the Atlantic. The auxiliary cruiser war had begun.

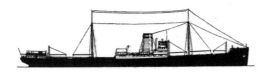

CHAPTER 2
THE *ORION'S* ATLANTIC WAR

The first nine months of the period of cruiser warfare inaugurated early in April by the departure of the *Orion* and *Atlantis* was therefore marked by considerable successes to the enemy and, except for the occasional interception of supply ships, total lack of success to our counter-measures.[1]

Captain Stephen Roskill
The War at Sea 1939–1945

THE *ORION* DEPARTS

On 18 March 1940 *Grossadmiral* Raeder inspected the *Orion* in Kiel, wishing Weyher and his men good luck. As the crew, twenty officers and 356 sailors, made their final preparations, the last men returned from shore leave as a cold north-westerly breeze engulfed the ship. After departing Kiel, the raider hid in an isolated inlet where the crew disguised her as the Holland-America Line freighter *Beemsterdijk*, painting her hull black with a yellow band, the superstructure white and the masts yellow.

The *Orion* carried six 5.9-inch guns, camouflaged as deck cargo and a deckhouse; a 75-mm gun mounted at the bow; anti-aircraft weapons disguised as cranes, cargo and deckhouses; and six torpedo tubes; a hold full of mines; and an Arado seaplane. (AUTHOR'S COLLECTION)

The *Orion*'s six 5.9-inch guns, camouflaged as deck cargo and a deckhouse, could not be seen.[2] A 75-mm gun was mounted at the bow and her anti-aircraft weapons, a twin-mounted 37-mm gun and four quad-mounted 20-mm guns, were disguised as cranes, cargo and deckhouses.[3] Six above-water torpedo tubes, in two triple mountings, were installed near the stern and her holds contained 228 mines and an Arado seaplane, a reliable aircraft suited to high seas.[4] On the supporting beam in the wheelhouse, Weyher, recently promoted to *Fregattenkapitän*, inscribed his maxim: 'We sail with eagle eyes, a hand on the rudder — and luck.'[5]

On 6 April Weyher assembled the crew and announced their imminent departure. The *Orion* would enter the Pacific via Cape Horn, the southern tip of South America, before operating in Australian waters and the South Pacific. To evade the Royal Navy's blockade of the North Sea and break out into the Atlantic, Weyher decided to transit the Denmark Strait between Greenland and Iceland.

The *Orion* departed in clear weather and the crew experienced relief as their voyage commenced. The *Seekriegsleitung* simply noted, 'Ship "36" (Weyher) sails according to plan as the second auxiliary cruiser.'[6]

DETECTING RAIDERS

To prevent the breakout of raiders, the Royal Navy's Home Fleet at Scapa Flow focused on intercepting large German warships while the cruisers and armed merchant cruisers of the Northern Patrol guarded the Denmark Strait. By February 1940 the Admiralty had converted fifty-six liners into armed merchant cruisers and twenty joined the Northern Patrol, but they had inferior armaments compared with raiders, as Captain Stephen Roskill explained: 'none of the fifty liners which the Admiralty had fitted with a few obsolete guns . . . was capable of dealing with the well-armed and highly efficient German raiders.'[7]

The Admiralty accurately foresaw the auxiliary cruiser menace as pre-war studies warned they would constitute the greatest surface threat.[8] As accurate intelligence would be vital to assist counter-raider operations, the Admiralty's Operational Intelligence Centre (OIC) gathered intelligence on enemy warships, the Government Code and Cipher School at Bletchley Park attempted to break German codes and radio direction-finding posts tried to locate raiders. In 1939 the Royal Navy had ten direction-finding stations in Britain, three in the Mediterranean and two in the Far East, but these could not provide effective coverage across the great expanses of ocean where raiders might be hiding.[9]

Aircraft could detect raiders, but the British had only a small number of obsolete reconnaissance planes. Coastal Command wanted regular patrols between Scotland and Norway, but its planes did not have the range to reach the Norwegian coast, so the Royal Navy used submarines to fill this gap.

Ultimately, the British did not have an effective means of detecting raider departures and knew nothing about German plans.[10] They did not know which freighters had been converted into raiders, when they would depart or which routes they would take.[11] The Royal Navy, unprepared for the onslaught, remained in the dark.

IN THE NORTH SEA

The *Orion* proceeded alone, leaving behind the red cliffs of Heligoland. Two friendly planes appeared overhead to protect her from British submarines and two torpedo boats escorted her through the Ems minefields before departing after completing their mission. The raider maintained full speed while the engineering officer *Kapitänleutnant* Erwin Kölsch struggled to keep her oil-fired boilers working without emitting columns of black smoke, which would be seen for miles. He kept a careful watch on the funnels and increased the air flow into the injectors to reduce the smoke when it got too thick. The crew braved the cold without heating as all available power had been diverted to the propeller.

The *Seekriegsleitung* ordered *U-64* to escort the *Orion* through the Heligoland Bight and Denmark Strait, but after the raider arrived at the rendezvous location, the U-boat failed to appear, and the *Seekriegsleitung* informed Weyher that the meeting would now occur west of the Ems minefields.

On 7 April the bulk of the *Kriegsmarine* headed towards Norway as an invasion fleet while a Royal Navy force intended to mine Norwegian waters.[12] Weyher, caught between the two fleets, realized that something was going on from unusual wireless traffic: 'It appears from W/T [wireless traffic] that our own Fleet has sailed and that the enemy has reacted to it.'[13] Radio news soon announced the German invasion of Norway. The raider continued north through turbulent seas but *U-64* again failed to appear as she had been diverted to Norwegian waters.

The *Orion* headed north-west midway between the Shetland Islands and Norway and the lookout spotted drifting mines, stark reminders of the expanding war. Weyher avoided a fishing boat in case she was an enemy spy ship. After sunset the raider avoided two neutral ships, brightly lit by their peacetime lights.

At sunrise the *Orion* continued north-west through overcast skies and, after the lookout spotted a British destroyer, Weyher ordered hard to starboard. The raider retreated south until the warship disappeared and, shortly afterwards, she evaded another destroyer. In the afternoon the *Seekriegsleitung* informed Weyher that two enemy battlecruisers were proceeding on a parallel course only 60 miles away. He altered course to avoid them, but shortly afterwards the lookout spotted a large vessel and four British destroyers emerging from a rain squall about 10 miles away. The *Orion* headed towards a dark patch of mist, but the destroyers turned and followed. She could not outrun the destroyers and a single shell could detonate her mines, resulting in a tremendous explosion that few could hope to survive.

The *Orion*'s fate rested upon the plausibility of her Dutch disguise, but if the Royal Navy saw through the ruse Weyher would fight. He might be able to sink at least one destroyer, but his career would almost certainly come to a spectacular end in the cold waters of the North Sea. Tension in the bridge escalated as the four destroyers surrounded the raider and, as they approached closer, the gunnery officer *Oberleutnant* Hans-Reimer German relayed the distance to his men who adjusted the sights on their hidden weapons. Crewmen dressed as Dutch merchant sailors positioned themselves on the deck and bridge in plain sight and, to complete the illusion, the cook wearing a white apron stuck his head out of the galley while a sailor walked across the deck and emptied a bucket of rubbish into the sea. The destroyers resumed their original course, either believing the charade or they had more important considerations with battles occurring off Norway.[14] The *Orion*'s crew felt relief and Weyher's strong nerves won their respect.

Given the Royal Navy's strong presence in the North Sea, Weyher could either proceed on a longer course than originally planned or wait for a more favourable time to break out. As the *Orion* had already passed the narrowest waters between the British Isles and Norway, he decided to proceed on the longer route.

On 9 April the *Seekriegsleitung* ordered the *Orion* to rendezvous with *U-37* only to later redirect the U-boat towards Norway, although a reconnaissance report from the submarine stated that no enemy warships had been spotted near Iceland.[15] Weyher took this news cautiously as the submarine may have failed to spot enemy vessels in bad weather.[16]

As the *Orion* headed towards Greenland on a course between Jan Mayen Island and Iceland, the conflict off Norway began working in Weyher's favour because the British had depleted the Northern Patrol to meet their Norwegian commitments. He also had a good understanding of the Norwegian campaign courtesy of the *B-Dienst* codebreakers, which helped him avoid Royal Navy warships.

Weyher decided to disguise the *Orion* as the Russian freighter *Soviet* because Dutch ships did not frequent these waters. Although the *Soviet* was listed in international shipping registers, they contained no description so the crew improvised a realistic design: a black hull, red and white edges on the amidships and a red band on the funnel with a hammer and sickle.

As the *Orion* continued through miserable arctic winds, ice formed outside and coffee froze in flasks. After the lookout spotted the icebergs off Greenland, she turned south-west towards the Denmark Strait and navigated through a maze of icebergs. In the morning mountainous waves struck the raider; it was perfect weather to avoid being seen, but she made slow progress. On 14 April the *Orion* triumphantly entered the Atlantic as an ominous aurora borealis with a blue veil of light appeared overhead.

THE PHANTOM BATTLESHIP

Although the *Orion* had reached the North Atlantic, Weyher did not have authorization to engage enemy ships until he reached the Pacific. He decided to disguise his raider as the Greek freighter *Rocos* because Soviet vessels rarely ventured into these waters. While hidden in a fog bank, the crew lowered the masts, raised the funnel and altered the superstructure. They also added rust colouring to the hull to give authenticity to the image of a Greek tramp ship.

On 15 April the *Orion* headed south through the misty seas of the Grand Banks near Newfoundland. The crew enjoyed the warm morning sun and many sunbathed on the deck, a pleasant contrast to the recently experienced arctic freeze. The successful breakout and agreeable weather caused morale to soar as their voyage towards the equator continued.

As the *Orion* continued south, the *Seekriegsleitung* assigned Weyher a special mission to trick the British into believing a German pocket battleship was active in the North Atlantic by broadcasting deceptive signals.[17] If successful, this would disrupt the North Atlantic convoy system and force the Royal Navy to divert warships from Norway. Weyher accordingly decided to sink an enemy freighter and broadcast a fake warship warning, and hopefully the British would assume a pocket battleship had been responsible. With this plan in mind, Weyher ordered a westerly course towards the intersection of the New York–Gibraltar–Panama routes, where he hoped to find a suitable victim. As this area was beyond the range of U-boats, sinking a vessel there would give credibility to the notion of a pocket battleship.

The *Orion* headed south-east through rain and overcast sky. Weyher avoided three vessels as they could not be identified and, after arriving at the intersection, the lookout spotted only neutral ships. Weyher spent two more days patrolling the area without success before deciding to try his luck east of Bermuda.

Weyher started receiving improved intelligence reports as the *B-Dienst* had recently cracked more British naval codes following the capture of documents in Norway.[18] He noticed a weakening of Royal Navy strength in the Atlantic as it concentrated in the North Sea and used this intelligence to avoid enemy warships.[19]

On 19 April the lookout sighted a vessel heading in an opposite direction but, as she approached, they saw a red funnel, which caused disappointment as she was most likely Soviet. As the distance closed, Weyher identified a passenger ship with a blue funnel — the red-like appearance had been caused by rust — and several stern guns confirmed her enemy status. He relented, not wishing to start a duel with a well-armed adversary possessing superior speed.[20] The vessel passed the raider at 4000 metres (4374 yards) without incident.

As the *Orion* approached Bermuda on 24 April, the lookout spotted a ship that appeared only as a shadow in the pre-dawn darkness, and nobody could determine if she was a merchant vessel or a warship. Weyher concluded that she must be an enemy as neutral ships proceeded at night with their peacetime lights on, and the shadow transformed into the silhouette of a freighter.

The *Orion* turned west and hid in the darkness and, at sunrise, Weyher could clearly see the freighter in the light of the emerging day. He still had not positively identified her as an enemy so he feigned a boiler problem as an excuse to drift east to get a better look and place his guns in a better attack position. The *Orion*'s funnel emitted thick black smoke as she changed course, while the freighter maintained her course, seemingly unaware of the threat. No neutrality markings could be seen, but two stern guns confirmed her enemy status.

Weyher let his prey pass astern before turning to follow, hoping to settle the matter quickly before her wireless could broadcast a raider warning. True to the requirements of international law, he ordered 'decamouflage'. The crew raised the *Kriegsmarine* flag and hid the Greek letters and colours behind canvas as the gunners readied their weapons. Weyher ordered the

On her first voyage the *Orion* reached the Atlantic, but *Korvettenkapitän* Kurt Weyher did not have authorization to engage enemy ships until he reached the Pacific. However, near Bermuda he attacked the British freighter *Haxby*, taking her crew prisoner and sinking the ship.
(AUTHOR'S COLLECTION)

freighter to stop and his 75-mm gun fired a warning shot across her bow. The *Orion* had just fired the first shot of the German auxiliary cruiser war.

Tension escalated as Weyher waited to see how the Allied captain would respond. The freighter quickly changed course, increased speed and broadcast an RRRR warship warning, stating the location and her name 'Haxby'. Ironically, the wireless operator signalled 'RRRR' instead of a QQQQ auxiliary cruiser warning, and as this implied the freighter had encountered a pocket battleship, the *Orion*'s wireless operators did not jam the entire message.

The small 5207-ton British freighter *Haxby* had been proceeding from Glasgow to Corpus Christi in ballast, hoping to return with scrap metal. Although she was only armed with a 4.7-inch cannon and an anti-aircraft gun, her master Captain Cornelius Arundel had no intention of surrendering. He ordered his stern gunners to their action stations and despite the terrible odds he would fight.

Weyher, annoyed that the *Haxby* had not stopped, ordered his guns to open fire and the first salvo of 5.9-inch shells smashed into her hull. The gunners displayed great skill in manually keeping their aim with sights dating from 1916 while compensating for the roll of the sea. The *Haxby*'s stern guns returned fire but failed to hit the raider while German shells pounded the freighter, causing several fires. Eventually a shell hit a stern gun, igniting nearby ammunition and putting the second gun out of action, but Captain Arundel refused to stop as he still had a duty to keep broadcasting his raider warning until another wireless acknowledged the message.

The *Haxby*'s radio went silent after a shell struck her bridge and Weyher ordered a ceasefire even though the freighter had not stopped. Bright flames engulfed the *Haxby* and she eventually stopped after fire destroyed her engine room. Her crew attempted to lower lifeboats but one caught fire and another sank after hitting the water. Weyher sent across three boats to rescue the survivors and upon their arrival the British lowered their wounded from the stern. To the horror of all onlookers a sailor jumped overboard and died after getting caught in the exposed propeller.

Captain Arundel and twenty-four men became prisoners on the *Orion*. Guards helped move eleven wounded to the hospital and gave the remainder, to their surprise, dry clothes, blankets, cigarettes and tea before escorting them to the prison quarters below deck. Sixteen *Haxby* sailors had been killed.

Weyher decided to sink the blazing hulk of the *Haxby* as the huge clouds of black smoke could be seen for miles, potentially attracting the Royal Navy. The torpedo officer *Oberleutnant* Klaus Thomsen fired a torpedo and the explosion broke the freighter in two, forcing her masts inwards as she disappeared beneath the waves. The *Seekriegsleitung* later noted: 'the sinking of this steamer is the first success to be achieved against merchant shipping by German raiders in the war.'[21]

Weyher asked Captain Arundel why he disobeyed his order to stop. Arundel replied that he was merely carrying out orders.[22] This conversation set the grim tone for the struggle that followed. During World War I, freighters normally stopped after a warning shot, followed by an orderly boarding party with no loss of life. In this war, history would not repeat itself because all vessels had radios and their captains had a duty to broadcast raider warnings.[23] This vastly increased the level of violence, and many brave Allied sailors would die gallantly trying to send a desperate signal to the outside world. Captain Arundel's reply shocked Weyher's romanticized expectations:

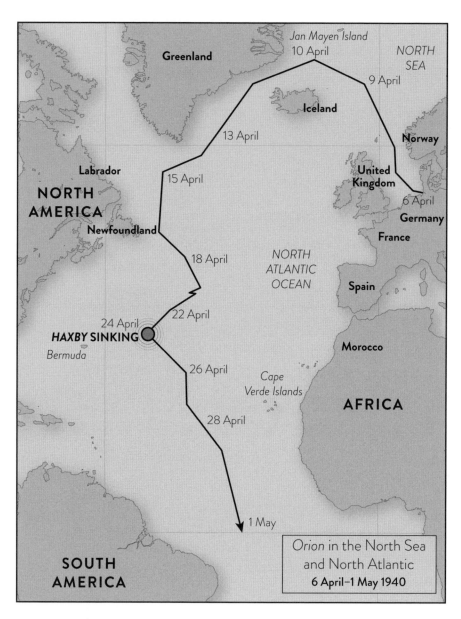

A scrupulous observation of the unwritten laws of the chivalrous code of sailors would in many cases have been equivalent to suicide; in the age of radio the hunter so easily became the hunted. Thus had technical progress in naval warfare too become a Moloch [god] that threatened to devour all fairness and humanity.[24]

In the afternoon four British sailors placed the body of boatswain Robertson, a wounded *Haxby* sailor who died onboard the *Orion*, in a coffin. At sunset the raider stopped and her crew assembled on the deck in their best uniforms along with Captain Arundel and the other prisoners. The sailors covered Robertson's coffin with a Union Jack while guards stood by with fixed bayonets. Weyher gave a tribute, Captain Arundel recited a prayer and the guards presented arms. The boatswain piped 'overboard' and Robertson's body was given to the sea. After the ceremony several prisoners gathered near the steward's room to drink spirits, but a few minutes later the war again became the priority.

Weyher decided to disguise the *Orion* as the Brazilian freighter *Mandu* because Greek ships did not frequent the Central Atlantic. The prisoners meanwhile adjusted to captivity. Although they suffered from discomfort and poor ventilation, they received fair treatment and could exercise on the deck twice each day. They also consumed the standard German ration of black bread and sausage.

The *Orion*'s wireless later broadcast several broken messages stating, 'RRRR 3020 hours . . . by pocket battlesh. . .' as the *Haxby*'s garbled signal may not have been received.[25] In this way the British might believe that a second ship had been attacked, but in the end the deception plan failed because the Admiralty did not receive these messages. Weyher decided against attacking further ships in the Atlantic and the raider resumed her course towards Cape Horn.

RENDEZVOUS WITH *WINNETOU*

On 30 April the crew experienced their first tropical rain, causing many to run to the deck for showers. The men, wearing their summer uniforms and gym clothes, spent their free time trying to sleep in hammocks in the sweltering heat.

The *Orion* crossed the equator the next day, entering the South Atlantic, and in accordance with maritime tradition King Neptune inspected the crew during a crossing of the line ceremony, but Weyher did not allow the customary baptism for sailors who had not previously passed the equator.

After the *Orion* crossed the Bahia—Freetown route, Weyher became

An Arado seaplane, a reliable aircraft suited to high seas.
(BUNDESARCHIV, BILD 101I-524-2270-19A)

worried as the *Atlantis* had recently been active in this area and enemy patrols might be searching for suspicious ships; therefore, he intended to transit the South Atlantic as quickly as possible. On 3 May the raider passed Ascension Island and three days later Weyher calculated that his fuel supply would last fifty-seven more days. The *Orion*, an ill-suited raider, consumed 40 tons of fuel each day, five times more than the diesel-powered *Atlantis*. Weyher requested more fuel, and the raider continued south while he waited for a response. After repeating the request three more times, he received a clear message. The *Orion* would rendezvous with the tanker *Winnetou* at location 'Max', 660 miles north of South Georgia.

On 12 May the *Orion* reached 'Max', but after the *Winnetou* did not appear the raider searched the area, although poor visibility and rough seas made the task difficult. The next morning the weather improved and Weyher ordered his pilot *Oberleutnant* Klaus von Winterfeldt to find the tanker. The Arado seaplane struggled to take off in the rough South Atlantic swell and it took an hour to get it airborne. Winterfeldt soon spotted the *Winnetou* and signalled the *Orion*'s location by lamp while the tanker's crew looked upon the surreal sight of a German seaplane so far from home.

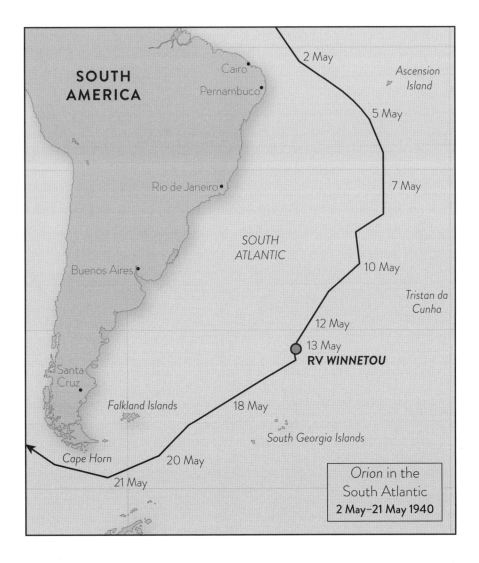

Orion in the
South Atlantic
2 May–21 May 1940

The *Winnetou* had been at Aruba in the Lesser Antilles at the start of the war. After an unsuccessful attempt to get home, she found refuge in the Spanish Canary Islands where she became a raider supply tanker under the *Etappen* organization. She left port with Captain Fritz Steinkrauss in command, a former *Kaiserliche Marine* sailor who had served on a cruiser at Jutland, and proceeded at 7 knots, her top speed due to poor maintenance.

The *Orion* rendezvoused with the *Winnetou* and Steinkrauss boarded the raider to discuss the transfer of fuel and provisions. After being introduced to Weyher, Steinkrauss responded to all his suggestions and requests by saying 'all right' in English, and he became affectionately known as 'Captain Allright'. The two ships came alongside and fuel from the tanker soon flowed into the *Orion*'s tanks.

Weyher and Steinkrauss discussed future plans and agreed to rendezvous again in the South Pacific on 18 June, the earliest time *Winnetou* could arrive given her slow speed. On 16 May the ships parted company and the *Orion* proceeded south-west towards Cape Horn.

As the *Orion*'s voyage continued the raider war escalated. The *Atlantis* sank the *Scientist* in the South Atlantic and mined the approaches to Cape Agulhas, South Africa, but caused no damage. The *Widder* and *Thor* both departed Kiel and entered the Atlantic, but the *Seekriegsleitung* knew little about auxiliary cruiser operations. As raider captains rarely broke radio silence, Berlin often only learned details from decoded British signals.[26]

Weyher recorded his plans: 'My intention had been to round Cape Horn in order to carry out the mine laying during the moonless night of 6th/7th June. After this I intended to raid New Zealand waters until the arrival of the "WINNETOU".'[27] On 21 May the *Orion* passed Cape Horn and entered the Pacific, and nobody in Australia or New Zealand knew the war was coming their way.

CHAPTER 3
THE HAURAKI
GULF OPERATION

But now, here we are in sight of New Zealand. There a special job awaits us; to sow mines at the entrance to Auckland Harbour. As the English are far from suspecting that such an operation is to be feared, because they know that no mine-layer of the usual type would be able to venture so far from Europe. We are able to set about it at night in all tranquility.[1]

War Correspondent
German Raider *Orion*

THE AUSTRALIA STATION

Australia is strategically located near major maritime trade routes and the Admiralty, in recognition of this importance, established the Australia Station in 1859, an operational area encompassing the seas surrounding the continent. In 1939 the station extended westwards for 1500 miles into the Indian Ocean and eastwards past New Zealand and Fiji, while its northern boundary included the Solomon Islands and its southern border touched Antarctic waters. This vast body of water covered one-quarter of the southern hemisphere.

The Australia Station had great economic importance, as numerous Pacific trade routes converged at Sydney and Melbourne, and Indian Ocean trade at Fremantle, Western Australia. The British war economy needed imports from Australia and New Zealand and, as the freighters carrying this cargo normally voyaged alone until joining the North Atlantic convoys, they would be vulnerable targets for raiders. The Allies faced a challenging prospect in protecting shipping in the Australia Station, given a lack of warships and the area's vastness.

The Royal Australian Navy (RAN) correctly concluded that raiders would enter the Australia Station, and Commander Henry Burrell, Director of Operations and Plans, concentrated on protecting key areas:

> With such a small navy, however, we were forced to concentrate our forces in focal areas and the entrances to main harbours. Ships outside this protection were routed evasively by our control service to, it was hoped, confuse the enemy.[2]

Lieutenant-Commander Rupert Long, Director of Naval Intelligence, RAN, was haunted by the failure to stop the raider *Wolf* during World War I.[3] Therefore, he wanted coastwatchers on the isolated islands near Australia to prevent raiders using them as bases as the *Wolf* had done:

> German commerce-raiders may make use of harbours in New Guinea as refuelling bases from which to launch attacks upon shipping on the Australian coast; New Guinea and the Solomon Islands, with their numerous and little frequented harbours being admirably suited for this purpose.[4]

Long expanded his coastwatcher network in New Guinea and the Solomon Islands to cover the north-eastern approaches to Australia. Lieutenant-Commander Eric Feldt, head of naval intelligence in Port Moresby, organized this expansion by travelling extensively in New Guinea and the South Pacific to recruit new coastwatchers. In October 1939 Feldt informed Long that his coastwatchers had only a 5 per cent chance of spotting raiders, but Long optimistically replied that 'these arrangements are noted with considerable satisfaction, and it is pleasing to find that you were able to cover so much territory in so short a time'.[5]

In May 1940 the *Atlantis'* mines convinced the RAN that raider activity would soon reach the Australia Station.[6] The Naval Board decided that the three cruisers and two armed merchant cruisers in the Australia Station would be sufficient insurance against raiders, so it released the heavy cruisers *Australia* and *Canberra* for service in other stations.[7] Burrell viewed this depletion as a calculated risk: 'We realised that reducing forces on our Station carried with it a certain degree of risk, particularly to unescorted ships. However, fighting the known enemy justified this risk.'[8]

Meanwhile in New Zealand Commodore William Parry, Chief of Naval Staff, warned:

> As in the last war, there is nothing to prevent this vessel, or other armed raiders, laying mines off the coasts of New Zealand. The four minesweepers in commission were totally inadequate to ensure even reasonable security from enemy minelaying activities. The first warning of an enemy minefield was likely to be the destruction of one or more ships.[9]

The home-based squadrons of the Royal New Zealand Air Force (RNZAF) conducted maritime patrols to protect shipping, but as it had no long-range aircraft in New Zealand, the Tasman Empire Airways flying boats *Awarua* and *Aotearoa* began patrolling out to the Chatham and Kermadec islands. Numerous uneventful flights made the New Zealand aircrews complacent, but the tranquillity of the Tasman Sea would soon be shattered.

THE WAR REACHES NEW ZEALAND

The *Orion*, after passing Cape Horn, continued west across the Pacific, keeping south of the normal trade routes to avoid detection, and the lookout only spotted cape pigeons and albatrosses. The crew initially experienced milder than expected weather but soon felt cold Antarctic winds. As the raider continued through empty ocean wastes, Weyher relaxed strict naval discipline to create a greater sense of comradeship. Some sailors founded a club to teach lessons based on their collective knowledge, and the men also spent their spare time in the cinema, library and chapel.

Weyher planned to mine the approaches to Auckland during the darkness of the new moon period, but the *Orion*'s slow progress against the Pacific head winds ruined his timetable. However, he calculated there would still be sufficient darkness at night to continue his mission.

The *Orion* continued towards the Hauraki Gulf, the gateway to Auckland, disguised as an anonymous Dutch–Africa Line freighter with a red funnel and brown-yellow masts. On 13 June 1940 the raider entered New Zealand waters while the mechanics prepared their moored contact mines by inserting soluble plugs, screwing in the horns and adjusting the depth settings. The men also readied the mine-launching platform, concealed beneath camouflage at the stern.

Weyher, to his astonishment, overheard the schedule of RNZAF reconnaissance flights on local radio news and discovered that no flights would be conducted that afternoon.[10] He also learned that the New Zealand cruiser *Achilles* and the armed merchant cruiser *Hector* were in Auckland Harbour.

In the afternoon as the sun set behind the volcanic peaks visible in the distance, the mining officer *Kapitänleutnant* Warnholtz informed Weyher that all mines were ready. That night visibility in the moonlight extended out to 10 miles and the meteorologist Doctor Geil predicted that it would not improve.

As the *Orion* approached her first target area, the crew saw a signal station and the fully lit Cuvier Lighthouse. Weyher observed that 'it was not possible to approach closer than eight German nautical miles to the Cuvier lighthouse without being sighted by the Signal Station'.[11] At 1926 h the first mine slid down the launching rails into the sea and further mines descended as the raider proceeded on a carefully planned zigzag course. The mines floated until their anchors, attached to cables, pulled them down, and when the anchors reached the seabed the mines remained in position just below the surface. The crew held their breath as the lighthouse routinely lit up the raider's port side, causing some men to instinctively duck for cover. As far as Weyher could tell his activities had not aroused suspicion and soon fifteen mines had been laid south-east of Cuvier Island.

The *Orion*, after passing Cape Horn, continued west across the Pacific, entering New Zealand waters on 13 June 1940 to lay mines in the approaches to Auckland. (AUTHOR'S COLLECTION)

The *Orion* began laying her second minefield east of Great Barrier Island and forty-five more mines descended into the sea. The raider avoided the dark shadows of two ships before proceeding towards the northern entrance of Hauraki Gulf. After reaching the passage between Great Barrier Island and the Mokohinau Islands, the crew dropped fifty-seven mines overboard.

After midnight the *Orion* laid fifty-two mines in a semicircle pattern north of the Mokohinau Islands while the navigation officer *Kapitänleutnant* Hertz used its lighthouse as a beacon. The raider next headed north-west towards the Maro Tiri Islands, where the men would push the final fifty-nine mines overboard. The weather became overcast with light rain, providing additional concealment, and as the last mines slid into the sea the lookout spotted a ship heading directly towards the minefield. Although it took forty-eight hours for the mines to arm, faulty mechanisms could instantly arm them and an early detonation would endanger the raider. Weyher held his breath as the vessel proceeded through the minefield, but no explosion followed and the ship continued towards Auckland.

After laying 228 mines without being detected, the *Orion* fled north-east at full speed towards the Kermadec Islands. Weyher intended to patrol the Auckland–San Francisco and the Sydney–Samoa–Honolulu routes, but first he needed to rendezvous with the tanker *Winnetou* to refuel.

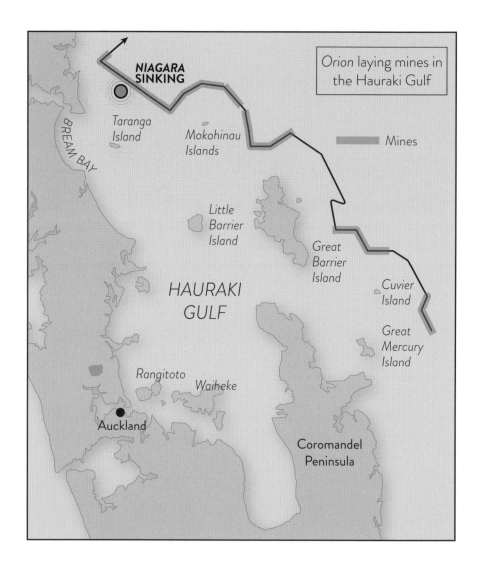

NIAGARA
SINKING

Orion laying mines in
the Hauraki Gulf

BREAM BAY

Taranga
Island

Mokohinau
Islands

Mines

Little
Barrier
Island

Great
Barrier
Island

Cuvier
Island

HAURAKI
GULF

Great
Mercury
Island

Rangitoto

Waiheke

Auckland

Coromandel
Peninsula

On 15 June the *Orion*'s wireless room listened for news about the mines, but there were no reports. In the afternoon the lookout spotted the Kermadec Islands and a large steamer, but Weyher did not give chase as the *Orion* was still in range of enemy planes. The Arado conducted a reconnaissance flight the next day, but after the seaplane landed a wave pushed it underwater, although the pilot *Oberleutnant* Winterfeldt and his observer Passler escaped unharmed. The seaplane's floats prevented the plane from sinking and it could be repaired. Weyher signalled the *Winnetou*, ordering her to a new rendezvous south of the Cook Islands but received no reply.

On the evening of 18 June the engineering officer *Kapitänleutnant* Kolsch informed Weyher that the *Orion*'s speed had to be reduced to 5 knots for a few hours so he could make urgent repairs, but before Weyher had time to respond the lookout spotted the light of a freighter. Normally only neutral ships voyaged with their peacetime lights on at night, but in these remote waters many Allied vessels also did the same. Kolsch informed Weyher that full speed would be restored by midnight and the *Orion* slowed down so the repair work could be carried out.

After the mechanics repaired the engines, the *Orion* increased speed on an intercept course towards the freighter on a gradual approach to avoid suspicion. Weyher retired to his chartroom to consider tactics, but at 0344 h the signals officer *Leutnant* Vellguth interrupted him with an urgent message. The wireless room had overheard: 'SOS Niagara. . . . Explosion in No. 2 hold, Position Maro Tiri. . . . Engines disabled, No. 2 hold full of water. Vessel going down by head. Putting into boats.'[12] The *Orion*'s minefield had claimed a victim.

The Lloyd's Register informed Weyher that the *Niagara* was a Canadian Australasian Line passenger ship but he temporarily ignored this achievement to focus on the freighter. He sipped his morning coffee in the fresh breeze while the raider reduced speed to come astern of her prey. An hour later the Germans obtained a better view as both vessels came abreast at 3000 metres (3280 yards) and no neutral markings could be seen.

The 5781-ton Norwegian freighter *Tropic Sea* had departed Sydney bound for Panama carrying wheat. Captain Ostberg did not sense any danger, but this abruptly changed when he saw the *Kriegsmarine* flag being raised. A warning shot followed with an order to stop and maintain radio silence. Captain Ostberg ignored this order and the *Tropic Sea* maintained her course, but after a salvo landed just short of the freighter, he decided to stop. Chief Officer Dravik recalled the encounter:

> I was in the chart-room at the time, and as I was also the Wireless Operator on the *Tropic Sea* I thought it was better to take no chances, so I shut down the wireless. The Raider fired two shots which fell all round our ship and we therefore stopped the engines.[13]

Lifeboats from the 13,415-ton liner *Niagara*, which struck two mines between Bream Head and the Mokohinau Islands on 19 June 1940, on its way from Auckland to Vancouver. (AUTHOR'S COLLECTION)

A boarding party led by *Oberleutnant* Raschke seized the *Tropic Sea*. Captain Ostberg told Raschke that he was transporting wheat to America and claimed neutral status. As the boarding party searched the freighter, a launch took Captain Ostberg and Dravik to the *Orion*, despite the protests of Mrs Ostberg, a stewardess on board. After the Germans discovered documents proving the ship operated under British charter, Weyher formally captured the vessel:

> According to the manifest the loader was the Australian Wheat Board, accounting executed by the Commonwealth Bank of Australia, and, according to the contract, the charterer being the British Government. The cargo was obviously bound for England and could be considered contraband.[14]

Weyher placed *Oberleutnant* Eichorst in command of the *Tropic Sea* before focusing his attention back to the *Niagara*. The enemy would now be alerted to his presence and would certainly despatch all available warships to hunt him. As the *Tropic Sea* had not broadcast a raider warning, the Allies had no way of determining the *Orion*'s current location, but nevertheless she would be hunted.

THE *ORION'S* MINES

At 0340 h on 19 June, the 13,415-ton liner *Niagara* struck two mines between Bream Head and the Mokohinau Islands. The ship had been proceeding from Auckland to Vancouver and her cargo included eight tons of gold ingots from South Africa valued at £2,500,000 and small arms ammunition. Able Seaman Ray Nelson remembered waking up after the mines exploded:

> I got out of the cabin as fast as possible. There was a lot of confusion naturally. There was quite a lot of damage to the fo'ard part of the ship. The number two hold had taken the blast of the explosion. The deck in that area was splintered.[15]

Captain William Martin ordered Nelson to close all the portholes in the forward accommodation area, but flooding prevented him from doing so. As the liner was sinking fast by her bow, Captain Martin decided to abandon ship. The crew remained calm and helped the passengers into the lifeboats. Sister Munroe, a nurse on board, described her ordeal:

The *Orion's* remaining mines eventually broke free from their moorings and drifted, with many washing up on the New Zealand and Australian coasts in 1940 and 1941. This mine was found in the Manukau Harbour.
(AUTHOR'S COLLECTION)

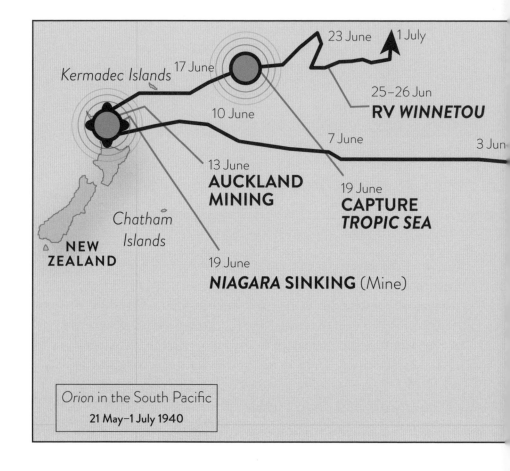

23 June   1 July

Kermadec Islands 17 June

25–26 Jun
RV WINNETOU

10 June

7 June

3 Jun

13 June
**AUCKLAND
MINING**

19 June
**CAPTURE
TROPIC SEA**

Chatham
Islands

△ **NEW
ZEALAND**

19 June
NIAGARA SINKING (Mine)

Orion in the South Pacific
21 May–1 July 1940

The lifeboats were gradually drifting apart all around the stricken
Niagara. The great old ship seemed to have steadied, and the hope
of all was that she would survive. At the end of half an hour the
watertight bulkheads must have collapsed under the strain, for she
slowly stood on end and slid under the surface. Sorrow was the
predominant feeling for the passing of that fine old ship.[16]

After Wellington Radio intercepted the *Niagara*'s distress signal the *Achilles*
left Auckland and headed towards the liner's reported location. The cruiser
found eighteen lifeboats and the liner *Wanganella* rescued all 349 passengers.
The minesweepers *James Cosgrove* and *Thomas Currell* arrived and found
German mines.

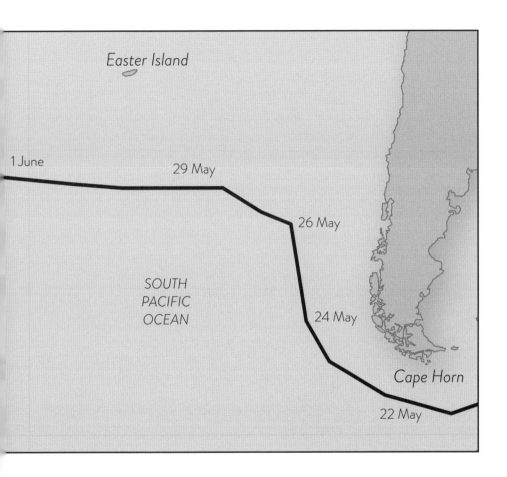

Prime Minister Peter Fraser announced the sinking, as the *Seekriegsleitung* noted:

> An announcement was made by the New Zealand Prime Minister, Fraser, that the [*Niagara's*] loss was caused by a mine. . . . Thus Ship '36' [*Orion*] (Weyher) reached her minelaying area according to plan at the earliest possible moment and has achieved a very pleasing success.[17]

The Naval Board closed New Zealand ports and switched off all coastal navigation lights. Maritime trade ground to a halt and as waterfront warehouses ran out of space, cargo piled up on the quays. New Zealand radio stations stopped broadcasting information about reconnaissance flights, and across the Tasman the RAN confined the liner *Strathmore* with over 400 troops on board to port.

The minesweepers *Wakakura*, *James Cosgrove*, *Thomas Currell* and *Humphrey* swept the approaches to Auckland, and the *Futurist* and *Nora Niven* later swept the approaches to Wellington and Lyttelton. Two weeks later the Naval Board reopened the main shipping channels and by September the minesweepers had discovered 131 mines.[18]

The *Orion*'s remaining mines eventually broke free from their moorings and drifted, with many washing up on the New Zealand and Australian coasts. In August the fishing boat *Ahuriri* found a drifting mine near Richards Rock at the Mercury Islands and it was towed into Mercury Bay and safely detonated. The steamer *Period* sighted three possible mines off Botany Bay in August, which closed Sydney Harbour while minesweepers searched the area.[19]

Mines continued to be found during 1941. In January a mine drifted ashore near Coromandel Harbour on New Zealand's North Island, where a naval team disposed of it, and in March the *Thomas Currell* destroyed a mine near Flat Rock, off Kawau Island.

The *Orion*'s minefield caused one more tragedy. On 14 May 1941 the New Zealand minesweepers *Gale* and *Puriri* swept the waters near Bream Head.[20] The *Puriri* struck a mine and sank quickly. Five sailors perished, but the *Gale* rescued the survivors. A board of inquiry concluded the *Puriri*'s loss was attributable to the *Gale*'s senior officer since 'he did fail to carry out an organized search and to take proper charge of HMS *Puriri*'.[21]

By June 1941 twenty-four mines from the *Orion* had been discovered in New Zealand waters since the beginning of the year, but more mines continued to appear. After the minesweepers *Matai*, *Gale*, *Rata* and *Muritai* found ten mines near Bream Head and seventeen near Maro Tiri, the Naval Board remarked: 'Very creditable piece of minesweeping, often carried out under very adverse weather conditions.'[22]

The *Orion*'s mines would only sink the *Niagara* and *Puriri*, but Weyher formed a different impression. A New Zealand radio station reported that the *Port Bowen* was a total loss.[23] Prisoners later incorrectly told him that this vessel had struck a mine but she had actually run aground.[24] Prisoners also incorrectly told Weyher that the steamer *Baltanic* had been sunk in the Colville Channel after hitting a mine.[25]

As the *Niagara* rested at a depth of 60 fathoms, the Bank of England asked the Admiralty to recover her valuable cargo of gold. Captain John Johnstone led a remarkable salvage operation from the *Claymore* in late 1941. Divers made more than 300 descents, returning with 555 of the 590 bars of gold in an operation Captain Stephen Roskill praised:

> The subsequent recovery of the greater part of the ten tons of gold, from deep inside a big ship sunk in a depth of 438 feet in strong tidal currents where many mines were still present, was one of the most remarkable feats of salvage ever carried out.[26]

After the war in May 1953 Johnstone returned to the *Niagara*'s resting place on the salvage vessel *Foremast* to search for the remaining thirty-five bars of gold.[27] This time his divers recovered thirty bars, but five remain somewhere inside the liner.

THE HUNT FOR THE TASMAN RAIDER

The sinking of the *Niagara* alerted the Allies to the presence of a raider and ships, aircraft and coastwatchers searched for the intruder. RNZAF planes patrolled the approaches to Auckland, Cook Strait, Lyttelton and Otago; however, as they lacked range the civilian flying boats *Awarua* and *Aotearoa* conducted long-range patrols but failed to spot the now infamous 'Tasman Raider'.

The *Hector* left Auckland and patrolled the eastern approaches to Cook Strait while the *Achilles* and the *Awarua* searched the waters near the Kermadec Islands. The *Achilles* arrived off Raoul Island before heading towards the southern Kermadec islands of Macauley and Curtis and patrolling the Stella Passage between Curtis and Cheeseman islands. Having sighted nothing, the *Achilles* returned to Auckland, and the *Hector* headed to Wellington after finding no trace of the raider.

Operations in Australian waters concentrated on protecting the Bass Strait; the cruiser *Perth* patrolled the western approaches and the armed merchant cruiser *Manoora* guarded the east, while Royal Australian Air Force (RAAF) Hudsons and Ansons patrolled the skies above the strait.

The *Orion* and *Tropic Sea* had meanwhile continued towards their rendezvous with the *Winnetou* south of the Cook Islands, although no confirmation signal from the tanker about the new location had been received. The wireless eventually received a weak acknowledgment and the rendezvous took place on 25 June, causing both crews to cheer loudly. The *Winnetou*, having completed a long journey around Cape Horn, refuelled the raider and her prize ship.

The prisoners on the *Orion* adjusted to their new lives as Captain Arundel from the *Haxby* remembered:

> Yes, they turned out to be human enough in spite of the murder they had committed. The ship's prison officer gave me a carton of American cigarettes and a tin of British ones, and he politely apologised to me for not having a bottle of whiskey to give me. But the food! We had hardly anything but German sausage, and it was terrible.[28]

Captain 'Allright' Steinkrauss and half the *Winnetou*'s crew boarded the *Orion* to watch a film, but Weyher had an ulterior motive and offered Steinkrauss command of the *Tropic Sea* for her voyage to Europe. Steinkrauss characteristically replied by saying 'all right', and the *Winnetou*'s first officer Danneil took command of the tanker.

The *Tropic Sea* received fuel and supplies and her prize crew, eleven men from the *Orion* and seventeen from the *Winnetou*, stripped her of all useful items such as wheat, flour, paint and radios, which was transferred to the raider. The fifty-five Allied prisoners on the *Orion* boarded the prize ship after Captain Arundel gave Weyher a letter:

> I wish to show on behalf of myself, Officers and crew appreciation of the treatment received during our stay as prisoners on board your vessel. We have always received the best of attention under the circumstances and have in no way complaints whatsoever. Also I would like to thank the doctors for their best and kindest attention to the wounded and sick.[29]

On 1 July 1940 Weyher and the *Orion* left New Zealand waters, heading north into the South Pacific, looking for fresh victims.
(AUTHOR'S COLLECTION)

On 30 June the *Tropic Sea* departed while the *Orion*'s crew gave three cheers. Weyher headed towards the South Pacific, and if he experienced no luck there he would enter the Coral Sea. The raider parted company with the *Winnetou* the next day, and the *Orion* headed north looking for fresh victims.

CHAPTER 4
THE *PINGUIN'S* FIRST VICTORIES

The most enterprising and successful of all the raider captains was
Captain Krüder in the *Pinguin*.[1]

Vizeadmiral Friedrich Ruge
Commander of Security West

THE BREAKOUT

In June 1940 the *Pinguin*'s crew of twenty-six officers and 375 sailors completed
their final preparations. Krüder had orders to attack enemy shipping in the
Indian Ocean before mining Australian waters and attacking the Norwegian
Antarctic whaling fleet.[2] The raider was armed with six 5.9-inch guns,
hidden behind steel shutters that opened with the help of counterweights, as
well as a 75-mm gun, a twin-mounted 37-mm gun and four quad-mounted
20-mm cannons, hidden inside false ventilators, water tanks and packing
cases.[3] Her four twin-mounted torpedo tubes were mounted on the deck on
both sides of the bridge and her holds contained 300 mines and two obsolete
Heinkel seaplanes.[4]

The *Pinguin* departed Gotenhafen disguised as a freighter on 15 June. She arrived off the Danish Island of Lolland two days later and rendezvoused with *Sperrbrecher IV*, a pathfinder vessel designed to detonate mines ahead of convoys, and two torpedo boats that would escort the raider through the Danish Great Belt. In the morning the small flotilla arrived in the Kattegat between Denmark and Sweden.

After *Sperrbrecher IV* departed, the *Pinguin* and torpedo boats rounded the Jutland Peninsula and entered the Skagerrak between Norway and Denmark before heading towards the North Sea, while an escorting Dornier 18 flying boat and two fighters appeared overhead. Two minesweepers reinforced the escort and the flotilla proceeded north along the Norwegian coast before reaching Bergen. The torpedo boats retired while the *Pinguin* and the minesweepers continued north and entered Sorgulen Fjord, where Krüder disguised his raider as the Soviet freighter *Petschura*.

On 23 June the crew battled gale-force winds and the minesweepers returned home as they could not withstand the weather. A short time later the lookout spotted a periscope and briefly saw a submarine as a wave rose and fell. As the *Seekriegsleitung* had directed all U-boats away from the *Pinguin*'s route, the submarine had to be British. Krüder hoped the Soviet disguise would be believed as the raider headed towards North Cape. The submarine surfaced and gave chase while disappearing and reappearing from view in the heavy seas.

A sailor on the submarine's conning tower signalled 'what ship?', which Krüder ignored, followed by 'heave to or we open fire'. Krüder also ignored this message, hoping that bad weather would prevent the submarine from being stable enough to effectively use her weapons. The submarine fired three torpedoes that missed the *Pinguin* and she chased the raider for an hour before disappearing.

The *Pinguin* turned north-west towards Jan Mayen Island as Krüder planned to hide in the fog banks near the island until bad weather developed in the Denmark Strait, and once in the Atlantic he would resupply *U-A* near the Cape Verde Islands off north-west Africa.[5] The U-boat's commander, *Korvettenkapitän* Cohausz, had recently sunk the armed merchant cruiser *Andania* south-west of Iceland. The Royal Navy had reduced the Northern Patrol to provide additional warships for the Dunkirk evacuation, and with the *Andania* gone, the British had no warships guarding the Denmark Strait.[6]

On 24 June the lookout spotted Jan Mayen Island, but improved weather prevented fog banks from forming. However, as the *Pinguin* approached Greenland, fog appeared and Krüder ordered a south-westerly course towards the Denmark Strait.

The fog lifted the next day and as a *Kriegsmarine* weather ship predicted a warm front approaching, which would create bad weather, the *Pinguin*'s meteorologist Doctor Ulrich Roll recommended waiting. Krüder agreed and three days later the warm front arrived, producing low clouds and heavy rain. The raider resumed her course towards the Denmark Strait through freezing rain, rolling seas and a maze of icebergs.[7] On 1 July the *Pinguin* entered the North Atlantic and Krüder celebrated this achievement by opening a box of cigars and passing them around the bridge.

IN THE ATLANTIC

On 6 July the lookout spotted a liner east of Newfoundland while the *Pinguin* headed south towards the Canada–Liverpool route. The navigation officer *Kapitänleutnant* Michaelson believed she was the armed merchant cruiser *Carmania* and the raider evaded the suspected warship.

The *Pinguin* approached the main Atlantic convoy routes in pleasant weather and clear visibility. After passing the Azores, Krüder decided to disguise the *Pinguin* as the Greek freighter *Kassos*, as Soviet ships did not frequent these waters. The *Seekriegsleitung* meanwhile ordered him to rendezvous with *U-A* in remote waters north-west of St Peter and St Paul Rocks.[8]

On 17 July the *Pinguin* reached the rendezvous and *U-A* arrived the next day. The U-boat had recently sunk two Norwegian ships but had no more torpedoes and needed fuel. The U-boat crew boarded the raider to bathe and help themselves to better food, and the submariners gave a tour of their U-boat to a group from the raider. Strong winds convinced Krüder and Cohausz to head south to conduct the transfer in calmer seas and two days later they rendezvoused again. The raider's crew transferred eleven torpedoes and other supplies to *U-A* on rubber rafts, the first time an auxiliary cruiser had resupplied a U-boat.

On 25 July the *Pinguin* towed *U-A* south-east towards Africa to conserve

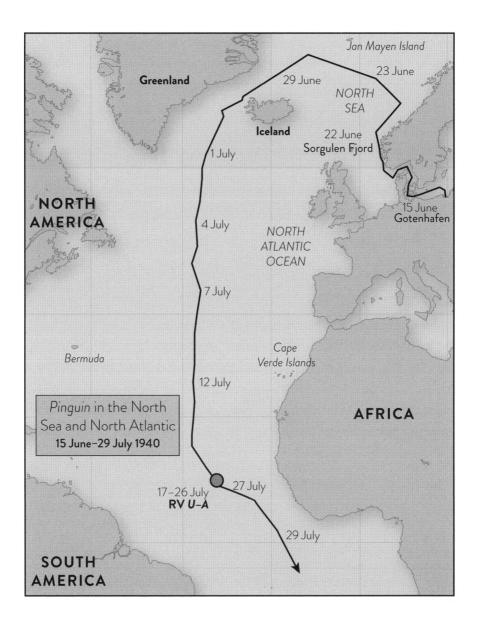

her fuel. At night the lookout spotted lights and the U-boat proceeded alone to investigate, returning at midnight. Cohausz had fired a torpedo at an enemy tanker but missed, and after this disappointment the raider resumed her southerly course with *U-A* in tow until they reached the latitude of Freetown, the assembly point of convoys. The U-boat proceeded alone

ABOVE Pet penguins in the swimming pool aboard the *Pinguin*.
(AWM: NAVAL HISTORICAL COLLECTION)

BELOW Sailors on the *Pinguin* playing with the ship's pet dog in the swimming pool.
(AWM: NAVAL HISTORICAL COLLECTION)

towards Freetown but faulty machinery forced Cohausz to head home, although he sank four freighters with torpedoes from the *Pinguin* before reaching Kiel.[9]

The *Pinguin* continued south-east and entered the South Atlantic. Krüder learned from a signal that an engagement was taking place between the armed merchant cruiser *Alcantara* and the *Thor* south-west of Rio de Janeiro, 1300 miles away. The *Thor*, commanded by *Kapitän* Otto Kähler, had previously captured the Dutchman *Kertosono* and sank four freighters near Brazil. The raider shelled the *Alcantara*, which lost speed and allowed Kähler to escape.

On 31 July the *Pinguin*'s lookout spotted a freighter in clear weather 300 miles north-west of Ascension Island, proceeding on a parallel course in the opposite direction. If she was an enemy vessel, Krüder would attack without jamming her wireless, as a raider warning would draw Allied warships away from the *Thor*. Krüder assumed the Allies would not suspect that two auxiliary cruisers would be operating so close to each other, and in this way he could help the *Thor* escape.

The 5358-ton British freighter *Domingo de Larrinaga* had been heading from Bahia Blanca to Freetown carrying grain, intending to join a convoy bound for Newcastle. Captain William Chalmers spotted a ship, but relaxed after seeing a Greek flag and only became concerned when she began to turn. He examined the ship again and concluded that she was too well painted to be Greek, so he ordered full speed and hard to starboard. Thick black smoke emerged from the freighter's funnels, while the wireless officer Neil Morrison broadcast a raider warning and the stern gun crew ran to their obsolete 4-inch cannon.

The *Pinguin* maintained her intercept course and after a two-hour chase the distance closed to 2½ miles. Krüder could see enemy stern gunners observing his raider but they did not open fire. He raised the *Kriegsmarine* flag, fired a warning shot and ordered the *Domingo de Larrinaga* to stop. As the freighter continued to flee and kept broadcasting raider warnings, the German gunners opened fire and a salvo struck her near the bridge, causing multiple fires. The stern gunners fought back, but all their shells missed and the freighter eventually drifted to a halt and Captain Chalmers decided to abandon ship.

Krüder ceased fire and a boarding party led by *Oberleutnant* Erich Warning

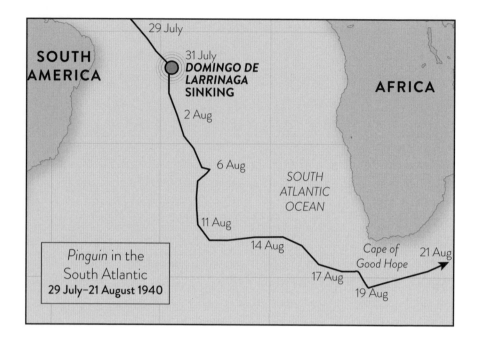

SOUTH
AMERICA

29 July

31 July
DOMINGO DE
LARRINAGA
SINKING

2 Aug

6 Aug

SOUTH
ATLANTIC
OCEAN

AFRICA

11 Aug

14 Aug

Cape of
Good Hope

21 Aug

17 Aug

19 Aug

Pinguin in the
South Atlantic
29 July–21 August 1940

searched the burning freighter and Doctor Wenzel assisted wounded sailors. The Germans evacuated the survivors before placing demolition charges with a timer set for nine minutes. The boarding party returned to their motorboat but could not start its engine. Boatswain Rauch frantically tried to fix the engine as the countdown to detonation approached and, with only two minutes left, the men tried to row away but the heavy seas prevented progress. No explosion eventuated and, after the engine came to life, the shaken boarding party returned to the raider.

Krüder sank the *Domingo de Larrinaga* with a torpedo and all thirty-two survivors became prisoners on the *Pinguin*, including the radio officer with two broken legs. Eight sailors had died and four had been injured.

The *Pinguin*'s radio room overheard busy radio traffic as the *Domingo de Larrinaga*'s raider warning had been received by the South Atlantic Station. The cruiser HMS *Dorsetshire* proceeded to the reported position while the cruiser HMS *Cumberland* patrolled north-east of Tristan da Cunha. Krüder's plan to help the *Thor* succeeded as the Allies believed one raider was responsible for both incidents.[10] The *Pinguin* headed south and the British cruisers hunted her without success.

On 12 August the *Pinguin* neared Tristan da Cunha and the crew experienced the cold southerly gales of the Roaring Forties. Krüder correctly believed his prospects of finding lone merchantmen in the Indian Ocean would be good. The Italian declaration of war had forced the Royal Navy to divert most of its warships on anti-raider operations to the Mediterranean, significantly reducing its presence in the Indian Ocean. The British also closed the Suez Canal and re-routed shipping around the Cape of Good Hope, forcing merchant vessels to head towards the *Pinguin*.

'SECTION 19'

The Admiralty, increasingly concerned about raiders, tasked Sub-Lieutenant Patrick Beesly to analyze information on enemy auxiliary cruisers.[11] Beesly, an intelligence officer at the OIC, had joined the Royal Navy in June 1939 after being educated at Cambridge. In the shadowy world of the Naval Intelligence Division he became friends with Ian Fleming, the personal assistant of Rear-Admiral John Godfrey, Director of Naval Intelligence.[12]

Beesly's team — 'Section 19' — knew almost nothing about auxiliary cruisers, whose existence could not be confirmed as overdue ships could have fallen victim to conventional raiders, U-boats or natural hazards. On 18 July Beesly confirmed their existence after a lifeboat landed in the West Indies, containing victims of the *Widder* commanded by *Kapitän* Hellmuth von Ruckteschell. After intercepting the *Krossfonn*, *Davisian* and *King John*, Ruckteschell abandoned forty Allied sailors in a lifeboat 240 miles from the Lesser Antilles in a savage but foolish action that gave Beesly the first eyewitness account of an auxiliary cruiser.[13]

The *Widder* later sank the Norwegian tanker *Beaulieu* and Ruckteschell refused to rescue her crew from their lifeboats, but fortunately a tanker later found them. After the raider sank the *Anglo Saxon*, Ruckteschell again refused to rescue survivors. One lifeboat reached the Bahamas seventy days later but only two of its eight occupants had survived and the other lifeboat was never seen again. After the *Widder* captured the *Antonios Chandris*, Ruckteschell abandoned her crew of twenty-nine in their lifeboats. Although a Portuguese freighter rescued them, seven men had died. On 31 October the raider arrived at Brest, ending her barbaric voyage.[14]

'Section 19' had great difficulty tracking auxiliary cruisers given the vast dispersion of their operations and their almost total wireless silence. Beesly recalled: 'The first attempts to pin down the positions or track movements of ships like *Thor* or *Penguin* [*Pinguin*] looked heartbreakingly inadequate.'[15] He faced the tragic reality that most of the time he had to wait for doomed merchantmen to broadcast warnings before raiders could be located. Over time, however, the gradual accumulation of information enabled him to form a picture of raider operations:

> The first approach could only be an historical one; the assumption that certain incidents were the work of the same ship, while others, because of the time and distance factor must be associated with a second or third raider. . . . As the existence of each fresh raider was established she was given a distinguishing letter, for of course at this stage their German designation was not known.[16]

The *Orion* became known to the British as 'Raider A', the *Komet* as 'Raider B', the *Atlantis* as 'Raider C', the *Widder* as 'Raider D', the *Thor* as 'Raider E' and the *Pinguin* as 'Raider F'. Beesly's raider reports slowly became more detailed as Commander Donald McLachlan from Naval Intelligence noted:

> Every issue of the Weekly Intelligence Review prepared for the Fleet by Beesly's colleagues in Section 19 contained the latest facts, silhouettes, possibilities; biographies of each raider were gradually built up, their captains identified, their tactics described.[17]

The usefulness of these reports was primarily of historical value, as anticipating a raider's next move remained pure guesswork. McLachlan recalled: 'There was no more painfully accumulated or more frequently revised mosaic in NID [Naval Intelligence Division] than the one concerned with raiders'.[18]

The battle between the *Alcantara* and the *Thor* made it clear that German auxiliary cruisers completely outgunned their British counterparts. Although only conventional cruisers had a good chance of sinking raiders, the Royal Navy did not have enough warships to effectively hunt them due to commitments in the North Atlantic and Mediterranean, and the few available cruisers concentrated on patrolling focal points.[19] Captain Agar described these inadequate measures:

> The best counter-measure is to organise in each Area 'Hunting Groups' of warships powerful enough to deal with a well-armed Raider; but this takes time. In the meanwhile, our Merchant ships had to take their medicine, and gallantly they did, often at great sacrifice of life.[20]

The Royal Navy waited for a QQQQ signal that just might provide an opportunity to sink a raider.

A MADAGASCAN NIGHT

On 19 August 1940 the *Pinguin* rounded the Cape of Good Hope, entering the Indian Ocean. During free time the crew often visited the cinema and *Oberleutnant* Friedrich Gabe described one occasion:

> In one of the recent films there was a floozie doing a strip tease. The Old Man [Krüder], who was present, indignantly ordered her to put her clothes on again, which was quite simply arranged; all the projectionist had to do was to run it through backward. The general opinion is that the Old Man who isn't as old as all that just wanted to see it all over again.[21]

The *Pinguin* headed north-east towards Madagascar, keeping clear of the *Atlantis'* operational area. Rogge had recently achieved great success in the Indian Ocean, capturing the *Tirranna* and *City of Bagdad* and sinking the *Kemmendine* and *Talleyrand*. As the *Pinguin* neared Madagascar on 26 August, Krüder ordered *Oberleutnant* Werner to fly a reconnaissance mission. The Heinkel seaplane painted with British markings took off and in the afternoon the observer *Oberleutnant* Walter Müller spotted a tanker.

The unarmed 7616-ton Norwegian tanker *Filefjell* had been heading to Cape Town from the Persian Gulf, carrying aviation fuel, with a crew of thirty-nine sailors. Captain Josef Nordby had been warned about a raider in the Indian Ocean following the sinking of the *Kemmendine*. Two days earlier his wireless intercepted a raider warning from the *King City*, another victim of the *Atlantis* which had been sunk 600 miles north-east of the tanker. Captain Nordby continued with increased caution, but believed the danger to be far away.

Captain Nordby stood on the *Filefjell*'s bridge and spotted a seaplane. When the seaplane passed overhead he saw British markings and waved. He felt relief, believing a British cruiser must be nearby, and the aircraft disappeared.

An hour later the Heinkel returned and after circling the *Filefjell*, Müller fired a flare to get her attention and dropped a message, which Captain Nordby read:

> On account vicinity of enemy raider alter course to 180 degrees distance 140 miles. From that point take up course direct to 31 degrees North 37 degrees East. Thence you get further information. Do not use wireless. Signed Hopkins, Commander HMS Cumberland.[22]

Captain Nordby complied and the *Filefjell* turned directly towards the *Pinguin*, 140 miles away. Werner observed the tanker's change of course and flew away confident he had accomplished his mission. However, Captain Nordby soon wondered why a British cruiser would want to rendezvous with his tanker. After re-reading the message and noting its poor English, it no longer seemed authentic so he changed course hoping to reach a safe port.

After the Heinkel returned to the *Pinguin*, Krüder set a course towards the *Filefjell*, but in the late afternoon he became concerned as the tanker had not yet been sighted. Werner once again took off but failed to locate her and returned to the raider.

At 1720 h Captain Nordby felt safe enough to broadcast a raider warning, but the *Pinguin*'s wireless intercepted the signal and direction-finding suggested the tanker was fleeing to Africa. With only an hour till sunset, Krüder formulated a daring plan. Werner would locate the vessel by flying in the direction of the signals bearing and tear down the tanker's radio aerial before landing and ordering her to stop at gun point. Krüder justified the risks:

I appreciated what I was asking of the aircraft and its crew when I sent it out just before dark with the order to land in the dark, in a swell alongside an unknown, possibly enemy steamer, and keep in contact with her until the ship arrived, but it was the only way to make sure of the tanker by night.[23]

The Heinkel took to the skies and Werner found the *Filefjell* and tore down her aerial with a grappling hook on his first attempt. On the second pass he dropped a bomb near the ship and strafed the tanker, which persuaded Captain Nordby to stop. Werner, almost out of fuel, landed in front of her and signalled: 'Remain stopping here. Cruiser Cumberland will proceed with you. Show your lights.'[24] Captain Nordby obeyed, fearing the seaplane's machine gun might ignite the aviation fuel. The tense standoff lasted two hours until the *Pinguin* arrived and Werner signalled: 'We are both lying here. Hi Hi.'[25]

A boarding party led by *Oberleutnant* Warning captured the tanker, finding her secret papers and code-books. A prize crew came aboard and the Norwegians transferred to the raider. Krüder decided to leave the area and the raider headed south, followed by the *Filefjell*.

At 0303 h the lookout spotted a black shadow and the profile of a tanker became visible. Krüder ordered an intercept course while the *Filefjell* remained behind. The *Pinguin* passed astern and took up an attack position on the tanker's port quarter. Krüder ordered her to stop and fired a warning shot.

The 6901-ton tanker *British Commander* had been proceeding in ballast from Falmouth to Abadan via Cape Town with a crew of forty-six sailors. She was armed with a 4-inch gun, a 12-pounder cannon and machine guns. Captain John Thornton had been asleep in his cabin until a knock on his door informed him that Second Officer Mitchison needed him on the bridge. As he climbed the stairs, he heard a shell land in the water and after reaching the bridge he saw a ship about 2 miles away that signalled 'stop instantly'. The radio officer Watson meanwhile ran to the wireless room and broadcast a raider warning, which the Walvis Bay shore station acknowledged.[26]

After the *Pinguin*'s searchlights exposed sailors standing near the stern guns, Krüder ordered his gunners to open fire, but their first salvo missed the *British Commander*. Captain Thornton ordered hard to starboard and full speed but decided against returning fire, hoping to discourage further aggression. Watson sent another signal stating his vessel was being shelled, which the Cape Town station acknowledged. In response the cruisers HMS *Colombo* and *Neptune*, as well as the armed merchant cruisers HMS *Arawa* and HMAS *Kanimbla*, converged on the area.

The *Pinguin*'s guns pounded the *British Commander* and Captain Thornton, knowing his warnings had been received, decided to abandon ship. Krüder ceased fire and signalled the tanker: 'I will sink your ship and will give you fifteen minutes to abandon.'[27] The tanker's crew lowered two lifeboats from the starboard side, which could not be observed from the raider, and the men rowed westwards, hoping to avoid capture in the darkness.

After fifteen minutes a torpedo struck the *British Commander*, causing her foremast to collapse. She listed to port but remained afloat. After the *Pinguin*'s gunners sank the stricken tanker, the Germans found the two lifeboats, and forty-six sailors became prisoners. Krüder introduced himself to Captain Thornton:

He called me to his cabin and asked me why I had sent a wireless message after he had told me not to. . . . He seemed to be very concerned at the likelihood of distress messages being transmitted and told me that merchant seaman were not soldiers, they had no right to endanger their lives, and it would have been my responsibility had any of my crew been killed.[28]

Krüder had misjudged the willingness of Allied sailors to risk their lives in order to broadcast warnings and, as his romantic notions of a gentlemanly 'prize war' faded, the war took on a grimmer tone.

The *Pinguin* fled south-east but five minutes later the lookout spotted yet another ship. The raider turned to port and crossed her stern before approaching from starboard. The 5008-ton Norwegian freighter *Morviken* had been heading in ballast to Calcutta from Cape Town with a crew of thirty-five sailors. Krüder ordered her to stop and fired a warning shot. Captain Anton Norvalls raised the Norwegian flag and his vessel came to a halt. The boarding party found the Norwegians to be highly co-operative

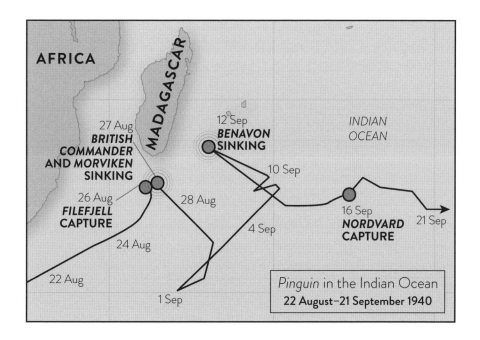

AFRICA

MADAGASCAR

INDIAN OCEAN

27 Aug
BRITISH COMMANDER AND MORVIKEN SINKING

12 Sep
BENAVON SINKING

10 Sep

26 Aug
FILEFJELL CAPTURE

28 Aug

16 Sep
NORDVARD CAPTURE

21 Sep

4 Sep

24 Aug

22 Aug

1 Sep

Pinguin in the Indian Ocean
22 August–21 September 1940

and when they told Captain Norvalls that his ship would be sunk, he offered to take her to Germany rather than see her lost. Krüder, however, did not have enough time to organize a prize crew with the Royal Navy in pursuit, so the Norwegians transferred to the raider and the boarding party scuttled the *Morviken*.

Kapitänleutnant Michaelson was an old friend of Captain Norvalls and he talked to the prisoner in his cabin. At first Captain Norvalls became angry as Michaelson had not prevented the scuttling of his ship; however, Michaelson pleaded that he tried to persuade Krüder not to but his captain had the final word. Captain Norvalls accepted this and the two friends shook hands.[29]

One hour later the *Filefjell's* prize crew informed Krüder that a large enemy freighter had been sighted, but he decided against pressing his luck for a fourth time. He also decided to scuttle the *Filefjell*, as he did not have enough time to make preparations for her voyage to Europe. After demolition charges failed to sink the tanker, the raider's guns ignited her aviation fuel, causing a fireball to rise into the night sky, and the raider fled south-east.

South African planes from Durban and Maputa searched the approaches to the Mozambique Channel and Ansons conducted patrols from Cape Town but failed to spot the *Pinguin*.[30] The *Kanimbla* reached the *British Commander*'s reported position but only found an oil slick. The Royal Navy failed to locate the raider and the East Indies Station lamented: 'Unless they are in very close proximity to the scene of action, A.M.C.s [armed merchant cruisers], with their slow speed, stand little chance of making contact.'[31]

Krüder believed the Allies would assume that he was fleeing the area outright, so he decided to lie low in nearby remote waters before returning to Madagascar, as it would be the last thing the enemy would expect.

RETURN TO MADAGASCAR

On 31 August the *Pinguin* avoided a large Blue Funnel liner that Krüder suspected was an armed merchant cruiser. He decided to disguise his raider as the Norwegian freighter *Trafalgar* after Captain Norvalls told him 'the Greeks have a few good ships, and those good ships are not in the East'.[32]

The *Pinguin* headed north-east towards Madagascar and the Heinkel attempted a reconnaissance flight five days later, but the swell caused its engine to fall out, igniting the fuel and forcing Werner and Müller to jump into the water. The crew rescued both aviators, but the seaplane had been destroyed. Although there was another Heinkel in the hold, it could only be assembled in good weather.

On 9 September Krüder learned from a distress signal that the *Atlantis* was attacking the freighter *Benarty* elsewhere in the Indian Ocean. This news pleased him as it would focus enemy attention away from his raider. The *Pinguin* continued towards Madagascar and shortly after dawn on 12 September the lookout spotted a freighter.

The 5872-ton Scottish Ben Line freighter *Benavon* was headed to London with a cargo of rubber and hemp from Manila and Singapore. In line with company tradition, the ship's forty-eight sailors consisted of Scottish officers with Chinese stewards and engine room workers. Captain Thomson knew a raider was active in the Indian Ocean but, after hearing the *Benarty*'s distress signal, felt secure as the incident occurred 600 miles away.

As the *Benavon* headed west-south-west at 12 knots, Cadet Graham Spiers spotted an approaching ship. Chief Officer James Cameron, in command on the bridge as Captain Thomson was asleep in his cabin, relaxed when he saw the Norwegian flag. Although both vessels were converging, he maintained his course since, under the International Collision Regulations, the *Trafalgar* had to turn. However, she made no attempt to correct her course and when the distance closed to a mile the *Benavon's* whistle signalled danger. Captain Thomson arrived on the bridge and ordered hard to starboard to avoid a collision. The British sailors then saw the *Kriegsmarine* flag being raised. Captain Thomson sounded the alarm and the stern gunners ran to their 4-inch cannon and anti-aircraft gun.

The *Pinguin* fired a warning shot but Captain Thomson decided to fight. When Krüder saw the stern gunners preparing their weapons he ordered his gunners to open fire. The stern guns returned fire and one shell hit the raider and penetrated her hull through the crew's quarters, passing close to the mines before ending up in the stoker's mess. As it failed to explode, Petty Officer Streil threw it overboard through the hole it had made.

A salvo struck the *Benavon's* bridge, killing Captain Thomson and several officers, including Cameron, and most of the stern gunners met the same fate. Shells also destroyed her main mast and radio aerial while the funnel collapsed onto the deck. The *Benavon's* fires could not be extinguished and, after coming to a stop, Krüder ceased fire and sent boats to rescue the survivors. Doctor Wenzel and Warning boarded the burning ship to help the wounded and received burns.[33] After the rescue operation the *Pinguin's* gunners finished off the stricken freighter. Seven British and eighteen Chinese sailors became prisoners while twenty-three men had been killed. Krüder conducted a burial at sea for three Allied sailors who died on the raider.

The *Pinguin* headed south-east towards Australia and on 16 September the lookout spotted the 4111-ton Norwegian freighter *Nordvard*, carrying wheat from Australia to Port Elizabeth. After the *Pinguin* fired a warning shot, Captain Henry Hansen offered no resistance and the Germans captured the *Nordvard* without incident. Krüder placed a prize crew on board under the command of *Oberleutnant* Hans Neumeir. All the *Pinguin's* prisoners transferred to the prize ship except for Captain Thornton, Captain Chalmers and a few other key personnel. The raider replenished her prize with fuel, water and food as well as letters home from the crew. The *Nordvard* departed and arrived safely in Bordeaux on 21 December.[34]

CHAPTER 5
THE NORTHEAST PASSAGE

The prisoner alleged that he was told on board '45' [the *Komet*] that she had reached the Pacific by going north round Russia. He was told that at one period the raider had run fast in the ice and had had to be freed by Russian ice-breakers. . . . This story, which seems highly improbable, was repeated by other prisoners.[1]

Royal Navy Interrogation Report
May 1941

THE ARCTIC ROUTE

The Nazi–Soviet Pact created interesting opportunities for the *Kriegsmarine*, and *Grossadmiral* Raeder wanted to take advantage of this change in diplomatic alignment, seeking access to Russian naval bases in exchange for superior naval technology.[2] He also wanted the Soviets to support the auxiliary cruisers and, as such, his naval attaché in Moscow, *Kapitän* Norbert von Baumbach, raised this possibility with Soviet naval officials, who agreed to help.[3]

In January 1940 Baumbach informed Berlin about a promising new opportunity. German freighters stranded in the Far East might be able to return home through the Northeast Passage, the Arctic waters north of Siberia that linked Europe and Asia.[4] This passage was closed most of the year due to heavy ice, but in the summer vessels could attempt the route with the help of icebreakers. A secure sea-route to the Pacific would allow freighters to return home from Japan carrying vital cargoes, and raiders from Germany could bypass the British blockade, as the *Seekriegsleitung* well understood: 'A northeast passage "postern gate" on the outward and homeward passage would therefore be most useful. The merchant raiders are already being fitted provisionally with the necessary reinforcement against ice.'[5]

On 18 March Baumbach formally requested permission for an auxiliary cruiser to transit through the passage:

> We brought the matter up at a period beginning about the middle of March, which was politically unfavourable. For this reason, I was not able to risk bringing the information to the notice of Molotov, but was obliged on the advice of the Ambassador, to use my direct contacts with the Soviet Navy. In this way the announcement was not 100% legitimate.[6]

The Soviets agreed and told Baumbach that an icebreaker would rendezvous with the raider at Vaygach Island in the Barents Sea on 15 July in return for 850,000 roubles. The *Seekriegsleitung* selected the *Komet* to attempt the voyage.[7]

THE ARCTIC RAIDER

In June 1940 the *Komet* completed her trials, and her crew of twenty officers and 250 sailors made preparations for their voyage through the Northeast Passage. Eyssen's main operational area would be waters near Australia and New Zealand, as well as the Indian Ocean, but he could also operate in the wider Pacific and South Atlantic. He also had orders to mine the approaches to Australian, New Zealand or South African ports.

The *Komet* was armed with six 5.9-inch guns and a 60-mm gun mounted at her bow.[8] Her anti-aircraft weapons consisted of one twin-mounted

The *Komet* was armed with six 5.9-inch guns and a 60-mm gun mounted at her bow, five anti-aircraft weapons and six torpedo tubes. The raider's holds held thirty magnetic mines, a high-speed minelaying launch *Meteorit* and an Arado seaplane. (AUTHOR'S COLLECTION)

37-mm gun and four quad-mounted 20-mm cannons.[9] She also had four above-water torpedo tubes in twin mounts installed on both sides of the bridge and two single underwater tubes. The raider's holds contained thirty magnetic mines, a high-speed minelaying launch *Meteorit* and an Arado seaplane. As the largest Soviet ship to transit the Northeast Passage was 4000 tons, the *Komet*, being the smallest raider at 3287 tons, was ideally suited to attempt the voyage.[10] Her bow had been strengthened and she had a special propeller designed for Arctic conditions, while extra gas cylinders and heaters would protect the crew from the freezing Siberian weather.[11]

On 3 July the *Komet* departed Gotenhafen disguised as the freighter *Donau*, and two minesweepers escorted her through the Danish Great Belt. The raider proceeded through the Skagerrak between Norway and Denmark before heading north along the Norwegian coast. Eyssen had orders to rendezvous with the tanker *Esso*, which would accompany the raider, carrying additional fuel and provisions. However, the tanker's voyage ended after she ran aground on 4 July, forcing her to return to Bergen. The *Komet* had to make the journey alone, but Eyssen first stopped at Bergen to load Arctic equipment from the *Esso*.

On 12 July the *Komet*, now disguised as the Soviet freighter *Deynev*, passed

North Cape and headed east across the Barents Sea towards the rendezvous with the icebreaker. Baumbach had deliberately not confirmed arrangements with the Soviets to deny them any opportunity to cancel the operation and 'the sudden appearance of Ship "45" [*Komet*] at the pre-arranged meeting place took them completely by surprise'.[12]

As the Northeast Passage was not yet open due to a colder than expected winter, the *Komet* waited in the Barents Sea. Eyssen used this time productively, training the crew and making additional preparations to ready the raider for the ice. He gained a reputation as a strict disciplinarian, and the crew knew there would be trouble if the ship was not functioning properly.[13] While not on duty, the men watched films, listened to records and read books. The officers and NCOs also organized their own social gatherings, and at times invited Eyssen.[14]

On 1 August the Soviets announced the raider would accompany the second convoy from Murmansk.[15] However, after this convoy departed without the *Komet*, Baumbach observed:

> The reasons for making these deliberately false statements were presumably that the Russians wanted to keep Ship '45' completely isolated from other traffic. In future, it should be remembered that all Russian information is completely or partly untrue.[16]

On 13 August the Soviets informed Baumbach that the *Komet* would rendezvous in Matochkin Strait with the icebreaker *Lenin*, which would escort the raider through the Kara Sea. The raider, again disguised as the *Donau*, rendezvoused with the icebreaker on 21 August.[17] After the Soviet captain advised haste, as the passage could close at any time due to shifting ice, the two ships proceeded through the Kara Sea towards the Vilkitsky Strait. The *Lenin* created a path for the raider through partially melted and loose ice, while Eyssen and his crew found themselves in a bleak world of dense ice and cold winds. The men became unnerved by the screeches that echoed through the hull as the raider brushed past icebergs.

The *Komet*, following the *Lenin*, covered 12 miles through the Kara Sea the next day but, as she had to wait for the icebreaker *Stalin* to escort her through the next stage of the passage, the crew ventured ashore under the

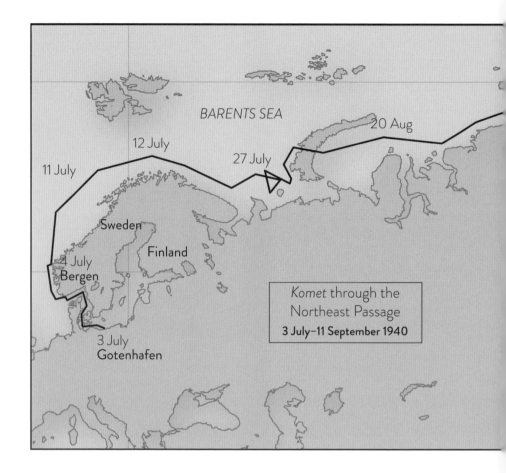

BARENTS SEA

20 Aug

12 July

27 July

11 July

Sweden

Finland

4 July
Bergen

Komet through the
Northeast Passage
3 July–11 September 1940

3 July
Gotenhafen

watchful gaze of the *Lenin*'s crew. Before the *Stalin* arrived, the *Lenin* received new orders to escort the *Komet* to a new rendezvous beyond the Vilkitsky Strait in the Laptev Sea. On 25 August the two ships entered the strait and, after passing Cape Chelyuskin, the most northerly point of Siberia, they rendezvoused with the *Stalin*. Eyssen boarded the *Stalin* and discussed the passage with Captain Belonsov, who showed him the latest charts and ice forecasts. After the conference the Soviets celebrated by drinking vodka and, as the Germans operated on Central European Time, Eyssen found himself drinking at what was for him 0600 h in the morning!

The *Lenin* departed and the *Komet* followed the *Stalin* south-west towards the Laptev Sea. The raider made slow progress through thick fog, which in the evening reduced visibility to almost zero. At times the Germans lost

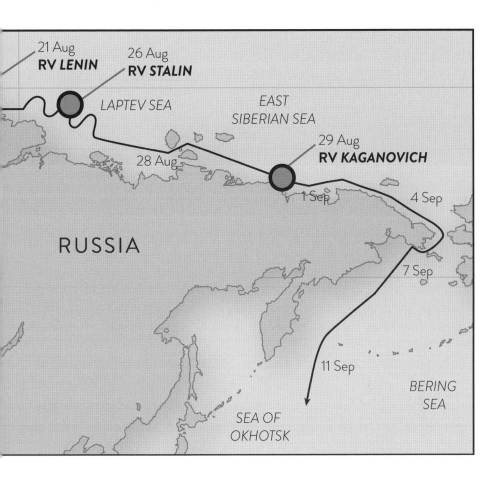

sight of the icebreaker, forcing them to follow the sound of her foghorn until glimpses of her searchlight could be seen. The *Stalin* also left behind a trail of oil for the raider to follow. Eyssen admired the cold reserve of the Soviet sailors and Karl-Herman Müller, a sailor on the *Komet*, observed: 'The Russians were quiet, calm and factual. The relationship was good. . . . We liked them. We saw they were good people.'[18]

On 27 August the two vessels entered the open waters of the Laptev Sea and made good progress travelling through 170 miles of ice in twenty-four hours. The *Stalin* departed and Eyssen signalled a message of gratitude. The *Komet* continued alone, but once past Bear Island she would rendezvous with the icebreaker *Kaganovich*, which would escort her through the final stage of the passage.

The *Komet* entered the ice-free Sannikov Strait before heading south-east through the East Siberian Sea and rendezvoused with the *Kaganovich* on 29 August. The icebreaker escorted the raider through heavy ice, and Eyssen recalled the deteriorating conditions:

> Everything that can happen to the seaman in those northern latitudes happened to us . . . a strong wind with snow squalls, strong drift and, occasionally, darkness, which could only be penetrated by searchlights. We were continually caught fast in frightening masses of ice.[19]

The crew battled against strong winds and freezing snow squalls, and in the dark they could see only a faint yellow light emanating from the *Kaganovich*. The *Komet* repeatedly became stuck, making Eyssen completely dependent on the icebreaker to free his raider.

On 1 September the weather improved and the *Komet* had an open sea all the way to the Bering Strait, the gateway to the Pacific. The *Kaganovich*'s captain Meleshov boarded the raider and informed Eyssen that new orders from Moscow instructed him to escort the raider back through the ice passage to European waters due to concerns about the United States Navy in the area, but Eyssen had no intention of complying:

> I took it very calmly without showing any excitement or disappointment but inside me I felt totally different. To go through all this and now very soon there will be free water in front of me. Only 400 sea miles and I would be through! And now to turn around! This is no option, even if I have to act on my own against an order of the High Command of the Navy.[20]

Eyssen suggested clarifying their orders and Meleshov agreed. The next day Eyssen informed Meleshov that as he had not received new orders, he would continue east alone, but Meleshov pleaded with him for more time to confirm his orders. Eyssen knew that Soviet assistance would no longer be necessary and suspected the 'new orders' to be a diplomatic ploy to allow the Soviets to deny their involvement if the *Komet*'s voyage through the ice passage became known to the world. The Soviet attitude had actually changed because the

Foreign Ministry became aware that the *Komet* was a raider and attempted to sabotage the operation.

The *Komet* resumed her voyage without interference from the *Kaganovich*, which followed the raider for a short time. The raider entered the Chukchi Sea before reaching the Bering Strait. After finally reaching the Pacific Ocean on 10 September, Eyssen ordered a southerly course towards Australia.

The *Komet* had made an epic arctic voyage of 3300 miles through the Northeast Passage, and Eyssen reflected: 'This trip has been enough for me; I would not do it again voluntarily a second time.'[21] Meanwhile, in Moscow, Baumbach thanked Admiral Kusnezow for getting the *Komet* through the ice passage.[22] Baumbach had also been deeply impressed with the Soviet sailors:

> One must specially admire the Russian crews who have been making the voyage by this route for eight years, generally, with little assistance and sometimes without help of any kind, with unquenchable optimism and great nautical dash.[23]

The *Komet* was the only German ship to voyage through the ice passage during the war, and the expectation of a secure route to the Far East never materialized as German–Soviet relations soon deteriorated.

The Soviet assistance remained secret, although in May 1941 the Royal Navy captured a German sailor who knew about the *Komet*'s voyage, but the British did not believe his story.[24] After the German invasion of Russia, Rear-Admiral Kharlamov, Head of the Soviet Military Mission in London, informed the British that 'there is no foundation for the assertion' that the Soviet Government assisted a raider through the ice passage.[25] The British initially accepted Soviet assurances, but Royal Navy intelligence later confirmed the rumours of an Arctic voyage.[26] The British ultimately turned a blind eye to the role the Soviet Union had played in supporting the *Komet* for the sake of the 'Grand Alliance'.

CHAPTER 6
THE TASMAN RAIDER

Many stories of individual heroism and endurance will emerge from this tale of the British Merchant Service in conflict with the enemy at sea. . . . They tell of the gallant battle the British steamer 'TURAKINA' fought against overwhelming odds in the Tasman Sea. . . . It is a story that will live in the glorious annals of the British at sea, and of the British Merchant Navy in particular.[1]

Alfred Nankervis
Australian Navy Secretary

THE SOUTH PACIFIC

In July 1940 the *Orion*, after escaping from New Zealand waters, headed towards Tahiti and the Society Islands. The crew experienced the Tropic of Capricorn's heat and as this increased tension on board, Weyher allowed officers to drink with their men to reduce friction between the ranks.

The *Orion*, plagued by engine troubles, stopped for repairs, causing Weyher anxiety as the mechanical problems seriously restricted his operational freedom. The raider patrolled the Tonga, Samoa and Phoenix islands routes for two weeks, only encountering small sailing boats, and despite being close to exotic tropical locations the crew lived in a world of near empty sea.

In July 1940 the *Orion* left New Zealand waters. On 28 July the raider rendezvoused with the *Winnetou* between the Gilbert and Ellice islands and the tanker refuelled the raider.
(AUTHOR'S COLLECTION)

On the evening of 21 July the lookout sighted a lighthouse on Fiji's northern coast beneath a silver moon. Weyher planned to use his Arado to investigate Suva Harbour, but in the morning the rough seas prevented the seaplane from taking off. Weyher considered landing a shore party to destroy Suva's installations and shipping, but felt this would be an unwise reaction to the current inactivity. After intercepting a signal indicating an enemy cruiser was nearby, Weyher decided to head north-west along the Suva–Yokohama route.

On 28 July the *Orion* rendezvoused with the *Winnetou* between the Gilbert and Ellice islands and the tanker refuelled the raider. Weyher informed Captain Danneil that the *Winnetou* would accompany him as a scout ship, and both ships proceeded south-west towards the Santa Cruz Islands.

THE NAVAL ATTACHÉ

Grossadmiral Raeder asked the Japanese Navy for permission to allow supply ships to use anchorages in Japanese-controlled territory.[2] The Japanese replied that they wanted friendly relations within a strict policy of neutrality and, as such, Germany could not establish bases in its territory, but they would provide supplies.[3] However, Japanese authorities later agreed to allow German vessels to use Japanese-controlled islands in the Central Pacific as anchorages.[4]

Konteradmiral Paul Wenneker, the German naval attaché in Japan, had previously commanded the pocket battleship *Deutschland* in the North Atlantic before arriving in Tokyo via the Trans-Siberian railway, courtesy of the Nazi–Soviet Pact.[5] He oversaw the *Etappen* supply network and prepared raider supply ships for their voyages.[6] The liner *Scharnhorst* in Kobe became a depot ship, and shipments of supplies and equipment for the raiders began arriving from Germany through the Soviet Union. The *Kriegsmarine* also despatched to Japan Captain Dau, who had commanded the supply ship *Altmark* during the *Graf Spee*'s cruise, to train the supply ship crews.[7]

Wenneker prepared the raider supply ships *Regensburg*, *Elbe*, *Kulmerland* and *Anneliese Essberger* and Japanese support became more forthcoming. Captain Ichimaya informed Wenneker that the *Elbe* and *Regensburg* would be allowed to depart without prior declaration to the port authorities and also warned Wenneker that Allied armed merchant cruisers had been active in waters south of Japan.

Wenneker learned about raider operations in the Pacific from newspapers reporting the *Orion*'s exploits:

> I hear for the first time — and indirectly at that — of the presence of a German auxiliary cruiser in Australian waters. I believe it essential for the Naval Attaché in Tokyo, who will ultimately be responsible for the supply of these ships, to be informed <u>officially</u> as well about how many and what sort of auxiliary cruisers are currently at sea, or at any rate, about those operating in the vicinity of East Asia.[8]

Wenneker did not appreciate that the *Seekriegsleitung* also knew little about raider operations as the captains rarely broke radio silence.

THE CORAL SEA

On 4 August the *Orion* and *Winnetou* entered the Coral Sea. The tanker refuelled the raider three days later, but as her engines would soon break down, she headed for Japan. Weyher, concerned as Berlin had not acknowledged his message detailing the route his prize ship *Tropic Sea* would take to France, signalled the German Embassy in Tokyo.[9] Wenneker received this message and his staff accordingly relayed signals between the *Orion* and Berlin.[10] After the *Winnetou* arrived in Kobe on 1 September, Captain Danneil proceeded to Tokyo and gave Wenneker a copy of the *Orion*'s war diary and Weyher's list of supply requirements.[11]

The *Orion* headed towards Brisbane as Weyher planned to attack shipping on the New Caledonia, Fiji, Honolulu and Panama routes. As the raider approached, the wireless room noticed increased radio traffic between reconnaissance planes and ground bases. Weyher, after listening to a radio news interview with an RAAF officer, noted: 'The Australian Air Force controls coastal waters by continuous patrol flights up to 100 miles out to sea. Ships were escorted up to 20 miles. Bomber flights were in a state of continual readiness.'[12]

On 10 August the lookout spotted a freighter and Weyher ordered a gradual intercept course. The bridge officers identified her as the *Triona* owned by the British Phosphate Commission. In the afternoon the *Orion* turned to port to get into an attack position, but the *Triona* changed course and disappeared into a rain squall. Her captain did not broadcast a raider warning and was most likely following routine orders to avoid other ships, without realizing the genuine danger. Weyher relented, not wishing to continue the chase, which would almost certainly result in a raider warning.

Weyher decided against operating near Brisbane and the *Orion* headed north-east towards Noumea. The wireless room overheard a RAN signal asking an American steamer if she had seen a missing plane. As this message implied that air patrols now flew 150 miles from the coast, Weyher reflected that 'the decision to remain in the vicinity of Brisbane only for a brief lapse of time proved to be justified'.[13] On 13 August the raider arrived off Noumea and the crew saw the island's mountains and the lights from the town. The Arado flew over the harbour the next day and *Oberleutnant* Winterfeldt spotted four ships alongside the pier and public gatherings in the streets and squares. Weyher learned from radio news that the civil unrest was a Free French protest against the Vichy regime.

In the afternoon of 16 August the lookout spotted a steamer heading towards Noumea and Weyher ordered an intercept course. After sunset the freighter turned to port and her navigation lights indicated that she was most

The French cargo vessel *Notou* was sunk by the *Orion* south-west of Noumea on 16 August 1940. In the right background is the auxiliary minesweeper HMAS *Tongkol*. (AWM: NAVAL HISTORICAL COLLECTION)

likely neutral. When the *Orion* came abeam Weyher signalled 'what ship?' and the freighter replied 'Notou'.

The small 2489-ton steamer *Notou* had departed Newcastle bound for Noumea carrying coal. Captain Louis Jego thought the *Orion* was another freighter until he received an order to stop. He ignored this order but a warning shot persuaded him to obey. The Frenchmen only realized they were dealing with Germans after the boarding party arrived. Although France was ruled by the Vichy regime, Weyher seized the *Notou* since she had departed an enemy port and also because Noumea seemed certain to rally behind the Free French.[14]

Weyher decided to sink the *Notou*, and her crew of thirty-seven sailors and a passenger, Paul Vois, director of the Paris-Noumea Nickel Company, boarded the *Orion*. After demolition charges exploded the freighter refused to sink so the gunners opened fire as Alphonse Villa, a New Caledonian sailor, witnessed:

> Half of the crew was taken over to the German ship while some officers took over the log book, papers etc. The other half of the crew came in the second boat. They locked us in the cabins and hatches and we heard at 2000 the guns firing and were told our ship was sunk.[15]

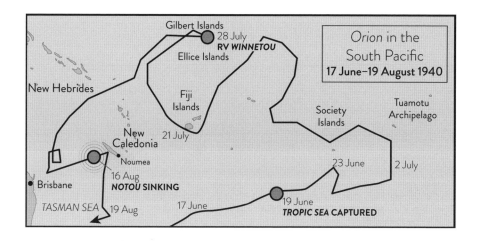

The Germans gave Captain Jego and Vois a cabin and placed the eight officers in another cabin while the men quartered in the hold. Weyher decided to leave the Coral Sea after his wireless room intercepted signals intended for the *Notou*. RAAF Hudsons searched for the *Notou* one week later after she became overdue but found no trace.

THE TASMAN SEA

After entering the Tasman Sea the *Orion* continued south towards New Zealand. On 20 August, while 350 miles west of Wellington, the weather became cold and the sea rough. In the afternoon the lookout spotted a freighter emerging from a rain squall. Weyher planned to slowly overtake her before dark, and as the distance closed a large stern gun became visible. The raider slowly approached the freighter, which frequently disappeared in rain squalls only to reappear a short time later.

The 8706-ton New Zealand Shipping Company freighter *Turakina* had left Wellington for Sydney carrying lead, wheat and wool.[16] Captain James Laird spotted the *Orion* and became suspicious as he had been informed that no other ships would be nearby. He decided to flee and the *Turakina* turned hard to starboard.

The *Orion* followed the *Turakina* and when the distance closed to 5500 metres (6014 yards), Weyher ordered her to stop, but Captain Laird

On 20 August 1940 the *Orion* attacked the New Zealand Shipping Company freighter *Turakina*, in what was the first naval duel in the Tasman Sea.
(AUTHOR'S COLLECTION)

continued to flee. The raider's guns opened fire as the freighter presented a good target, silhouetted against the setting sun. First Radio Officer Sydney Jones broadcast a raider warning, which the Brisbane and Chatham islands stations received.[17]

Captain Laird ordered his 4.7-inch stern gun to return fire and Seaman Mander directed its aim from the top of the foremast. This duel became history's first naval battle in the Tasman Sea. Slater, an engineer, remembered the engagement:

> I think we gave 'Jerry' quite a shock. They tried to blind our gun's crew by turning a searchlight on them. They had no sooner swept the deck with the beam and settled it on the gun than we fired and the Germans switched it off.[18]

The *Turakina*'s stern gun only narrowly missed the *Orion* while the raider's gunners concentrated their fire on the freighter's wireless room, but their first shells missed as the rough seas made aiming difficult. Nevertheless, their shells soon struck the freighter as Slater recalled:

> One shell brought down the fore topmast with the lookout, one hit the bridge, one hit the galley, just forward of the funnel, another burst in our quarters and yet another hit the cadets' house at the roof of the mainmast.[19]

Jones, despite being wounded, continued to broadcast raider warnings until a shell hit the aerial and the radio went dead. The stern gun ceased firing after the foremast collapsed as Mander could no longer direct their aim from his vantage point.

The *Turakina* had been reduced to a blazing hulk. Weyher ceased fire and approached closer but the stern gun resumed firing. The *Orion* returned fire and more shells struck the doomed freighter, but her stern gunners hit the raider's hull. The raider's 20-mm anti-aircraft guns poured rapid tracer fire into the stricken vessel, and by this time half her crew of fifty-seven sailors had been killed. Captain Laird, suffering from head wounds, went to the main deck and ordered his gunners to keep firing, but Third Officer John Mallet reported that his gun could no longer target the raider. Captain Laird reluctantly decided to abandon ship.[20] The two port lifeboats had been destroyed, but the crew lowered a starboard boat, which soon sank. Some sailors placed Jones, now severely wounded, into the last boat while others jumped overboard.

Weyher fired a torpedo, which struck the *Turakina*'s stern without detonating, but a second torpedo hit her hull and exploded. The freighter sank two minutes later. The *Orion*'s only damage was dented camouflage plates.

The *Orion*'s crew rescued fourteen men from the lifeboat. Weyher spent six hours searching for others even though enemy warships would almost certainly be in pursuit and, when some crewmen complained, he scolded them and stated that it was the duty of sailors to rescue others in peril.[21] The high seas prevented the launch from assisting the rescue, but when the crew heard cries for help they dropped a rubber raft attached to a rope overboard to fish survivors from the sea. They saved seven more men before Weyher ended the search close to midnight. However, as the raider departed, the crew heard another cry for help and they rescued a sailor who asked, 'Where are all the hits? We were shooting very well.'[22] The *Orion* fled south at full speed towards the Great Australian Bight.

The crew rescued twenty-one survivors, including seven wounded, who received treatment from Doctor Raffler. When Edward Sweeney boarded the *Orion* he experienced surprise after the Germans gave him hot tea.[23] Thirty-six men had been killed, including Jones, and it is believed that Captain Laird died in the torpedo explosion. Slater explained Captain Laird's reasons for fighting to the bitter end:

Captain Laird had kept the vow he was said to have made that he would fight his ship to the last if he were attacked by a raider. His conduct might be regarded as Quixotic, but Captain Jock Laird was a dour Scot. He had been given a gun with which to defend his ship; he was resolved to use it, no matter what the odds.[24]

Sweeney also remembered the German reaction to their courage: 'Our attackers praised our courage for fighting against overwhelming odds, but considered us mad English.'[25] The next morning Mander died from his wounds and Weyher gave him a burial at sea. Captain Laird and Jones were later commended for good service while Mallet was made a Member of the Order of the British Empire. Jones and Mallet were also awarded the Lloyd's War Medal for Bravery at Sea.

After receiving the *Turakina*'s raider warning, the Australian and New Zealand authorities suspended trans-Tasman shipping and ordered all nearby merchant ships to head to the nearest port. The RAN postponed the departure of troop Convoy US 4 to the Middle East while its escorts, the *Achilles* and *Perth*, hunted the intruder. The *Achilles* departed Wellington and headed towards the *Turakina*'s reported position. The flying boat *Awarua* flew towards the reported location while the *Aotearoa* and Australian Empire flying boats patrolled waters to the north. After the *Achilles* found no sign of the *Turakina*, Commodore Parry headed towards the Three Kings Islands. Naval intelligence staff in Wellington concluded from direction-finding reports that a raider was near Campbell Island and Commodore Parry accordingly headed south; however, in the morning he learned the fix more likely originated from the North Atlantic, convincing him the raider had escaped northwards.[26] The *Achilles* patrolled the approaches to Auckland before returning to Wellington. The 'Tasman Raider' had disappeared.

THE GREAT AUSTRALIAN BIGHT

The *Orion* continued south-west and on 22 August a de Havilland bomber spotted her, circled and flew away without incident. Over the next two days the raider pitched and rolled in the Roaring Forties before rounding

Tasmania, 200 miles south of Hobart, and entering the Great Australian Bight. The raider voyaged through forty-foot waves and a storm that lasted five days. Several patrol planes passed overhead, but the raider remained hidden from sight by rain squalls and low clouds.

On 30 August the *Orion* neared the South Australian coast before turning west towards Albany, Western Australia. Australian radio stations entertained the crew as Weyher remembered:

> When the ship's radio-room had worn out its stock of gramophone records, it turned on the Australian stations. . . . To the men's amazement, it was German folk songs, military marches and classical music, all over again.[27]

No enemy ships had been encountered since the *Turakina*, and Weyher recorded: 'Again and again the shipping-lanes from Capetown to South Australian ports and from Aden and Colombo via Cape Leeuwin to South Australia were crossed without sighting a ship.'[28] However, he decided to transform five steel beer kegs into fake mines to drop in the approaches to Albany.

On 2 September the *Orion* headed towards Albany while the crew prepared the dummy mines by filling the kegs with enough cement to enable them to float just below the surface. They used lead to make horns and each mine contained explosives that would ignite if the horns were touched. As the crew assembled the mines, the roll of the ship caused an engineer to drop a spanner, detonating a mine. The explosion wounded Lambert Harders and Karl Putz. Harders' forearm was blown off and he died from a lack of blood, the first death of a crewman. Putz lost his left eye and a fragment of steel became lodged in his right eye, which the doctors could not remove.

At 2030 h the crew began laying the dummy minefield in sight of the Eclipse Island Lighthouse, 20 miles outside Albany Harbour. After they dropped the mines overboard, the *Orion* fled south-west.

The *Orion* headed towards Fremantle as Weyher intended to approach the port hidden in the bad weather. On 3 September an RAAF Hudson appeared overhead and circled the raider twice while a group of 'civilians' waved at the plane from the deck and the aircraft departed. The Hudson had been patrolling the route of Convoy US 4 and Australian naval authorities correctly assumed the vessel was a raider.[29]

The *Orion*'s radio detection unit picked up six aircraft taking off from Busselton that appeared to be searching for the raider. Weyher, having lost the element of surprise, urgently needed to reach safe waters, but he had 40 miles to cover before his ship would be beyond the range of enemy planes. Shortly before noon an aircraft approached while the raider hid in a rain squall. At midday the crew heard two planes that could not be seen and in the afternoon two more aircraft could be heard, but dense rain concealed the raider. The crew relaxed as the raider proceeded beyond the range of the RAAF.

On 4 September the *Orion*, 350 miles south-west of Cape Leeuwin, headed north-west, deeper into the Indian Ocean. Weyher decided to disguise the *Orion* as an anonymous British freighter. This transformation took five hours and Weyher rewarded this work by slaughtering three pigs, and the crew enjoyed their first fresh meat since leaving Germany, a meal washed down with brandy.

THE DUMMY MINE

On 8 December a fisherman, Frederick Douglas, found a metal object on a beach near Esperance and reported his discovery to the police. Constable John Brown of the Western Australian Police, who was also a coastwatcher, investigated and informed naval intelligence in Fremantle.[30] Constable Brown warned locals not to approach the object, but inquisitive people came to look and two people even scratched their initials on it. Chief Petty Officer Claude Choules and an RAAF photographer arrived from Fremantle to identify the object and Constable Brown drove them to the beach.[31] Choules concluded it was a mine but could not identify the type:

> We were driven to Eleven Mile Beach, where we found the mine and took several photographs. It was not one of our own and I concluded it was German from the serial number: the figure seven was written in the European fashion, with a dash through the stem.[32]

The Naval Board ordered Choules to bury the mine in a secret location pending instructions on how it should be disposed, and he returned one month later and destroyed it with explosives.[33] The public heard nothing about the incident as censorship prevented a local newspaper from publishing a story.[34] Unfortunately for Weyher his dummy mines caused no disruption to shipping, and as a member of his crew had been killed preparing them, it was a high price to pay for no result.

'SHELTERING PLACE A'

On 7 September radio news informed Weyher that the British submarine *Truant* had intercepted his prize ship *Tropic Sea* in the Bay of Biscay. After the submarine challenged the vessel Captain 'Allright' Steinkraus ordered his men to scuttle their vessel. The *Truant* rescued the *Haxby* survivors, Captain Ostberg and his wife, but they left behind the Germans and Norwegians in lifeboats. A Sunderland flying boat rescued the Norwegians the next day, and the Germans later landed in Spain.

The *Seekriegsleitung* ordered the *Orion* to rendezvous with the supply ship *Regensburg* at Ailinglaplap Atoll (Sheltering Place A) in the Japanese-controlled Marshall Islands. The *Komet* also received orders to proceed to Ailinglaplap as did the supply ship *Weser* in Mexico. The *Norddeutscher Lloyd* freighter *Regensburg* had become a raider supply ship in Japan, and she would replenish the *Orion* and provide her with machinery to help overhaul her engines. Charles Noack, a sailor on the *Regensburg*, described preparing for the voyage: 'All this went on with a goodly amount of secrecy, with specific instructions to make no mention to anyone.'[35] On 27 September the *Regensburg* left Yokohama and headed south disguised as a Japanese freighter.

Weyher planned to return to the Pacific via the Great Australian Bight, hoping to intercept enemy shipping south of Adelaide before heading north towards Ailinglaplap. As the *Orion* headed east, the crew assembled on deck and Weyher awarded thirty Iron Crosses, which had been allocated to the raider in recognition of the Hauraki Gulf mining operation. After the raider rounded Tasmania and entered the Tasman Sea, the crew experienced warmer weather, and the prisoners exercised on deck and enjoyed fresh air. The *Turakina* prisoners passed their time playing bridge

A dummy mine, fashioned from a beer keg, laid by the *Orion* and found near Albany, Western Australia, in 1940.
(AWM: NAVAL HISTORICAL COLLECTION)

while Vois taught the *Notou* crewmen star navigation.

On 21 September the *Orion* passed midway between Sydney and New Zealand, and Weyher patrolled the area for five days without any luck. After this disappointment the raider headed towards the Kermadec Islands, arriving there on 27 September when the crew spotted Macauley Island with its large vertical cliff and grassy top, where a hut had been built to provide emergency shelter for shipwrecked sailors.

On the other side of the Pacific, the Canadian armed merchant cruiser HMCS *Prince Robert* captured the *Weser* near Mexican waters. As she had been heading towards Ailinglaplap, the *Seekriegsleitung* feared the rendezvous may have been compromised, and ordered the other ships to instead proceed to Lamotrek Atoll in the Caroline Islands (Sheltering Place Y). The supply ship *Kulmerland* replaced the *Weser* and departed Kobe under the cover of an air raid drill arranged by the Japanese.

Weyher had to first rendezvous with the *Regensburg* in the Marshall Islands to refuel before heading to the Carolines. After passing Santa Cruz, Weyher decided to disguise the *Orion* as the Japanese freighter *Maebasi Maru* and the crew painted characters on the hull copied from a Kodak advertisement produced in Yokohama. On 10 October the raider arrived at Ailinglaplap and rendezvoused with the *Regensburg*. The *Orion* anchored alongside her against a backdrop of white beaches, green jungle and native huts. Doctor Raffler led a shore party on a mission to gather coconuts, the first time any sailors had stepped ashore since the beginning of the voyage. The raider received fuel and other stores, including Japanese beer and cigarettes. The injured sailor Putz transferred to the *Regensburg* so he could undergo surgery in Japan.

The *Orion* and *Regensburg* left the atoll two days later and headed south-east towards Lamotrek. The *Regensburg*, which had greater speed, went ahead and Weyher patrolled nearby shipping routes hoping to intercept fresh victims before arriving at the rendezvous.

On 14 October the *Orion* approached the Carolines and in the pre-dawn darkness the lookout spotted a red light. The ship's peacetime lights indicated she was most likely American or Japanese, but after approaching closer no neutral markings could be seen under the moonlight. Weyher ordered her to stop, but the vessel did not reply. After the raider fired two warning shots, the ship identified herself as the 'Ringwood'.

The 7302-ton Norwegian vessel *Ringwood* had been proceeding from Shanghai to Ocean Island to load phosphate. Captain Alfred Parker believed he had been stopped by a British warship so he lowered a rope ladder for the boarding party. After the men climbed on board the radio operator opened the door to his cabin and the light from inside illuminated the deck. The Norwegians then suddenly realized they were dealing with Germans. Captain Parker surrendered and the boarding party seized his documents and radio. Captain Parker protested but the *Ringwood* had intended to load phosphate bound for the British colony of Jamaica. The *Ringwood*'s thirty-five sailors became prisoners on the *Orion*. Captain Jego and Vois told Captain Parker that they had been prisoners for two months but their treatment had been fair. The boarding party scuttled the *Ringwood*.

The *Orion* chased a steamer the next day, but boiler problems reduced her speed and a disappointed Weyher let her go. He could no longer delay the planned engine overhaul, and the raider continued towards 'Sheltering Place Y'.

OBTAINING INTELLIGENCE

While the *Orion* terrorized the Pacific, 'Section 19' began producing more sophisticated reports on the raiders:

> The raiders are converted merchantmen and probably have a number of characteristics in common. They would appear to be of between 7,000 and 9,000 tons, of the cargo liner type, with a speed of at least 16 knots. They have a heavy armament of two or more 5.5-in. and four or more 4-in. guns, as well as dual purpose pom-poms [20-mm guns] and machine-guns. . . . The guns are very well concealed, and outwardly the raiders present a completely innocent appearance, being disguised as Swedish or other neutral vessels.[36]

The British underestimated their firepower and overestimated their speed. Some of the intelligence had been obtained from the survivors rescued from the *Tropic Sea*.[37] The British also learned more about the raider

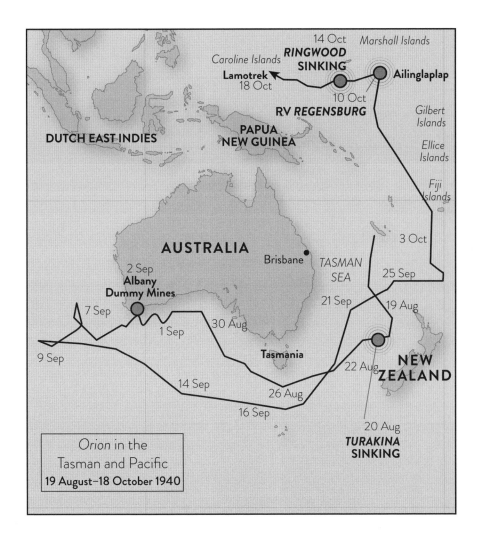

Orion in the Tasman and Pacific
19 August–18 October 1940

supply ships and their relationship with Japan, correctly concluding that the tanker *Winnetou*, now in Kobe, had replenished the *Orion*.[38] Nevertheless, the raiders continued to terrorize the high seas before vanishing and the Allies seemed powerless to stop them.

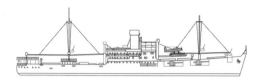

CHAPTER 7
THE FAR EAST SQUADRON

These Nazi prison ships [*Orion* and *Komet*], which masqueraded under Japanese names, were not 'hell ships'. We could not complain of our treatment, but with a crowded ship, food was short. At first, we could not eat the raw bacon or sausage, but it's amazing what you'll eat when you're hungry.[1]

Anonymous Allied prisoner

SHELTERING PLACE Y

After entering the Pacific in September 1940, the *Komet* headed south-west towards Japan disguised as the Soviet freighter *Deinev*. The crew, no longer under the gaze of the Russians, resumed combat training. Strong winds and a nearby typhoon created rough weather, but the raider sustained only minor damage and she set a course towards the Marshall Islands to rendezvous with the *Orion*, *Kulmerland* and *Weser* at Ailinglaplap Atoll (Sheltering Place A).[2] Eyssen decided to disguise his raider as the Japanese freighter *Manyo Maru* because Russian ships did not frequent these waters.

After the *Komet* passed the Mariana Islands on 27 September, Eyssen

In Hamburg, Germany, the cargo vessel *Kulmerland*, which acted as a supply ship for the auxiliary cruisers *Komet* and *Orion* in the Pacific, accompanying them on the raid on Nauru in December 1940. In October 1941 she supported the *Kormoran* in the Indian Ocean.
(AWM: NAVAL HISTORICAL COLLECTION)

learned the rendezvous would now occur at Lamotrek Atoll in the Caroline Islands (Sheltering Place Y) because the *Weser*'s capture had compromised Ailinglaplap. The raider reached the Carolines three days later, but as Eyssen had arrived early, he decided to patrol the Bismarck Archipelago, north of New Britain. The raider headed south and her Arado seaplane flew a patrol mission but crashed into the sea and could no longer fly. After arriving off New Britain, the *Komet* spent several days patrolling the area without success and morale declined.

On 14 October the *Komet* arrived at Lamotrek and the next day rendezvoused with the *Kulmerland*, disguised as the Japanese freighter *Tokyo Maru*, in a lagoon. The *Hamburg-Amerika* freighter had sought refuge in Kobe at the start of the war, where she became a raider supply ship under the command of Captain Wilhelm Pschunder. She replenished the *Komet* with fuel and supplies.

The *Orion*, disguised as the *Maebasi Maru*, and the *Regensburg* arrived at Lamotrek on 18 October. As the two ships approached the lagoon, the lookout spotted the Japanese passenger ship *Palau Maru*. The German ships followed her inside the lagoon where they also sighted the *Komet* and *Kulmerland*. The *Palau Maru* broadcast an unreadable signal and passengers began photographing the German vessels.

The *Palau Maru* left the lagoon, but a short time later a Japanese sailing ship arrived and anchored alongside the *Komet*. A Japanese official boarded the raider and declared that Japan would not tolerate any infringement of her neutrality. Eyssen claimed that the German vessels were blockade runners on their way home but had stopped to exchange fuel and supplies. He explained that the Japanese markings were only intended to deceive the Royal Navy before stating that Germany and Japan were allies under the Tripartite Pact.[3] Furthermore, he produced authentic Japanese port clearance documents from the *Kulmerland* and *Regensburg* and the official departed, seemingly satisfied.

Weyher proposed to Eyssen that the *Orion* and *Komet* should operate together because, given the poor state of his engines, he would find it difficult to conduct cruiser warfare alone and this problem would be negated if both raiders worked together. Eyssen agreed and the *Seekriegsleitung* gave them permission to operate together until the end of 1940. The *Kulmerland* would also accompany the raiders as a scout ship.

When the *Regensburg*'s crew visited the *Komet*, Charles Noack asked to transfer to the raider:

> I was very surprised, and might I say, deeply moved, and momentarily emotionally put off balance by the camaraderie of the raider's crew, not only towards us but also among themselves. Equally impressive to me was the discipline and orderliness of the crew. Oh yes, I wanted to be part of that.[4]

Noack enlisted in the *Kriegsmarine* and joined the *Komet*'s crew along with other sailors from the *Regensburg*.

Eyssen, as the senior officer, named the small flotilla the 'Far East Squadron' in honour of Maximilian von Spee's cruisers from World War I. On 20 October the squadron departed Lamotrek and headed south, while the *Regensburg* headed north towards Yokohama. After arriving seven days later, *Konteradmiral* Wenneker, the naval attaché, thanked the crew for their efforts. Crewman Putz from the *Orion*, who had been injured in the dummy mine explosion, disembarked and, after undergoing surgery, recovered.

THE *RANGITANE* INCIDENT

The Far East Squadron headed south-west towards the New Zealand–Panama route in a line-abreast formation with the *Komet* to port, *Orion* to starboard and *Kulmerland* in the centre. The *Kulmerland* set the course and speed and at night the ships closed to visual distance to prevent accidental separation.

Weyher, worried about the photographs taken by the *Palau Maru* passengers, decided to alter the *Orion*'s disguise. The crew gave her a new coat of black paint, replaced the false deckhouse concealing the No. 5 gun with a false hatchway and lengthened the forecastle.

The squadron proceeded south between New Hebrides and Fiji. On the evening of 3 November the *Orion*'s lookout spotted a ship 250 miles north-west of the Kermadec Islands. Weyher signalled 'what ship?'. After receiving no reply he fired a warning shot and the vessel replied 'City of Elwood'. The searchlights revealed a freighter with a large American flag painted on her hull. The Germans relented and the neutral *City of Elwood* continued her voyage and broadcast a suspicious ship signal, but Eyssen saw a positive side as 'the fact that it is known that a German auxiliary cruiser is operating here will cause added anxiety'.[5]

The squadron spent four days patrolling waters 400 miles east of New Zealand without success, so the Germans decided to patrol the Wellington routes.[6] The squadron reached the Chatham Islands on 24 November without encountering any ships and Eyssen proposed attacking the enemy phosphate industry on Nauru. Weyher agreed and the squadron turned north.

On 25 November the *Komet*'s lookout sighted a ship in the pre-dawn darkness. The small 546-ton New Zealand steamer *Holmwood* had left Waitangi bound for Lyttelton with a cargo of sheep and wool. The *Komet* approached and a warning shot persuaded Captain James Miller to stop, and a boarding party captured the steamer without resistance. The Germans found the *Holmwood*'s code-books and divided the sheep between their ships, a welcome addition of fresh meat. The incident restored morale, as it was the first time the *Komet* had encountered the enemy. Eyssen scuttled the steamer and as she had not broadcast a distress signal, the Allies knew nothing about the German presence so close to New Zealand.

The *Holmwood*'s crew of seventeen sailors and twelve passengers, including four women and five children, began their new lives as prisoners on the *Komet*. Chief Engineer Abernethy recalled boarding the raider:

> We had to climb a rope ladder which was quite an ordeal for the ladies. We were met on deck by the complete ship's company, had our photos taken by many of the sailors. The children were drawn up in a basket very frightened, but they soon picked up courage and the German sailors were very kind to them, giving them chocolate and biscuits.[7]

Eyssen interrogated Captain Miller who later spoke highly of the Germans:

> I must say that during interrogation the officers of this ship were in every way exceedingly considerate, and conducted the whole proceeding in a most gentlemanly manner. At 7.30 p.m. I was taken along to interview the Commander [Eyssen] who expressed his regret at having had to sink my ship, but said it was a matter of war, and that as a seaman and gentleman, he trusted no personal ill-feeling existed.[8]

The squadron continued north towards Nauru. At 0300 h on 27 November the *Orion*'s lookout spotted a ship 300 miles north-east of East Cape, but in the dark rain she only appeared as a large shadow. The *Kulmerland* withdrew to allow the raiders to deal with the situation. Weyher and Eyssen believed they had encountered an enemy cruiser due to the vessel's large size and, as there seemed little hope of escape, they decided to attack.[9] The *Orion* slowly approached the suspected cruiser while the *Komet* approached from the opposite direction. After the *Orion* switched on her searchlights, Weyher saw a passenger liner with two stern guns and small anti-aircraft guns.

The 16,712-ton liner *Rangitane* owned by the New Zealand Shipping Company had left Auckland three days earlier bound for Liverpool via the Panama Canal carrying butter, pork, mutton, cheese, cocoa beans and forty-five bars of silver. On board were around 200 crew and 111 passengers, including thirty-six women, fifteen New Zealand Fleet Air Arm recruits and eighteen RNZAF airmen. After the bridge officers sighted two approaching vessels, they summoned Captain Lionel Upton, who arrived in his pyjamas, and he ordered full speed and a change of course away from the *Orion*.

As the *Rangitane* attempted to escape, both raiders fired warning shots. The liner's wireless operator Norman Hallett broadcast a raider warning and after the *Orion*'s signallers overheard this message, Weyher decided to open fire. The *Orion*'s first salvo struck the liner's stern, damaging the wireless room, and shells from the *Komet* severely damaged her steering and engines. After the crew repaired the main transmitter, Hallett signalled a raider warning, which shore stations in New Zealand acknowledged.

The *Rangitane*'s stern guns did not return fire because Captain Upton, knowing that his warnings had been received, feared pointless loss of life.[10] Two passengers, Betsy Sandbach and Geraldine Edge, British Red Cross nurses, described coming under attack:

> Suddenly there was a shattering noise as the first salvo of shells hit our side of the ship. Above the din of falling glass and the noise as the cabin walls fell in, rose a woman's piercing scream, and in the pitch dark a man called out pitifully, 'Can anybody come and help me? My arm is blown off.'[11]

Captain Upton decided to abandon ship: 'The bridge was wrecked, and the blazing glare of searchlights which were focused on us in the dawn made range-finding almost hopeless.'[12] The *Rangitane* came to a halt but as the raiders continued to fire, Captain Upton signalled that women and children were on board and the shooting ceased.

Weyher and Eyssen sent boarding parties to the *Rangitane*, which discovered an Admiralty report containing an accurate description of the *Orion* complete with a silhouette drawing. Weyher correctly guessed this information came from the *Tropic Sea* survivors. The boarding party took control of the evacuation and the liner's crew placed the wounded in lifeboats and lowered them into the water. Mertens observed the arrival of new prisoners on the *Komet*:

On 27 November 1940, some 300 miles north-east of East Cape, the *Orion* attacked the liner *Rangitane*, bound for Liverpool via the Panama Canal. On board were around 200 crew and 111 passengers, including thirty-six women.
(AUTHOR'S COLLECTION)

Most of the passengers were still in night attire, the women wrapped in blankets and overcoats over their negligees, and they were very cold and shaken. We did our best to cheer them up, but the *Komet* must have looked very grisly at first sight. The day before we had slaughtered 200 sheep that we took off the *Holmwood*, and our decks were still littered with blood, guts and scraps of hides and bones. It wasn't a pretty sight after the scenes in the *Rangitane*. Perhaps some of the passengers thought we were in the habit of massacring our prisoners.[13]

Elizabeth Plumb, a stewardess, attended to the female passengers despite being wounded, and guided passengers from their quarters to the lifeboats. Once on board the *Komet* she refused medical attention until others had received treatment. After she fainted, the doctors discovered her body had been riddled with splinters.[14] Plumb later received the British Empire Medal and Lloyd's War Medal for Bravery at Sea. William Francis, a cook, also received these medals for rescuing two women from their burning quarters

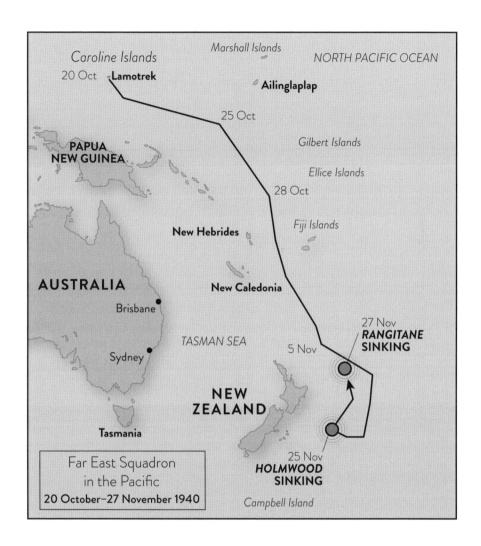

Far East Squadron
in the Pacific
20 October–27 November 1940

and helping a wounded passenger to a lifeboat, as did John Walker, a mechanic, for assisting two sailors to a lifeboat while under fire and saving a sailor after their lifeboat capsized.[15]

The Germans had no time to salvage the *Rangitane*'s cargo as they knew her signals had been received. As soon as the passengers and crew had been rescued, the *Komet* torpedoed the burning liner and finished her off with gunfire. The *Rangitane* capsized to port and vanished beneath the waves.[16]

After naval authorities in New Zealand received the *Rangitane*'s distress signals, the cruiser *Achilles* left Lyttelton and proceeded towards the reported position, while the armed merchant cruiser *Monowai*, on passage from Suva to Nauru, diverted towards the location. The minesweeper *Puriri* departed Auckland to search for survivors loaded with blankets, food and other supplies.

Since the sinking occurred outside the range of RNZAF aircraft, the flying boat *Aotearoa* took off from Auckland and searched until dark without seeing anything. After the *Awarua* arrived in Auckland, she took off in the early afternoon but also had no luck. The *Aotearoa* flew over the *Rangitane*'s location the next day and spotted an oil slick and debris, and the *Achilles* later found butter boxes and lifebelts.[17] The cruiser searched for survivors before heading towards North Cape to patrol the approaches to Auckland and the *Puriri* returned to Auckland. Once again raiders had terrorized New Zealand waters before vanishing.

PACIFIC PRISON SHIPS

The Far East Squadron fled north-east at full speed. The *Orion*'s lookout sighted a low-flying plane that evening and Weyher noted that 'the aircraft, in spite of good visibility through the light haze, had not seen the ships against the dark surface of the sea'.[18] This aircraft must have been the flying boat *Aotearoa* or the *Awarua*.

The *Orion* had ninety-two new prisoners, including sixteen women. The guards escorted Sandbach and Edge to their new quarters below the waterline. A few hours later an officer seated at a table interrogated the female prisoners, asking questions about their voyage and general shipping information. The interrogator asked Sandbach and Edge if they had heard anything about German raiders: 'One of our number replied to this question that we'd heard a good deal about a certain *Graf Spee* at one time, but he took the retort well and only laughed, saying "That was a long time ago".'[19] Not all the interrogations occurred in this manner. While under shock and after drinking whisky, the New Zealand Fleet Air Arm men described their bases and organization and the guards found a diary on an airman explaining how the RNZAF had been reorganized after the sinking of the *Niagara*.[20]

Doctor Raffler visited the *Orion* prisoners to patch up minor wounds, and asked the four nurses to help care for the wounded in the hospital. After they agreed he gave them a pack of cards to ease their boredom.

Miss Herbert-Jones, who had been returning home after evacuating British children to New Zealand, had been badly wounded with a splinter in her back, which tore one of her lungs. Raffler did all he could for her but she died. And another wounded prisoner, Seaman Dan Hantley, also died of his wounds. The *Orion* stopped for a burial service and the prisoners gathered on deck with the *Kriegsmarine* flag at half-mast. Sandbach and Edge recalled the service:

> Lined up on one side of the deck were roughly about one hundred and fifty sailors. They looked smart in clean white uniforms, and stood stiffly to attention in two rows; black ribbons from their caps floated in the breeze and bore the name *Krieg-Marine* in gold letters. In a long line in front of them stood some sixty officers, immaculate in dark uniforms, and all wearing grey gloves.[21]

During the service Weyher read the eulogy:

> We regard Miss Herbert-Jones as having fallen in the service of her country, just as a soldier falls with his arms in his hand. We regard her parting as a death of sacrifice such as that of many thousands of soldiers who have shed their life-blood for their country and their people. . . . We shall now place the deceased in the hands of our element, the eternal sea.[22]

A group of Polish stewardesses among the prisoners had been accommodated in the *Orion*'s middle deck without ventilation, making their conditions hot and damp. Weyher noted their attitude:

> Some of them lay all day on their hammocks, spread out on the floor, scorning the normal routine of a ship, doing no chores. For the guard-duty, whom the mixed effluvia of this compartment kept outside the doors, the more refined of these ladies showed their sympathy by presenting them their naked behinds.[23]

The squadron stopped so the prisoners could be more evenly distributed between the three ships. Most military prisoners boarded the *Komet* where they received toothbrushes, soap, towels and cigarettes. The guards gave them chess sets and books while senior officers received deckchairs and many prisoners spent their time playing card games. Abernethy began to admire the guards: 'The German officers are very decent chaps, always asking after our comfort, really we are surprised at their kindness.'[24] The female prisoners on the *Orion* boarded the *Kulmerland* where they found life less uncomfortable, although they could walk outside at certain times and play deck tennis. The guards also told them that they were being careful not to repeat the 'hell ship' *Altmark* public relations scandal. As the squadron continued north the prisoners waited to see what fate intended for them.

CHAPTER 8
THE AUSTRALIAN MINEFIELDS

For 12 months many Australians have regarded the war as being somewhat remote. These disasters on our shores have brought the war very near. There is, however, no cause for public alarm. The Navy has the matter well in hand, and with its characteristic thoroughness is leaving nothing to chance.[1]

Robert Menzies
Prime Minister of Australia
11 November 1940

THE *STORSTAD*

After the *Pinguin* terrorized the waters near Madagascar, Krüder planned to mine Australian waters, but his schedule had been delayed by the need to prepare his prize vessel *Nordvard* for her voyage to Europe. Therefore, he could not conduct the operation during the new moon period in late September 1940, but he would have another opportunity in late October. In preparation, Krüder and his navigator *Kapitänleutnant* Michaelson studied charts of Australian ports and developed a daring plan to conduct six co-ordinated mining operations that would throw shipping into total chaos.

However, the plan hinged on the need to complete all the minefields and escape before ships started to sink, a difficult endeavour as the mines could only be set with a 48-hour delay before being armed. Therefore, Krüder needed to capture another vessel to use as an auxiliary minelayer.

The *Pinguin* continued east across the Indian Ocean towards Australia, passing the Tropic of Capricorn. The mechanics assembled the spare Heinkel as Krüder wanted daily reconnaissance flights to maximize his chances of finding a minelayer, but over the next few days the seaplane failed to spot any other ships. During this quiet period the crew spent their free time reading books and watching films. Krüder created a recreation room with comfortable chairs where eight men at a time enjoyed one week's leave, being free from all duties except action stations.

After failing to find any victims Krüder headed towards Java, hoping to capture his prize on the Sunda Strait route. His search ended on 7 October after the lookout spotted a tanker south of Christmas Island. Krüder ordered her to stop. The unarmed 8998-ton Norwegian tanker *Storstad* had been proceeding from Borneo to Melbourne. Captain Egil Wilhelmsen obeyed Krüder's order and the boarding party captured the tanker without incident, finding the thirty-six Norwegian sailors to be highly co-operative.

The *Storstad* would make a suitable minelayer as she was expected in Australian waters and, as a tanker, would arouse less suspicion because the Allies were on the lookout for suspicious freighters. Krüder renamed her *Passat* (Trade Wind). The two ships arrived in isolated waters between Java and Australia, where the crew transformed the tanker's accommodation area into a mine deck and loaded her with 110 mines.

Krüder placed *Oberleutnant* Warning in command of the *Passat* with a prize crew of three officers and seventeen sailors, while five Norwegian volunteers ran the engine room. On 12 October the ships parted company and Krüder signalled: 'Auxiliary minelayer Passat proceed in execution of previous orders. Best of luck. Auf Wiedersehen.'[2] Warning replied: 'Message received. Thanks! Good luck to you, too. Orders will be carried out as instructed.'[3]

The *Pinguin* planned to approach the east coast via the Great Australian Bight before mining the approaches to Newcastle, Sydney, Hobart and Adelaide, while the *Passat* would mine Bass Strait between Tasmania and the mainland.

Members of the German prize crew on the Norwegian tanker *Storstad*. On 7 October 1940 the *Pinguin*, travelling east across the Indian Ocean, captured the tanker. *Kapitän* Krüder renamed her *Passat* and planned to use her to mine Bass Strait. (AUTHOR'S COLLECTION)

THE AUSTRALIAN OPERATIONS

The *Pinguin* entered the Great Australian Bight and continued east before rounding southern Tasmania. After entering the Tasman Sea she headed north before turning south-west on 28 October. That night Krüder planned to mine the approaches to Port Stephens, Newcastle and Sydney. The raider approached the coast during a dark, cloudy night. The crew saw the lights from Port Stephens and the Newcastle Lighthouse, and Krüder expressed 'surprise at seeing Newcastle and its navigational aids so well lit'.[4] At 2013 h the first mine dropped into the sea near Catherine Hill while Michaelson plotted the course, using the lighthouses as beacons, and soon ten mines had been dropped overboard.

The *Pinguin* approached closer to shore and laid ten mines west of Catherine Hill while the searchlights from Newcastle and Sydney illuminated the night sky. The raider turned west towards the Norah Head Lighthouse, and the men dropped another ten mines overboard, completing the Newcastle minefields. After Krüder set a southeasterly course towards Sydney at 14 knots, the *Pinguin* laid ten mines in the approaches to Sydney,

Prisoners on the foredeck of the captured Norwegian tanker *Storstad* being transported to France.
(AUTHOR'S COLLECTION)

directly east of Broken Bay, shortly before midnight. The raider fled south-east and soon the searchlights from Sydney could no longer be seen. The *Pinguin* headed towards Tasmania where Krüder planned to conduct his second mining operation in the approaches to Hobart.

On the night of 31 October the *Pinguin* rounded Tasmania and approached Bruny Island near Hobart in poor visibility and misty rain.[5] Doctor Werner Hasselmann observed the natural beauty of these waters:

> The sky was a little misty, but more colorful than we had ever seen it before on our voyage. Flashes lit up the horizon, and a blood-red sunset was reflected under thin white layers of cloud. The flashes of lightning seemed to conjure up arches, domes, and dizzy towers in the twilight.[6]

At 1900 h the lookout sighted the Cape Bruny Lighthouse and Krüder ordered action stations. An hour later Cape Bruny came into view and the crew saw searchlights on both sides of D'Entrecasteaux Channel. As the *Pinguin* approached, direction-finding equipment detected a patrol vessel inside Storm Bay and Krüder continued with increased caution. At 2120 h

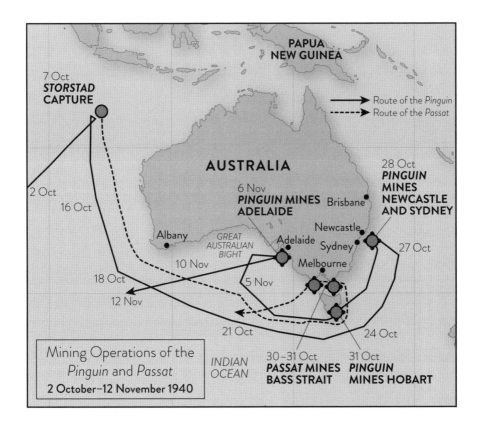

7 Oct
STORSTAD
CAPTURE

→ Route of the *Pinguin*
---→ Route of the *Passat*

PAPUA
NEW GUINEA

AUSTRALIA

28 Oct
PINGUIN
**MINES
NEWCASTLE
AND SYDNEY**

2 Oct

16 Oct

6 Nov
PINGUIN MINES Brisbane
ADELAIDE

Newcastle
Albany *GREAT
AUSTRALIAN
BIGHT* Adelaide Sydney
10 Nov Melbourne 27 Oct

18 Oct 5 Nov

12 Nov

21 Oct 24 Oct

Mining Operations of the
Pinguin and *Passat*
2 October–12 November 1940

INDIAN
OCEAN

30–31 Oct
PASSAT MINES
BASS STRAIT

31 Oct
PINGUIN
MINES HOBART

Mining Operations of the *Pinguin* and *Passat* 2 October–12 November 1940

the men dropped the first mine of the Tasmanian minefields in the entrance to the channel, and soon fourteen mines had descended into the sea.

The *Pinguin* headed east towards Storm Bay before turning north-east towards the coast, and laid sixteen mines south-east of Hobart, 6 miles from shore, under the gaze of two searchlights. After midnight the raider passed Port Arthur and laid ten mines near Fortescue before heading west towards Spencer Gulf, Adelaide.

On 3 November the *Passat* signalled Krüder, informing him that she had successfully completed her mission. The minelayer had passed Cape Leeuwin on 17 October before proceeding east through the Great Australian Bight. After rounding Tasmania she turned north towards Banks Strait, between Tasmania and Clarke Island. Warning struggled through bad weather and rough seas to reach his target area on schedule. On the night of 29 October the *Passat* headed north without flying a flag. Warning stood on the bridge dressed as a Norwegian captain, passing many ships and fishing boats while *Oberleutnant* Karl Schmidt and his men prepared their mines. After passing Eddystone Point, the minelayer turned north-west towards Banks Strait and laid five mines south of Cape Barren Island and twenty-five in the strait.

On the following night the *Passat* entered the eastern entrance to Bass Strait, the gateway to Melbourne, and laid ten mines north-east of Deal Island and another ten mines north of the island. Shortly after midnight the men dropped another ten mines overboard east of Cliffy Island. The minelayer headed west and, as she approached the Wilson's Promontory Lighthouse, a lamp from the naval signal station inside asked 'what ship?'. Warning replied: 'Tanker Storstad, Norwegian, from Miri to Melbourne.'[7] The lighthouse men had been expecting the *Storstad* earlier and commented on the bad weather, which presumably delayed the tanker. After this exchange the *Passat* laid ten mines south of the lighthouse.

On 31 October the *Passat*, after passing Melbourne, approached Cape Otway, the western entrance to Bass Strait. At night she laid five mines south of the cape and five mines south of Wattle Hill before turning south-west and releasing twenty more mines. Warning and his men saw lights from houses and passing cars but witnessing complacent normality made them homesick. At midnight the *Passat* dropped her last ten mines and escaped into the Great Australian Bight.

The *Pinguin* meanwhile approached Spencer Gulf, the gateway to Adelaide. On 6 November she approached the coast on a northerly course and waited for nightfall before proceeding east towards South Neptune Island. Michaelson used the South Neptune and Kangaroo Island lighthouses as beacons, while the raider dropped thirty mines off Cape Spencer and ten mines near Investigator Strait before escaping south-west. The *Pinguin* and *Passat* had laid 230 mines in Australian waters without arousing suspicion, but the minefields would not remain hidden for long.

THE WAR REACHES AUSTRALIA

On the night of 7 November the 10,846-ton Federal Steam Navigation Company freighter *Cambridge* proceeded towards Sydney from Melbourne carrying tin. While rounding Wilson's Promontory, an explosion rocked the

The Federal Steam Navigation Company's steamer *Cambridge*, which was sunk on
7 November 1940 by a mine laid by the *Passat* off the Victorian coast. The *Pinguin* and
Passat had laid 230 mines in Australian waters.
(AWM)

freighter after it struck a mine from the *Passat*. Captain Angell decided to
abandon ship:

> I was not shaken by the explosion, neither was anyone else who was
> amidships, but the stern of the ship was lifted up and started to go
> down immediately. It was very dark and very little could be seen, but
> some of the crew said afterwards that a considerable amount of water
> was thrown onto the deck.[8]

The *Cambridge* sank thirty minutes later. John Kinnear, a carpenter, drowned
after returning to his cabin to collect £30 that he had recently won in the
Melbourne Cup. The remaining fifty-seven crewmen boarded three lifeboats
and reported the sinking by lamp to the Wilson's Promontory Lighthouse.
The Naval Board warned all nearby ships to avoid the area due to possible
mines.[9] The minesweepers *Warrego*, *Swan*, *Orara* and *Durraween* proceeded

towards Bass Strait. The *Orara* rescued the *Cambridge* survivors and landed them at Welshpool.[10] The *Orara* and *Durraween* later sank two mines with rifles. The *Warrego* and *Swan* discovered two mines near Cape Otway while the *Beryl 11* and *Goorangai* swept the waters near Melbourne.

On 8 November the 5883-ton American Pioneer Line freighter *City of Rayville* proceeded towards Melbourne from Adelaide carrying lead, wool and copper. At 1930 h she struck a mine from the *Passat*, 6 miles south of Cape Otway. Captain Arthur Cronin decided to abandon ship. The vessel's forward section sank almost immediately, but her stern floated for about forty-five minutes before disappearing beneath the waves. The *City of Rayville* was the first United States ship sunk during the war and an engineer, James Bryan, became the first sailor to die on an American ship during the conflict. The men at the Cape Otway Signal Station witnessed the freighter sinking in the fading light, and fishing boats from Apollo Bay rescued thirty-seven survivors from their lifeboats. The *Warrego*, *Swan* and *Orara* arrived the next morning and discovered German mines.[11]

The Naval Board closed Bass Strait and declared the waters 30 miles from Wilson's Promontory and Cape Otway danger areas. The busy coastal steamers, a major means of civilian transportation, were confined to port as *The Argus* announced:

> Officials of Bass Strait passenger shipping services said last night that all services had been suspended until further notice. Passengers who had booked aboard the steamers would be permitted to cancel bookings and fly across [the strait].[12]

Bass Strait reopened on 14 November, but the *Kriegsmarine* had shut down a major focal point on the other side of the world for over a week. As the Bass Strait mines had been laid in busy waters without any alert being raised, Australia suffered a major humiliation.

THE RAIDER HUNT

The RAN initiated a raider hunt for the suspected minelayer and HMAS *Canberra*, *Perth* and *Adelaide* searched for the intruder while RAAF aircraft patrolled coastal waters. The failure to find the enemy prompted the RAAF to reassure a worried public:

> . . . it is impossible to ring the 12000 miles of Australia's coastline with a cordon of 'sky cavalrymen' through which a stray raider may not at times break. Taking advantage of dull or stormy conditions, a 'drop-it and run' raider may sneak through, but it must run the gauntlet of air-force patrols which have maintained a ceaseless watch since war broke out.[13]

Maritime patrols continued without success until 13 November. As the RAAF seemed powerless, the *Daily Telegraph* criticized the state of the air force:

> The mining of a British freighter and an American ship in Bass Strait is final and disastrous proof of the inadequacy of our coastal patrols. . . . Why wasn't the enemy minefield in Bass Strait discovered until after two valuable ships had been lost? The answer is that the tireless men of the R.A.A.F. simply cannot efficiently patrol because they haven't enough suitable planes.[14]

Growing public fears increased calls for continuous air patrols and Navy Secretary Alfred Nankervis explained to his Minister, William 'Billy' Hughes, the impossibility of such a proposal:

> A continuous patrol is the most uneconomic means of defence known, and it could only be done by diverting considerable forces from the offensive on which our victory must rest . . . the numbers involved are out of all proportion to the threat against which it is required to guard.[15]

Air Chief Marshal Charles Burnett, Chief of Air Staff, explained to the War Cabinet that at least 500 aircraft would be required to continuously patrol Australia's focal shipping areas. He also stated that only occasional patrols could be carried out due to other demands, but the lack of success could also be attributed in part to inexperienced crews and ground staff. The RAAF accordingly revised its reconnaissance methods based on the experience gained by RAF Coastal Command.[16]

The sinking of the neutral *City of Rayville* had diplomatic consequences, and the American Consul-General Albert Doyle reassured the Australian Government that American vessels would not be prohibited from trading in Australian waters. Prime Minister Menzies ensured the shipwrecked Americans received immediate relief and the sailors Cronin, Hart, Brooks and Thomas expressed their gratitude:

> Since the time of our rescue by the fishermen of Apollo Bay, through our stay at the Ballarat Hotel at Apollo Bay, and since our arrival in Melbourne, we have received every consideration and courtesy from our Australian friends. We cannot adequately express our deep appreciation of this kindness.[17]

Nobody in Australia could be certain how the mines had been laid, and press speculation included stories about mysterious submarines and phantom ships. Commander Long, Director of Naval Intelligence, believed neutral ships from nations friendly to Germany might have been responsible. Therefore, he organized searches of neutral vessels in Australian ports by Customs officials and disguised RAN intelligence officers, and these unfortunate men spent one year searching in vain for hidden mines.

THE MINEFIELD LEGACY

On 20 November 1940 the minesweeper *Goorangai* sank after colliding with the liner *Duntroon* and her full complement of twenty-four sailors perished. The minesweeper had been sheltering from bad weather in Port Phillip after conducting operations in Bass Strait. After departing she proceeded through the South Channel but the *Duntroon*'s lookout did not see her until it was too late. The *Goorangai* became the first RAN surface ship lost with all hands and the first RAN vessel lost during the war.

On 5 December the small 1052-ton coastal steamer *Nimbin* of the South Coast Steam Navigation Company headed to Sydney from Coffs Harbour.

The Australian cargo vessel *Nimbin*, which was sunk off Sydney on 5 December 1940 after hitting a mine laid by the *Pinguin*.
(AWM: NAVAL HISTORICAL COLLECTION)

She struck a mine from the *Pinguin* off Port Stephens about 8 miles from the coast. The explosion tore off her stern and she sank in less than five minutes, killing Captain William Bysantson and seven sailors. The twelve survivors found themselves in the water clinging to debris before the steamer *Bonalbo* rescued and disembarked them in Sydney.

The Naval Board closed the Port of Newcastle and suspended all voyages along the Sydney–Newcastle route. Five RAAF aircraft from Richmond patrolled the coast looking for an enemy minelayer and the minesweepers *Uki* and *Tongkol* swept the area.

On 7 December the 10,923-ton Federal Steam Navigation Company freighter *Hertford* proceeding to Adelaide from Fremantle struck a mine south-west of Cape Catastrophe in the Spencer Gulf. The blast disabled her engines and water flooded two holds. Captain Tuckett decided to abandon ship and a distress message reported their position. One lifeboat with key personnel followed the drifting ship and the three others headed for Neptune Island, landing safely the next day. At daybreak Captain Tuckett and the men in his lifeboat reboarded the *Hertford* and saved their ship. The tugboats

Wato and *Woonda* towed her to Port Lincoln and, although there had been no casualties, the *Hertford* remained out of commission until January 1942.

The Naval Board ordered all vessels to avoid the area and suspended nearby shipping. The *Warrego*, *Swan* and *Orara* swept the area and RAAF aircraft from Richmond, Laverton, Pearce, Darwin, Townsville and Archerfield patrolled coastal waters, searching for a long departed enemy.

On 4 January 1941 the *Warrego* discovered the Tasmanian minefield off Storm Bay near Hobart, resulting in the closure of Port Hobart. The Naval Board ordered all vessels to avoid the nearby channels, and minesweeping operations off Tasmania focused on clearing the channels.[18]

In early 1941 the undiscovered mines began breaking away from their moorings. The Bass Strait mines started to wash ashore near Cape Otway and the mines from the Newcastle–Sydney fields drifted north, mostly coming ashore on the Queensland coast. The minesweepers hurried from one area to another, causing a heavy strain on their crews. Passing merchant ships also destroyed many floating mines with rifles, and sailors from Rendering Mines Safe parties destroyed mines that had washed ashore.

On 26 March the tiny 287-ton trawler the *Millimumul*, while fishing off the New South Wales coast, struck a mine from the *Pinguin* and sank one minute later. Master Rixon and six sailors died, but the collier *Mortlake Bank* rescued five survivors from a lifeboat. The sinking occurred in an area that had been swept and it is likely that the mine's anchor had sunk into a depression and not been detected by minesweepers but later got caught in the *Millimumul*'s fishing nets.

On 14 July 1941 William Danswan and Thomas Todd, two RAN sailors from a Rendering Mines Safe party, died after a mine exploded at Beachport, south-east of Adelaide. The men had attempted to detonate it but their charge failed to explode. After waiting the required fifteen minutes, they proceeded to investigate, but it exploded as they approached. Danswan and Todd became the first servicemen killed in action on Australian soil and they were the final casualties from Krüder's mines, which claimed forty-three lives.

Five mines from Australia washed ashore in New Zealand. On 18 October 1942 Master Dawson on the fishing vessel *Britannia* found the first such mine in Pegasus Harbour on Stewart Island. Dawson tied a rope around it and dragged it up the rocks where a naval party led by Lieutenant Neale destroyed it. Minesweeping operations in Australian waters continued until 1946 and, in total, RAN minesweepers destroyed ninety-eight German mines.[19]

CHAPTER 9
THE INDIAN
OCEAN PURSUIT

As one seaman would another, both doing their duty to their country.
Krüder, in fact, did what he could for us — it was not much as there
seemed to be several Nazi officers amongst his men — but he showed
no bitterness toward us saying that his time would come someday.[1]

Captain Harry Steele
Prisoner on the *Pinguin*

WEST OF FREMANTLE

After their mining operations the *Pinguin* and *Passat* triumphantly
rendezvoused 750 miles west of Fremantle on 15 November 1940. The
ecstatic crews celebrated their spectacular success by drinking schnapps, and
the *Seekriegsleitung* declared their operation to be 'outstanding in its planning,
preparation and execution'.[2] *Grossadmiral* Raeder awarded fifty-five Iron
Crosses for Krüder to award at his discretion.

As the *Passat*'s engines were in a poor condition, Krüder decided against
transferring his seventy remaining mines to her for an envisaged minelaying
mission off India. Instead he would use the tanker as a scout ship, and she
again became the *Storstad*. *Oberleutnant* Warning returned to the *Pinguin* while

After mining Australian waters, the *Pinguin* (pictured), along with the *Passat* headed into the Indian Ocean in November 1940.
(AUTHOR'S COLLECTION)

eighteen Germans and twenty Norwegian volunteers remained on board and *Oberleutnant* Levit took command.

Krüder had time to hunt fresh victims before his planned sortie into Antarctic waters to attack enemy whalers. The *Pinguin*'s engines needed an overhaul and the mechanics achieved this without stopping by servicing one engine while the other propelled the raider at a cruising speed of 10 knots.

The *Pinguin* and *Storstad* proceeded deeper into the Indian Ocean. On 17 November the lookout spotted a freighter and within an hour the mechanics had both engines operating and the raider's speed increased to 15 knots. The freighter disappeared into the emerging darkness of a moonless night, but not long afterwards reappeared as a silhouette against the night sky. Krüder manoeuvred the *Pinguin* into an attack position and ordered the freighter to stop and fired a warning shot.

The 7920-ton British India Steam Navigation Company freighter *Nowshera* had been proceeding from Adelaide to Durban carrying zinc, wheat and wool with a crew of 113 men, mostly Lascars (East Indian seamen). Captain Collins, completely surprised by the *Pinguin*'s sudden appearance, had not expected a raider in these remote waters. Fifth Engineer Bellew and Cadet Simpson ran towards the 4-inch stern gun but Captain Collins, hoping to save lives, ordered them to stand down.[3] The *Nowshera* stopped and a boarding party led by Warning arrived. After inspecting the stern gun he expressed surprise at the surrender, especially since sandbags and steel plating had been installed in the bridge and wireless room. Before scuttling the freighter, the prisoners transferred to the *Pinguin*, but Second Engineer Philip tragically fell into the sea and drowned.

The *Pinguin* proceeded south-west while work on her engines continued. On the afternoon of 20 November the lookout spotted another freighter and, after the mechanics got both engines functioning, the raider approached at 14 knots, but the freighter suddenly changed course. Krüder did not pursue his prey as her radio remained quiet and she appeared to be following routine orders to avoid other ships. Instead, he planned to use his Heinkel to tear down her radio aerial. After the freighter disappeared, *Oberleutnant* Werner took off in the seaplane with *Oberleutnant* Walter Müller in the observer's seat.

The 10,123-ton British freighter *Maimoa* had been proceeding from Fremantle to Britain carrying steel, frozen meat, butter, wheat, textiles and eggs with a crew of eighty-seven sailors. Captain Herbert Cox spotted smoke and immediately suspected a raider and changed course, but did not broadcast a raider warning because he was not certain. After the smoke disappeared he felt safer, but a short time later he spotted a seaplane.

Werner flew over the *Maimoa* and unsuccessfully attempted to tear down her radio aerial with a grappling hook. On his next pass Müller dropped a weighted package containing a message: 'Stop your engines immediately. Do not use wireless, in case of disobedience you will be bombed and shelled.'[4] Captain Cox ignored this threat and his wireless broadcast a raider warning.[5] Werner dropped two bombs close to the freighter and her crew opened fire with rifles and a Lewis gun. The Heinkel circled and returned fire wounding sailors John Gillies and Malcolm Maclean. Werner finally tore down the aerial on his next pass. Captain Cox meanwhile spotted the *Pinguin* and altered course to the south-east. An epic chase had begun.

After gunfire damaged the Heinkel's fuel tank, Werner made an emergency landing. He expected the *Maimoa* to come towards him but the freighter passed by while men on the deck stared at the seaplane and one sailor waved. Apprentice Saddington climbed the funnel and rigged a spare aerial and the wireless resumed broadcasting raider warnings. One message included a description of the raider: 'Black Hull white band short funnel short topmasts.'[6]

Krüder could not spare the time to rescue Werner and Müller but sent a launch to stay with the seaplane. The *Storstad* meanwhile reported by radio that another ship had been sighted 10 miles away. At 1645 h the *Pinguin's* guns came within range and her salvos landed close to the *Maimoa*. As the freighter's 4-inch stern gun lacked the range to return fire, Captain Cox decided to abandon ship. Krüder ceased fire and a boarding party captured the freighter. The crew transferred to the raider and Krüder scuttled the *Maimoa* as she did not have enough coal to reach Europe. Despite the drama of the air attack there had been no fatalities on the freighter. Krüder recovered the Heinkel and rescue launch early the next day. Werner went below to the prison quarters to shake hands with the men who had fired at him and to congratulate them on their survival.[7]

After Perth Radio received the *Maimoa's* raider warning, the cruiser HMAS *Canberra*, which had been in Fremantle preparing to escort Convoy US 7, departed to hunt the intruder. Captain Harold Farncomb decided to investigate north-west of the *Maimoa's* reported location, believing the raider was heading towards the Cape Town–Singapore route.[8]

THE *PORT BRISBANE*

The 8739-ton Port Line freighter *Port Brisbane*, 60 miles north-east of the *Maimoa*, intercepted her raider warning. The freighter, armed with two 6-inch stern guns and one 3-inch anti-aircraft gun, was proceeding from Adelaide to Britain with frozen meat, butter, cheese and wool. Captain Harry Steele ordered a northerly course and doubled the watch. After the lookout sighted a tanker at 1700 h, he considered her to be harmless and she vanished over the horizon.[9] The vessel was in fact the *Storstad* and Levit shadowed the *Port Brisbane*, keeping out of view and signalling Krüder sighting reports. Captain Steele spotted smoke that disappeared and reappeared throughout the day, but concluded it came from a tramp ship. After sunset the freighter turned west towards Africa and Captain Steele felt safe enough to reduce his watch.[10] One hour later Fourth Officer Armitage reported the sudden appearance of a vessel and called Captain Steele to the bridge.

The *Pinguin*, guided by the *Storstad*, had approached the *Port Brisbane* on a parallel course, keeping her smoke just in sight. After sunset the overcast weather and moonless night hid the raider, and she manoeuvred ahead of the freighter before reducing speed to approach in silence. When the distance narrowed to just under a mile the raider's crew switched on their searchlights and readied their guns.

The *Pinguin* fired a warning shot across the *Port Brisbane*'s bow. Krüder ordered her to stop and a second warning shot followed. Captain Steele, however, ordered full speed and the stern gunners ran to their weapons while Wireless Operator Magee broadcast a raider warning: 'Port Brisbane suspicious vessel firing shots at us.'[11] Shore stations soon acknowledged his signals. The raider's guns opened fire and the first salvo struck the freighter. Captain Steele ordered his gunners to stand down:

> I soon realised it was useless having men at the guns, the first movement by anyone to load the guns the cruiser would have blown men and guns off the deck, so I called everybody away to safety. The Cruiser then concentrated his fire on the bridge, setting fire to same.[12]

A shell hit the wireless radio room, killing Magee, but the *Canberra* had received his signals and Farncomb changed course towards the action at 26 knots, dramatically increasing his chances of intercepting the *Pinguin*.

Shells pounded the *Port Brisbane* and fires raged across her upper deck and, with no hope of escape, Captain Steele decided to abandon ship. The doomed freighter stopped and the crew lowered three lifeboats. The *Pinguin* rounded up two lifeboats, capturing fifty-nine sailors and a female passenger, Nora McShane, who had been returning home to Africa after visiting relatives in Sydney. A friend had warned her against the voyage, but she insisted that the *Port Brisbane* was a 'lucky ship'.[13] The boarding party scuttled the freighter.

The third lifeboat commanded by Second Officer Edward Dingle escaped in the darkness after he convinced the twenty-six men on board to attempt an escape. Krüder searched for the missing lifeboat, partly on humanitarian grounds but also to leave no witnesses behind who could describe his raider. He gave up before daybreak and fled the area. Krüder told Captain Steele that he ended the search because a radio report indicated that an enemy cruiser was approaching.[14]

In the morning the men in Dingle's lifeboat found themselves alone on the open sea and Dingle formulated a plan:

> When daylight came I fixed our position and proposed that we make for Australia although in the prevailing wind conditions we had not much hope of getting there. That afternoon we decided to take advantage of the favourable winds and make for Mauritius instead. I warned the men to make up their minds to undertake a passage of about forty days.[15]

Dingle first searched for possible survivors and found the two empty lifeboats in the debris field, allowing them to redistribute themselves across three boats. He also found mail bags:

> In the bags we discovered parcels which contained small bottles of sauce pickles, Christmas puddings, chocolates and other edibles destined for Australian soldiers overseas. I know the Aussies, and know they would pardon the liberty taken with the gifts destined for them.[16]

The *Canberra* soon arrived, rescued the men and unsuccessfully searched the area before returning to Fremantle on 27 November.

THE SISTER SHIP

After sinking the *Port Brisbane*, Krüder decided to raid the Fremantle–Cape Town route before heading south towards Antarctica. The mechanics conducted engine work and the men painted the raider's hull and superstructure black.

On 30 November the *Pinguin* headed west and shortly before midday Krüder received a sighting report from the *Storstad*. The tanker had been scouting ahead of the raider when her lookout spotted a freighter 500 miles north of the Kerguelen Islands. Krüder decided to investigate and six hours later the lookout spotted smoke. He kept the smoke just in sight with the intention of striking at night without warning to destroy the wireless room. Krüder had long abandoned any fantasy of fighting a gentlemanly 'prize war' as silencing enemy radios demanded ruthless action. The raider

Seen from the cruiser HMAS *Canberra* (not visible), a lifeboat with survivors of the merchant vessel *Port Brisbane*, sunk by the *Pinguin* the previous day, comes alongside on 22 November 1940 in the Indian Ocean.
(AWM: NAVAL HISTORICAL COLLECTION)

followed the smoke until sunset and after dark no peacetime lights appeared, indicating the ship was enemy.

The 8301-ton freighter *Port Wellington*, the *Port Brisbane*'s sister ship, had been proceeding from Adelaide to Britain carrying meat, butter, cheese, steel, wheat and wool. The freighter was armed with two 6-inch stern guns and one 3-inch anti-aircraft gun. On board were eighty-two crewmen and seven female passengers, Salvation Army personnel returning to Britain after helping to evacuate children.

Upon realizing the *Port Wellington*'s identity, Krüder called Captain Steele to the bridge to inform him of his intention to sink her. Captain Steele replied that his brother-in-law, Chief Officer Bailey, was on board. He quietly hoped Bailey and the crew would survive the coming encounter.

After the distance closed to less than a mile, the *Port Wellington* suddenly turned hard to port as Fourth Officer Gilham had spotted the *Pinguin*'s silhouette. Krüder ordered his gunners to open fire and their first salvo hit the wireless room and the steering gear, causing large flames to rise against the night sky. First Radio Officer Arthur Haslam died before he could

Survivors from the *Port Brisbane* on board HMAS *Canberra* in the Indian Ocean,
23 November 1940.
(AUTHOR'S COLLECTION)

broadcast a raider warning and shrapnel wounded Captain Emrys Thomas'
leg. Bailey assumed command as flames reached the bridge. The explosion
had also forced a stern gun overboard and destroyed the anti-aircraft gun.
Bailey decided to abandon ship and the eighty-one surviving sailors and
seven passengers became prisoners on the raider. Captain Steele experienced
much relief after being reunited with Bailey.

Nurse MacLean, a passenger, attended to Captain Thomas' wounds but
he died on the *Pinguin*. The quartermaster Jim Waggott remembered his
death:

> Later that day we were informed of the death of our skipper Captain
> E.O. Thomas despite the very good medical attention he had received
> in the German ship's hospital bay. He was buried at sea the following
> day with full naval honours.[17]

Krüder had no time to transfer the *Port Wellington*'s cargo so he scuttled the
freighter and the *Pinguin* fled southwards.

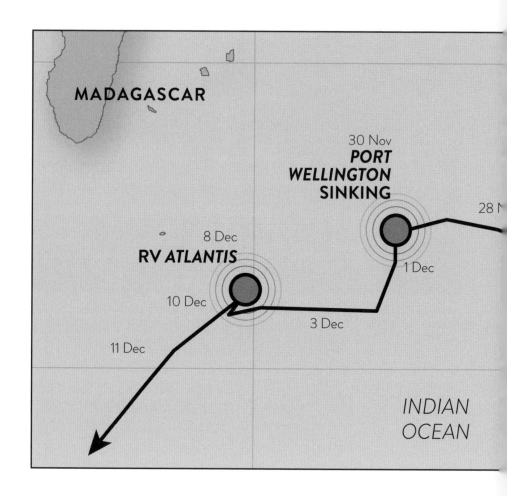

'TULIP'

Krüder decided to transport his 405 prisoners to France on the *Storstad* and signalled the *Seekriegsleitung*: 'Am detaching prize Storstad on course with orders to make for point Andalusia in Atlantic.'[18] Rogge in the *Atlantis* overheard this message and requested fuel from the *Storstad*. The *Seekriegsleitung* accordingly ordered Krüder to rendezvous with the *Atlantis* at 'Tulip', 900 miles south-east of Madagascar. On 7 December the *Pinguin* arrived and after the *Atlantis* appeared the next day, Krüder organized his men along the deck in their summer dress uniforms, but formality gave way to cheering. Krüder boarded the *Atlantis* as Rogge remembered: 'Krüder came on board — the first German outside my own ship's company to set foot on our decks

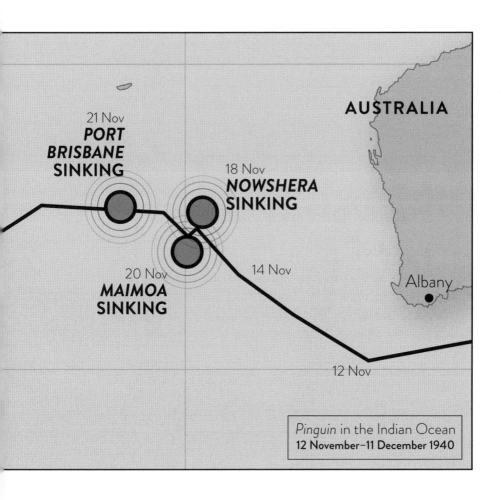

21 Nov
**PORT
BRISBANE
SINKING**

AUSTRALIA

18 Nov
NOWSHERA
SINKING

14 Nov

Albany

20 Nov
MAIMOA
SINKING

12 Nov

Pinguin in the Indian Ocean
12 November–11 December 1940

after three hundred days at sea. There was a tremendous reunion between our crews.'[19]

Rogge invited Krüder to his wardroom where they opened champagne. Rogge showed Krüder a captured map of the Admiralty's secret wartime routes.[20] At the same time both crews mingled to enjoy comradeship, food and drink. Rogge visited the *Pinguin* and gave Krüder a set of Antarctic charts, which had been captured on the Norwegian tanker *Teddy*, that indicated safe routes around Bouvet Island and would be extremely valuable to Krüder as he planned to enter those waters. While on the *Pinguin*, Rogge received a signal from Raeder: 'To Atlantis. Commanding Officer has been awarded Knight's Cross of the Iron Cross. I offer captain and crew my warmest congratulations on this recognition of the outstanding success achieved by the ship.'[21] Rogge's achievement caused the celebrations to begin anew on both raiders.

Rogge transferred 124 prisoners to the *Storstad* and the *Atlantis* received fuel, food and water. Krüder's prisoners also boarded the tanker. On 9 December the *Pinguin* departed and Krüder signalled the *Storstad*: 'Pleasant voyage and many thanks for everything. You have been our best prize to date.'[22]

THE VOYAGE OF THE *STORSTAD*

The *Storstad* headed towards Europe with 524 prisoners under the command of *Oberleutnant* Helmut Hanefeld. Krüder had given him a captured bottle of King George V whisky for luck and letters from the crew to their loved ones. The tanker had a prize crew of twenty Germans but Norwegian volunteers ran the ship, allowing the Germans to concentrate on guard duty. Hanefeld promised to do all he could to help the Norwegians return home, a vow he later kept.[23]

Overcrowding on the *Storstad* made life far worse compared with the raiders. In the forward hold 300 men used one toilet and slept on ropes laid on the floor. The Germans segregated the captains below the bridge, the female prisoners in the hospital and the Lascars in an aft compartment. The guards rigged the prison quarters with explosives and warned the prisoners that any attempt to take the ship would result in scuttling. They also set up two machine-gun positions on the bridge and carried rifles and grenades at all times.

The prisoners could exercise on deck for thirty minutes every second day. They received only one cup of water each day and vitamin pills every eleven days, but the guards gave each man a bottle of beer at Christmas. Apprentice John Smith from the *Port Wellington* recalled an aborted mutiny: 'There were two mad Australians up forward, and they were all for storming the bridge. There would have been terrible carnage.'[24]

The *Storstad* travelled far to the south to avoid the shipping routes and in the Antarctic cold one prisoner died of pneumonia. James Mason from the *Port Brisbane* remembered the voyage:

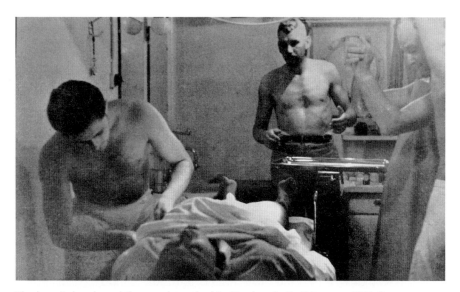

The hospital on board the naval supply ship *Nordmark*. On 6 January 1941 the
Storstad rendezvoused with the *Thor*, *Scheer*, *Nordmark* and *Duquesa* at 'Andalusia',
200 miles north-west of Tristan da Cunha.
(AUTHOR'S COLLECTION)

> There were 260 of us in this dungeon and we were battened down
> in semi-darkness for most of the voyage. They fed us and treated us
> as though we were dogs. Two tubs were made available for washing
> purposes but more often than not the men drank the water to try and
> quench their thirst.[25]

On 6 January the *Storstad* rendezvoused with the *Thor*, *Admiral Scheer*, *Nordmark*
and *Duquesa* at 'Andalusia', 200 miles north-west of Tristan da Cunha. The
Thor had recently sunk two freighters in the South Atlantic before engaging
the armed merchant cruiser *Carnarvon Castle* south of Rio de Janeiro on
5 December. After the raider opened fire at 12,800 metres (14,000 yards),
twenty-three shells struck the *Carnarvon Castle*, forcing her to retreat to
Montevideo with thirty-two dead and eighty-two wounded. The pocket
battleship *Scheer* had left Germany on 14 October on a mission to attack
North Atlantic convoys. After sinking the freighter *Mopan*, the raider attacked
Convoy HX 84 in the North Atlantic on 5 November, sinking the armed
merchant cruiser *Jervis Bay* and six merchant ships.

The *Storstad* refuelled the naval supply ship *Nordmark*, which had been assigned to support the *Scheer*. The prize tanker received eggs and beef from the prize ship *Duquesa*, a refrigerated freighter captured by the *Scheer*, resulting in a massive improvement to the prisoners' diet. The tanker departed the next day. Hanefeld kept the hatch covers open to improve conditions in the holds and allowed the prisoners on deck more frequently. Second Officer Buchan from the *Port Wellington* accurately plotted the *Storstad*'s course and correctly predicted she was heading for Bordeaux.[26]

The voyage continued without further incident until the *Storstad* reached the Bay of Biscay, when a Sunderland flying boat circled overhead. The Germans placed a Turkish flag across the deck and signalled meaningless messages until the plane disappeared and the tanker reached Bordeaux on 4 February.[27]

The Germans transported the prisoners to transit camp *Front-Stalag 221*, north-west of Saint Médard-en-Jalles, and news of their arrival reached home as *The Argus* reported:

Victor Raymond Jones, of Bakewell, Derbyshire, 15-year-old deckboy on the **Port Wellington**, which was sunk by a raider in the Pacific five months ago, has written to his mother that he is safe in a civilian internment camp in France. He asked for parcels, and said the menu was soup, coffee, and bread, so 'a few titbits would be very nice'.[28]

Ernest Howlett from the *Maimoa* planned an escape by digging tunnels and hoarding rations from French Red Cross parcels. However, on 11 March the guards told the prisoners that they would be leaving for Germany in the morning. Believing escape would be easier in France, Harper, Howlett, Ross Dunshea from the *Maimoa* and Robert Bellew from the *Nowshera* decided to escape from the train. After the prisoners boarded, the escapees discovered an unlocked door in their carriage. All four men jumped from the train as it slowed at a bend near Blois.[29]

The escapees travelled south-east through the woods, avoiding a nearby German Army camp before heading towards the border with Vichy France. They slept at night and travelled during the day to reduce suspicion. As the group passed through Blois, they crossed a guarded bridge over the

Loire alongside a party of French workers without being challenged by the Germans. In one village a German officer greeted them and in another a French policeman, realizing their identity, escorted them through the area. On 15 March the escapees reached the border and they eventually arrived in Spain via Marseilles with the help of sympathetic Frenchmen. At the British Consulate they met another escapee, Harry Rabin from the *Port Wellington*. The five men prepared a detailed report on their experiences, which was circulated around Allied naval circles, attracting great interest as it described the *Atlantis*, *Pinguin* and *Storstad*.[30]

CHAPTER 10
NAURU AND THE PHOSPHATE SHIPS

We are a very sorry crowd today. We are still all here, seem to be hanging about we think Nauru. . . . We cannot understand these ships hanging around after the slaughter here yesterday. . . . This all seems like a bad dream; it can't be possible that all this is going on.[1]

Chief Engineer Abernethy
Prisoner on the *Komet*

THE NAURU PLAN

After sinking the *Rangitane*, Eyssen became obsessed with attacking Nauru, an island in the north-eastern corner of the Australia Station and a centre of phosphate production, an industry vital for the supply of fertilizer. Nauru had been a German colony, but the Treaty of Versailles conferred her upon the British Empire. Australia became responsible for the island's administration, while control of the phosphate trade was vested in three commissioners from Britain, Australia and New Zealand. Under the League of Nations mandate military bases could not be established, so Nauru was undefended.

The British Phosphate Commission operated its own fleet of four vessels — the *Triadic*, *Triaster*, *Triona* and *Trienza* — but chartered vessels also frequented the island. As Nauru had no harbour, vessels would normally be moored off the island waiting to load phosphate from cantilevered jetties. Nauru produced almost a million tons of phosphate each year, so Eyssen's obsession had a sound foundation.

On 28 November 1940 the Far East Squadron neared the Kermadec Islands and Eyssen ordered a direct course towards Nauru. Weyher suggested taking the longer route through the Coral Sea as it would allow more opportunity to sink shipping but Eyssen, as the commander, overruled his advice. Eyssen planned to attack the ships near Nauru and a landing party would destroy the island's infrastructure.[2]

The squadron continued north, passing between New Caledonia and New Hebrides. After passing the Solomon Islands on 5 December, Eyssen declared his intention to land all prisoners on Nauru, but Weyher strongly argued that too many of them had valuable knowledge and insisted that only non-white prisoners should be released.

THE ATTACK

The squadron approached Nauru disguised as Japanese freighters. On the morning of 6 December the *Orion*'s lookout spotted a ship. The 4413-ton phosphate steamer *Triona* headed towards Nauru from Newcastle carrying food and piece goods.[3] Weyher concluded she would arrive at the same time as the squadron and, to prevent this, the raiders adopted an intercept course. The *Orion*, whose engines struggled to get beyond 10 knots, approached from the south under the cover of rain and the *Komet* headed north to cut off her escape. The *Triona* unknowingly became caught between both raiders.

After the *Triona*'s lookout spotted the *Orion*, Captain Hughes believed she was another phosphate ship, although he could not understand her changes in course. After the *Komet* fired a warning shot, the *Triona* attempted to broadcast a distress signal but the raider's wireless jammed this with a fake Japanese message. Both raiders fired salvos and several shells struck the freighter, which soon stopped, and her crew lowered lifeboats, as passenger Lorna Adams remembered:

The British cargo vessel *Triona*, which escaped an encounter with the *Orion* in the South Coral Sea on 10 August 1940, only to be sunk by that ship and the *Komet* on 6 December 1940 off Nauru.
(AWM: NAVAL HISTORICAL COLLECTION)

> I climbed down into the lifeboat which had been launched. . . . Our captain had got the radio of our distress away. He blew three blasts from our loved ship and reversed the engine and stopped her. As the blasts rang out — to me — it sounded like some stricken creature.[4]

A boarding party from the *Komet* captured the *Triona* and torpedoes from both raiders sank the steamer. Three men had been killed while sixty-one sailors and passengers, including six women and a child, became prisoners on the *Orion* and *Kulmerland*. On the *Orion* Doctor Raffler examined the prisoners before guards escorted them to their quarters, where they were given bread, jam, coffee, cards and cigarettes. Adams recorded her impression of the guards:

> The sailors themselves seemed to be merely boys. They were very kind and courteous to us. Their lives, too, had much sadness. They all spoke fair English. One fine looking fellow about 30 told us his wife had been killed in a bombing raid on her home town in Germany.[5]

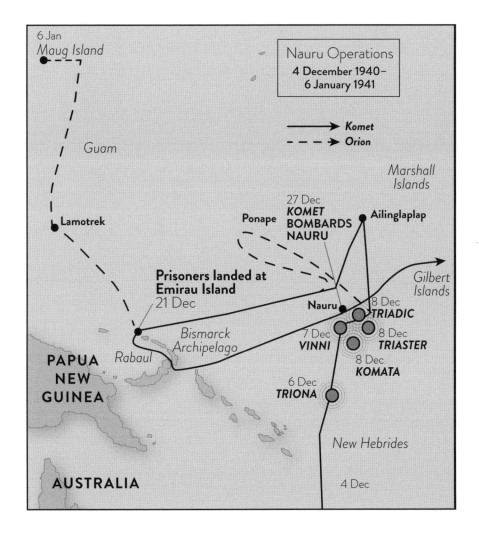

Weyher remembered the arrival of two prisoners; a mother and her eighteen-year-old daughter:

> At first they were genuinely afraid of the *Orion*, through the evil reputation which the ship had been given, but they soon discovered that they were being treated not merely correctly, but with real consideration, and they lost their reserve. They were particularly interested in what German women were wearing, and whether it was

all true about long skirts and no make-up. In the end the only way that their curiosity could be satisfied was by unearthing some copies of the smart set's monthly magazine *Die Dame*.[6]

The *Komet* proceeded ahead to investigate the waters closer to Nauru. On 7 December high seas and heavy rain prevented the seaplane from flying. At 1800 h observers on Nauru sighted a ship 4 miles offshore, but poor visibility prevented identification and the Harbour Master Anderson and the Nauru Administrator Lieutenant-Colonel Chalmers concluded that she must be a Japanese ship and took no action.[7]

At 1833 h the *Komet*'s lookout spotted the 5181-ton Norwegian vessel *Vinni*. After departing Dunedin she arrived off Nauru and had been drifting, waiting for calm weather to load phosphate. Captain Helmer Hendricksen spotted the *Komet* and noted the Japanese markings on her hull but, as she approached at high speed, he became suspicious and changed course. When the distance closed to 1½ miles the *Komet* ordered her to stop. Captain Hendricksen ordered his crew of thirty-one men to abandon ship and the raider captured the steamer without incident. After the Norwegians boarded the *Komet*, Eyssen scuttled the *Vinni* and since no warning had been broadcast, the remaining vessels around Nauru remained unaware of the approaching menace.

On 8 December the *Komet* and *Orion* rendezvoused. Eyssen reported that no ships were moored at the loading buoys but three ships had been spotted north-east of the island. The *Komet* would patrol north of Nauru while the *Orion* and *Kulmerland* would approach from the south, and both raiders would simultaneously attack any shipping at first light. Eyssen abandoned the plan to land a shore party due to bad weather.

At 0330 h the *Orion*'s lookout spotted a well-lit ship and the raider adopted an intercept course and the men soon sighted a second ship. Weyher maintained his course and closed the distance to 1300 metres (1420 yards) before signalling 'what ship?'. The 6378-ton phosphate ship *Triadic* had been drifting off Nauru waiting for the weather to improve. Captain Joseph Callender ignored the *Orion*'s signal while three RAN sailors, Enscoe, Mollross and Read, readied their 4-inch stern gun.

Weyher fired a warning shot and the *Triadic* switched off her lights and fled. After the *Orion*'s searchlights exposed her stern gun, Weyher ordered his gunners to open fire and their first salvo struck the *Triadic*, bringing down her derricks. Three more salvos pounded the freighter, destroying her wireless room and igniting fires. Seaman Ferguson witnessed the destruction:

> The lights had failed, the floor was covered with broken metal and fittings; the stairway to the saloon was a mass of smoke with a glow of fire at the bottom and the piercing scream of a woman passenger to the accompaniment of explosions on the port side.[8]

Captain Callender decided to abandon ship as 'the use of our gun could have resulted only in unnecessary loss of life'.[9] A Filipino sailor, Simeon Jiminez, had been killed and a boy, Jimmy Langer, had been slightly injured. After the *Triadic* stopped the crew lowered two lifeboats and the men rowed towards Nauru. As the *Orion* had to deal with the second ship, the *Kulmerland* captured the survivors.

The 6032-ton phosphate ship *Triaster* had been drifting off Nauru. Captain Rhoades heard gunfire and saw a ship on fire in the darkness and a second vessel. He correctly concluded that the *Triadic* had fallen victim to a raider so he switched off the lights and ordered full speed. At dawn, after losing sight of the suspected raider, a ship appeared astern, but he incorrectly guessed she was the *Triona* heading for safety.

The *Orion* opened fire without warning and her first salvo destroyed the *Triaster*'s radio mast. After three more salvos Captain Rhoades opted to abandon ship: 'I decided that there was no point in carrying on with a probably heavy loss of life, so I stopped *Triaster* and ordered everyone into the boats.'[10] The *Orion*'s boarding party searched the *Triaster* and scuttled the vessel.

The *Komet* had witnessed the shelling but Eyssen kept his distance to avoid friendly fire. Afterwards the raider captured some *Triadic* survivors from a lifeboat, including Chief Officer Low, who asked Eyssen why he opened fire without warning, and Eyssen replied: 'You were on an armed ship and I treat you as a warship. Why do you carry passengers on your ship with a gun on?'[11] The new prisoners included fourteen officers, nineteen Chinese, twenty-seven Filipinos and three passengers.

The 3900-ton phosphate ship *Komata*, owned by the Union Steam Ship Company, had arrived at Nauru two days earlier. Captain Walter Fish became concerned when his wireless operator reported unusual signals between Nauru and Ocean Island. He then sighted two ships about 1½ miles away; one appeared to be Japanese. He ordered full speed and hard to port.

The *Komet*'s lookout spotted the *Komata* and Eyssen ordered her to stop, but Captain Fish instructed Wireless Officer Ward to broadcast a warning which the raider's signallers attempted to jam. The Nauru and Ocean Island radios received the signal, but the message only stated that a raider was attacking a ship without any name, position or details. The Ocean Island wireless operator prepared to relay the message to Suva, but the *Komet* sent out a fake cancellation using the *Komata*'s call sign, which satisfied suspicions on Ocean Island and Nauru.[12] Weyher recalled his deception: 'The *Komet*'s wireless operator adroitly insinuated himself into this conversation and managed to reassure both islands that all was well, whereupon Nauru went so far as to apologise for getting panicky.'[13]

The *Komet*'s salvos struck the *Komata*, causing considerable damage and putting her radio out of action. The shells also destroyed the bridge, killing Chief Officer Tim Mack, while Captain Fish and several crew members received wounds. Fish decided to abandon ship and after the evacuation Ward found himself the only man on board. He entered the chartroom and threw a bag of confidential books overboard but failed to locate the key to the safe. The boarding party later removed the safe and discovered the *Komata*'s code-books.[14] Ward was later awarded the Lloyd Medal for Bravery at Sea. Thirty-two survivors became prisoners on the *Komet*, but Second Officer Hughes died on board and Eyssen gave him a burial at sea. Captain Miller from the *Holmwood* observed the arrival of Captain Fish:

> Captain Fish, master of the *Komata*, came on board looking very dishevelled and dressed like a No. 1 pirate — black silk handkerchief around his neck, old grey shirt with many small holes caused by splinter, khaki shorts and knee-high sea boots. He was showing very distinct signs of shell shock and excitement — quite understandable as he had been blown from his bridge to the decks below.[15]

The boarding party placed demolition charges in the *Komata*'s engine room, and after they exploded the ship remained afloat so the *Komet*'s gunner sunk the freighter. Seaman Ferguson from the *Triadic* witnessed her last moments:

> Very slowly she listed more and more, until the bottom appeared, then with a graceful and grand farewell, she slid down from sight with a fountain of spray blowing through the hole in her bottom. It was an awe-inspiring sight, such as I hope never to witness again and I remember wondering what thoughts passed through the mind of the 'Komata' Master, Captain Fish, as he stood in front of me and watched his ship make her last voyage to a watery grave.[16]

The *Orion* meanwhile finished off the *Triadic*. Her deck had been burned away and her phosphate cargo burned red hot, causing great clouds of steam. Weyher fired a torpedo, but after the explosion the proud ship refused to sink. Demolition charges placed by a boarding party eventually sank the *Triadic*. Nurses Sandbach and Edge from the *Rangitane* witnessed the sinking:

> During the afternoon the doctor asked if we would like to see a British ship sinking. Several of us peeped through his porthole. There was a small cargo-boat a number of yards away, ablaze fore and aft, sinking slowly. On the deck outside sat two German officers, gloating over the 'victory' that seemed so puerile and inglorious.[17]

On Nauru the weather had obscured the fighting, but the authorities could see the burning wreck of the *Triadic* and the *Komet* and *Kulmerland*, which they still believed was Japanese. Nauru's wireless operator tried without success to contact the ships before requesting all nearby Japanese ships to report. Two hours later Lieutenant-Colonel Chalmers signalled Australia that two Japanese vessels had been seen next to a burning ship and that contact had been lost with the phosphate ships.[18]

After visibility improved in the late afternoon, the authorities witnessed a vessel shelling another ship and the Nauru radio informed Australia.[19] In response the Naval Board ordered ships at or bound for Nauru and Ocean Island to disperse and make for Suva or Port Moresby, but nothing else could be done given the absence of nearby warships.[20]

The attack off Nauru was a major triumph for the *Kriegsmarine* as Eyssen and Weyher had sunk five ships, and the *Seekriegsleitung* noted: 'The operations on 7th and 8th December have earned recognition by reason of their systematic planning and execution. The combined efforts of several ships led to increased results.'[21] Weyher and Eyssen both fired salvos without warning because they feared enemy radios and, as the level of violence at sea escalated, the gentlemanly conduct of 'prize warfare' seemed a distant dream.

CHAPTER 11
HILFSKREUZER KORMORAN

How many times had I read descriptions of the exploits of such vessels [auxiliary cruisers] in the First World War and become enthusiastic at the way they did the job, cut off from the fleet and all its resources, completely on their own on the high seas! And I had been deeply impressed by the knowledge and skill of their commanders, the burden of responsibility that rested on their shoulders, and the courage and reliability of the men.[1]

Kapitän Theodore Detmers
Commander of the *Kormoran*

KORVETTENKAPITÄN DETMERS

On 4 June 1940 the *Scharnhorst*, *Gneisenau* and *Admiral Hipper* with four destroyers departed Kiel under the command of *Admiral* Wilhelm Marschall to bombard British positions around Narvik, but the evacuation from Norway prompted a change of mission and the force now hoped to intercept enemy troop convoys. On 8 June the Germans spotted the tanker *Oil Pioneer* and the armed trawler *Juniper*. The *Hipper* sank the *Juniper* before concentrating fire on the *Oil Pioneer* and Marschall ordered the destroyer *Hermann Schoemann* to finish off the crippled tanker.

Korvettenkapitän Theodore Detmers, commander of the *Hermann Schoemann*, was born on 22 August 1902. After joining the *Reichsmarine* in April 1921, he served on the battleships *Hannover* and *Elsass*, the sail training ship *Niobe* and the cruiser *Berlin*. He later worked in the Personnel Department in Berlin. In 1937 he became the executive officer on the destroyer *Leberecht Maass* before taking command of the *Hermann Schoemann*.

Detmers manoeuvred his destroyer towards the *Oil Pioneer* and sank her with a torpedo. The German force later sank the liner *Orama*, and the *Hipper* and destroyers headed home as they were running low on fuel.[2]

The *Hermann Schoemann* arrived in Wilhelmshaven on 17 June and as the crew prepared to take shore leave, Detmers received a telephone call from the Personnel Adjutant of Station North informing him that he would take command of 'Ship 41'. Detmers asked what this meant, but the adjutant replied that he would receive further orders in Hamburg. Detmers boarded the night train for Hamburg and after arriving became thrilled to discover that 'Ship 41' was an auxiliary cruiser. At thirty-eight years of age Detmers became the youngest raider captain.

THE SECOND WAVE

In mid-1940 *Grossadmiral* Raeder proudly briefed Hitler on the success of his 'first wave' of auxiliary cruisers:

> Two auxiliary cruisers [*Atlantis* and *Pinguin*] are in the Indian Ocean, one [*Orion*] is in Australian waters, one [*Thor*] is in the South Atlantic, one [*Widder*] in the Middle Atlantic; one [*Komet*] is outward bound via the northern route, and is now in the vicinity of the Bering Straits. . . . There are strong indications of concern on the part of the enemy, who is not in a position to carry out extensive search activity.[3]

Raeder also prepared his 'second wave' of raiders. The first ship selected, the 9400-ton *Hamburg-Amerika* freighter *Steiermark*, became 'Ship 41', officially a *Sperrbrecher* pathfinder. The *Steiermark* was launched in 1938 and *Hamburg-*

Captain Theodor
Detmers, Knight's Cross,
Iron Cross (First Class),
Commander of the
Kormoran.
(AWM: T. DETMERS)

Amerika intended her to serve on their Far East service, but she had only finished her first trials when war broke out.

In March 1940 dockyard workers in Hamburg began converting the *Steiermark* into a raider in an atmosphere of strict secrecy. The workers built a special corridor to enable the crew to quickly reach their action stations and additional tanks could store an extra 5200 tons of fuel, enabling her to cruise for a year before refuelling. Her holds contained two Arado seaplanes and a *Leichte Schnellboot* (light speedboat).

Detmers arrived and took charge of the conversion process. Fearing that major alterations would delay the voyage for months, he tended to overlook minor imperfections.[4] He had no say in selecting the twenty-six officers and 375 sailors assigned to his raider. Around 100 crewmen had been *Hamburg-Amerika* sailors, including all the engine-room personnel. The well-prepared crew quarters provided each sailor with an individual cabin containing a

ABOVE The 9400-ton *Hamburg-Amerika* freighter *Steiermark* was converted into a raider in Hamburg, becoming the *Kormoran*. Additional tanks could store an extra 5200 tons of fuel, enabling her to cruise for a year before refuelling. Her holds contained two Arado seaplanes and a light speedboat.
(BUNDESARCHIV, BILD 146-1969-117-48)

BELOW The raider *Kormoran* rendezvousing with a U-boat at an unidentified location.
(BUNDESARCHIV, BILD 146-1969-117-46)

bunk, a table and a cupboard. The less comfortable prisoner holds had been fitted out with hammocks, but better accommodation had been created for female prisoners and captains. Three refrigerated storerooms contained enough food to feed the crew and 100 prisoners for over a year.

During a visit to Berlin, *Korvettenkapitän* Gunther Gumprich, the head of the conversion department, asked Detmers what he was going to call his raider. Detmers had not considered the question and Gumprich suggested 'Kormoran'. Detmers instantly liked the name, recalling the gunboat *Cormoran*, which had gained fame in the South Seas and the World War I raider. He was also drawn to the bird's characteristics:

> The cormorant is a practical bird; it isn't much as far as looks go, but it knows its job. The Malays and the Chinese both use it for fishing. They put a ring round its neck, which does not interfere with its breathing but prevents it following its normal instincts and swallowing bigger fish. . . . I now hoped to catch a fish or two on the high seas so the name *Kormoran* seemed suitable.[5]

The dockyard workers completed the conversion work on 9 October. The *Kormoran* was the largest auxiliary cruiser, twice the size of the *Komet*, and her four diesel engines produced an impressive top speed of 18 knots and had excellent endurance.[6] The raider's main armaments consisted of six 5.9-inch guns, hidden behind counter-weighted steel plates and collapsible coverings.[7] The gunners performed regular training twice a week, including decamouflage drills. The starboard bow gun crew became an efficient team as they could fire the greatest number of shells in sixty seconds.[8] Detmers frequently oversaw the gunnery practice himself and questioned the gunners about their target priorities.[9] Two 37-mm guns were hidden behind sheet metal screens and five quad-mounted 20-mm cannons could be hydraulically raised from below deck.[10] The raider also had six torpedo tubes: two in twin-mounted, above-water tubes hidden behind flaps below the bridge and two single underwater tubes.[11]

On 9 October the *Kriegsmarine* commissioned the *Kormoran*, and Detmers organized a small celebration with shipyard representatives. The raider departed the next day and arrived in Kiel. That evening British bombers appeared overhead, targeting the oil tanks at Kitzeberg. As the night sky lit up with tracer flak, bombs detonated in the distance. The raider experienced her first taste of war, an event the officers celebrated with drinks in the wardroom.

As the crew loaded ammunition, fuel and other stores, a fire broke out in the power room, producing thick black smoke and, as fire fighters arrived to help, smoke filled the torpedo room, forcing the crew to open the flaps. The men quickly extinguished the flames but many curious onlookers noticed the vessel's strange features, making Detmers uncomfortable, so the raider moored as far away from the dock to regain privacy.

The RAF again bombed Kiel on the night of 15 October and one bomb fell 10 metres (32 feet) from the *Kormoran*'s stern, causing no damage, but the explosion made the ship shudder. The raider departed in a convoy three days later for Gotenhafen and, after arriving, the crew expressed amazement at the sight of bright peacetime street lights. Training intensified, but Detmers also granted generous shore leave in nearby Danzig.

On the night of 9 November, during weapons training in the Baltic, Able Seaman Erich Dembnicki fell through one of the torpedo flaps. The *Kormoran* searched for him but found no trace and, as the crew had lost a comrade, Detmers stepped up the training so they would be too busy to grieve.

The *Kormoran* returned to Gotenhafen for final preparations and the crew sensed their imminent departure. Raeder inspected the raider, wishing the crew good luck, as Detmers reflected:

> That was a memorable day for us. Once on board, the admiral was interested in everything, and wanted to know everything; and it was a real pleasure to show him round and explain just what had been done to turn an ordinary passenger ship into the best possible imitation of a warship.[12]

The *Kormoran* received her last stores, including 360 mines. Detmers decided against the option of hugging the French coast through the English Channel as he did not trust the *Luftwaffe* (German Air Force) to control the skies, so he opted for the Denmark Strait.[13] The *Kormoran* would break out during the new moon period, as there would be sufficient visibility to navigate around the ice.[14]

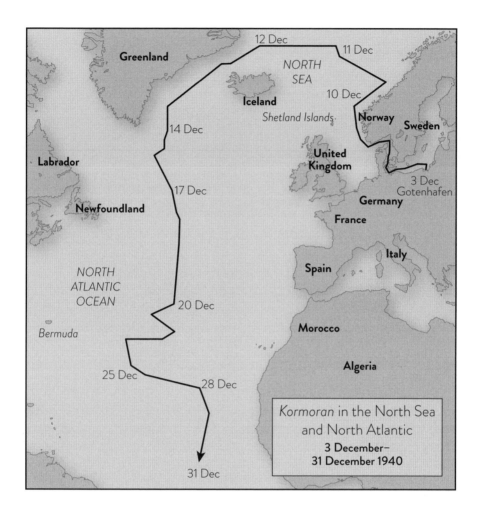

Kormoran in the North Sea
and North Atlantic
3 December–
31 December 1940

Detmers had orders to operate in the Indian Ocean while the South Atlantic and Pacific would be secondary operational areas.[15] The *Kormoran's* priority targets for minelaying were South African, Australian and New Zealand ports, but Detmers could also mine Indian waters. Detmers believed he could fulfil his deep ambition to become one of the greatest raider captains in history.

THE BREAKOUT

The *Kormoran* prepared to leave Germany at a fortuitous time. The Royal

Navy had established the Western Patrol to guard the approaches to Europe and North Africa but in doing so had depleted the Northern Patrol, which guarded the North Sea. The thinly dispersed armed merchant cruisers in severe winter weather could not effectively patrol the Denmark Strait.[16] The raider's breakout route was practically unguarded.

On 3 December the *Kormoran* departed Gotenhafen disguised as a *Sperrbrecher* pathfinder. She stopped near Hela to load two Arado seaplanes from the naval flying boat station at Danzig before rendezvousing with a genuine *Sperrbrecher*, which escorted her through the minefields of the Danish Great Belt. Strong winds slowed progress and Detmers feared he might not reach the Denmark Strait on schedule. On 7 December three escorting torpedo boats arrived and fighter aircraft appeared overhead. The raider proceeded through the Skagerrak between Norway and Denmark, but rolling seas forced the torpedo boats to return home as they could not maintain speed.

On the following night *Oberleutnant* Joachim Greter informed Detmers that four torpedoes had fallen off their racks in the rough seas. As they could not be secured, Detmers decided to stop to get the situation under control and the *Kormoran* approached Stavanger in the Tostenskjer Bight. As the raider approached the Norwegian coast, the alarm sounded after the lookout spotted a submarine in the dark. Detmers ordered evasive action in case torpedoes had been fired, but the 'submarine' turned out to be a rock formation and the raider safely dropped anchor in the harbour. *Oberleutnant* Heinz Messerschmidt went ashore and asked the port commander for a suitable location away from Norwegian eyes, and a pilot guided the raider to a channel between uninhabited islands.

After the crew completed the repair work, the *Kormoran* continued north while escorting aircraft appeared in the skies above. The men experienced a light breeze but the weather soon turned cold, reducing visibility to almost nothing. The raider hugged the Norwegian coast, appearing to be a freighter en route to Narvik before turning north-west. As the *Kormoran* headed towards Greenland, Detmers decided to disguise her as the freighter *Vyacheslav Molotov*, believing the Royal Navy would be reluctant to challenge a Soviet vessel.

On 12 December the *Kormoran* passed north of Iceland and a signal informed Detmers that the bad weather would not last and, therefore, the breakout should be postponed. The meteorologist Doctor Hermann Wagner confirmed its accuracy, and Detmers decided to continue as he could always turn around if the weather improved. The *Kormoran* headed south-west towards the Denmark Strait, but in the evening the predicted improvement materialized so Detmers retreated. However, he remained on the bridge hoping for a change in the weather. At 2200 h the wind began blowing stronger and he ordered a resumption of the breakout. The *Kormoran* headed south-west towards the Denmark Strait through the icy waters between Iceland and Greenland, and the next day she triumphantly entered the Atlantic under an overcast sky.

As the *Kormoran* continued south a storm reduced her speed to 3 knots but hid her from the outside world. She reached the North Atlantic trade route on 17 December, although Detmers did not yet have authorization to attack enemy shipping. The raider passed Newfoundland and after reaching warmer waters the crew began wearing their tropical uniforms. In the afternoon the lookout spotted smoke, and intelligence from the *B-Dienst* informed Detmers that his raider was between convoys HX 94 and HX 95.

The *Kormoran* headed south-west and, after avoiding a tanker, Detmers lamented: 'Pity that we are not allowed to do anything here yet.'[17] After passing the New York–Madrid Line, Detmers informed the *Seekriegsleitung* of his location and a reply authorized him to commence operations.[18] He patrolled the Azores–West Indies route but only spotted American ships. The raider had little ocean to hunt in due to the need to avoid nearby U-boat operational areas.

As the *Kormoran* continued south, the crew could spend their free time in a small swimming pool on the deck and every afternoon the cinema showed a film. Detmers ate in the mess with his officers as he wanted the 'close familiarity bred in torpedo boats and destroyers' so he could be in 'closer contact with the officers'.[19]

On 22 December the *Kormoran* passed Bermuda and the *Seekriegsleitung* assigned her to a new operational area in the North Atlantic to avoid a concentration of auxiliary cruisers in the Indian Ocean. Once inside the area, Detmers became increasingly disappointed as he had not yet encountered the enemy:

I have come to the conclusion that the Central North Atlantic is hardly travelled. Traffic probably goes on one of the two convoy routes and through the Panama Zone. One can count on a few irresponsibles who will take a short cut from the Cape Verde Islands.[20]

Detmers ordered a test flight on 30 December and the pilot, *Oberleutnant* Heinfried Ahl, successfully took off in his Arado. After landing, the winch used to raise the seaplane gave way and the plane fell into the sea. The Arado sustained damage but could be repaired; however, Detmers decided that it would be used only on rare occasions.

The year 1940 ended while the *Kormoran* headed south-west towards the Pan-American Neutrality Zone and Detmers reflected: 'Unfortunately we did not have the good fortune to obtain our first success in the old year; we look forward to the new one with greater hope.'[21]

An Arado seaplane from the *Orion* seen capsized in the ocean and being salvaged by the raider's crew.
(AUTHOR'S COLLECTION)

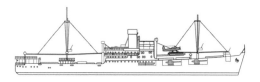

CHAPTER 12
THE CASTAWAYS OF EMIRAU ISLAND

The German Captain [Eyssen] in charge of the three ships was full of
his own importance — his egotism seemed to pervade the whole of
the crew and as often happens in these cases, let us hope that their
audacity will lead very shortly to their own destruction.[1]

G.R. Ferguson
Prisoner on the *Komet*

THE LAST DAYS OF THE SQUADRON

On 8 December 1940 the Far East Squadron reformed 20 miles off Nauru.
Seaman McHuley from the *Rangitane* died from his wounds on the *Orion*,
despite Doctor Raffler's best efforts to save his life, and Weyher gave him
a burial at sea. Eyssen could not land a shore party on Nauru due to bad
weather so the *Komet* and *Kulmerland* headed for Ailinglaplap to refuel, while
the slower *Orion* proceeded towards Ponape in the Caroline Islands, hoping
to attack enemy shipping. The squadron would rendezvous north of Nauru.

The *Orion*, after failing to find any victims, arrived at the rendezvous
on 13 December. As the *Komet* and *Kulmerland* had not yet arrived, Weyher

patrolled the area. The *Komet* and *Kulmerland* arrived three days later and Eyssen abandoned all hope of landing a shore party due to bad weather. As he could not release his prisoners on Nauru, what to do with his 675 captives became his most pressing problem.[2] The prisoners became aware of this as Sandbach and Edge noted: 'It was quite obvious that the prisoners were fast becoming too much for the enemy. The three ships were terribly overcrowded, rations were getting less and less and water a luxury.'[3] Despite the overcrowding and discomfort the guards treated the prisoners well, as Lorna Adams from the *Triona* expressed:

> The doctor on this ship is most kind and attentive to all the injured, and all the Germans from the chief captain to the steward boy, are kind to us women and to the little children. Mr Marks, the chief relieving engineer of this ship, is one of the finest men I have ever met in my life.[4]

Eyssen proposed landing all prisoners on Emirau Island in the Bismarck Archipelago, with the exception of key personnel. Weyher strongly argued that only non-whites, women, children and the disabled should be released since the others could provide useful intelligence to the enemy and return to duty. He suggested transferring these prisoners to the blockade runner *Ermland*, which had left Japan bound for France. Eyssen overruled Weyher and the squadron set a course towards Emirau. As the squadron approached, Eyssen told the Allied captains that they would be released on the island, and the *Orion*'s Arado seaplane conducted reconnaissance flights over the Bismarck Archipelago and the northern coast of New Guinea.

The squadron arrived at Emirau at dawn on 21 December. Two British families of plantation owners, the Colletts and the Cooks, lived there alongside the native population. The previous day Mr and Mrs Cook believed they had seen a German plane and after an anxious night they discovered that three ships had arrived. They drove to the beach in a Ford automobile and saw a motorboat approaching the jetty with officers in white dress uniforms. After seeing a *Kriegsmarine* flag the Cooks decided that friendliness would be the wisest policy, so they greeted the landing party. Eyssen asked Mr Cook if he would look after the prisoners. Mr Cook agreed and Eyssen told him

At Emirau Island in the Bismarck Archipelago on 21 December 1940. The German raiders *Komet* (as *Manyo Maru*), *Kulmerland* (with striped funnel) and *Orion* standing off the island.
(AWM)

that a lifeboat would be left behind so they could contact Kavieng on New Ireland, 70 miles away, to arrange rescue. Karl Mertens, a gunner on the *Komet*, recalled the meeting:

> When Eyssen went ashore in the first boat the astonished planter, named Cook, stood puffing at his pipe. . . . Eyssen explained that he had nearly 500 men, women and children to put ashore, and the planter shrugged his shoulders and said. 'Well. I can't chase you away with my shotgun.' Then he invited Eyssen into the house for a glass of beer.[5]

The prisoners began disembarking and the Germans also landed kerosene, food, cigarettes and rifles for them, but they also used a lorry to round up cattle, which they took back to their ships.

Chief Engineer Abernethy from the *Holmwood* witnessed the drama:

> Three raiders lying inside a coral reef, a big island covered with coconut palms, a seaplane in the water alongside our raider, motor launches going back and forward between the island and the boats bringing off fruit and coconuts.[6]

Eyssen gave a farewell address to the *Kulmerland* prisoners, which Sandbach and Edge described:

> . . . the Commodore came aboard and entered the dining saloon, followed by his usual retinue. He had come to bid us farewell, again treating us like something out of an asylum that has to be humoured. We felt like children leaving a party and that we ought to say 'Thank you for having me'.[7]

By noon 514 prisoners had landed. Eyssen disembarked all his prisoners except for some service personnel, but Weyher refused to land white males. The servicemen from the *Komet* signed a declaration before being allowed to leave:

> We the undersigned do herby give our word of honour and declare solemnly that on our release we will bear neither arms nor undertake military action against Germany and her allies during present hostilities. By breach of this promise we realise that we are liable to capital punishment.[8]

The Far East Squadron disbanded in the afternoon. The *Orion* headed north-west towards Lamotrek Atoll, where she would overhaul her engines and transfer her 183 remaining prisoners to the *Ermland*. Eyssen planned to mine Rabaul and bombard the oil facilities at Miri on Borneo before proceeding towards the Panama Canal Zone. The *Kulmerland* headed for Japan with copies of the raiders' war diaries, arriving there on 31 December.

THE CASTAWAYS

One group of castaways on Emirau walked 10 miles to the plantation, while the wounded and those who could not walk rode in a lorry. Adams described her reception:

> We women were sheltered in the mission house with Mr and Mrs Cook. They were excellent people. They have given us their home. Women and children sleep on the floor in rows — no bedding or mattresses. We just rest our heads on lifebelts and try to sleep with the many mosquitoes.[9]

The other white prisoners established a camp on the western side of the island and the remaining kept to the eastern end. The castaways built huts from palm tree branches and gathered tropical fruit. They also made soup from local vegetables, using coconut shells as bowls. Mr Cook slaughtered cattle and natives gathered coconuts, paw-paws and sweet potatoes for the new arrivals. Chief Officer Aslak Jensen from the *Vinni* recalled his newfound sense of freedom: 'We are again free to a certain extent and we enjoy it. It was chilly and uncomfortable in the bushes, but it was nothing compared with the prison rooms on board the raider.'[10]

Chief Officer Hopkins from the *Rangitane* hand-picked a crew to sail the lifeboat to Kavieng, but they decided to use a faster motor launch. On 23 December Hopkins, Collett, Barker and Jensen departed. John Merrylees, District Officer of New Ireland, remembered their arrival on Christmas Eve:

> I was awakened by Mr. Collett of Emirau bringing to my house four survivors of ships sunk by enemy action in the Pacific. At that time, Mr. Collett was unknown to me, although his name was familiar, and he stood in the background: the other four uniformed figures were strangers. . . . Feeling certain that they were genuine survivors, I invited Mr. Hopkins to tell his story.[11]

The *Leander* and *Shamrock* departed for Emirau with stores and medical supplies, arriving in the afternoon while two aircraft from Rabaul patrolled the area searching for the raiders. On Christmas Day the *Leander* returned

ABOVE Some of the passengers and crew among the 514 survivors who had been cast away on Emirau Island in December 1940 after their merchant ships were sunk by the *Komet* and *Orion*. They are standing outside their palm leaf shelter.
(AWM: NAVAL HISTORICAL COLLECTION)

BELOW Some of the survivors on Emirau Island after their merchant ships were sunk. There were 488 survivors rescued by the Australian steamer *Nellore*.
(AWM: NAVAL HISTORICAL COLLECTION)

to Kavieng with some women, children and wounded while the *Shamrock* embarked Captain Callender and 100 Filipinos and Chinese. A flying boat from Rabaul arrived with Lieutenant Hugh Mackenzie, a RAN intelligence officer, who interviewed the key survivors. Another flying boat evacuated the captains and others who could provide intelligence and, during an overnight stop at Port Moresby, RAAF personnel interviewed them. After arriving in Melbourne, intelligence officers further questioned the group.

The *Nellore* embarked the remaining 488 survivors at Emirau, which included eight Noumeans, seventy-two Chinese and ninety-five Filipinos. Upon arrival at Townsville on 1 January, the Chinese and Filipino castaways did not disembark, as they did not have permission to enter Australia, but two trains transported the other castaways to Sydney.[12] The press reported contradictory accounts of the treatment the prisoners had received. A Department of Air press statement gave a favourable view:

> The survivors were glad to get ashore, even though their treatment while on board the raiders had not been bad. The ships, however, were very crowded, and food was short. . . . Conditions and treatment on board the raiders were quite different from those experienced by prisoners aboard the Nazi hell ship *Altmark*, the survivors said.[13]

The Canberra Times took an opposite view in an article entitled 'Raiders Were Hell Ships':

> Conditions in which captives, including women, were held on board the Pacific raiders were worse than those of the *Altmark*, stated some survivors, who declared that the food was abominable and that machine-guns were trained down the holds. . . . The story told by these men duplicate that of the *Altmark* prison hell.[14]

The *Australian Women's Weekly* meanwhile expressed interest in the fashion sense of the female castaways:

> Youth and beauty had a special representative in Maureen White, typist, from Ocean Island, returning with her mother from Melbourne,

where she had been studying at a business college. Maureen was a passenger on the *Triona* when the ship was shelled, but she came through smiling, attired in cream slacks, a cream silk shirt, and an officer's cap perched on her curls.[15]

The Australian Government had to decide what to do about the men who had signed Eyssen's oath. The Australian Naval Board recommended that these men should not be compelled to serve. The War Cabinet ultimately decided that they should observe the oath but this should not prevent them from non-combatant duties or serving on merchant vessels.[16]

VALUABLE INTELLIGENCE

Eyssen's release of servicemen and merchant sailors was a major blunder. Lieutenant Mackenzie had been given two rolls of film on Emirau by Mr Steward who had taken pictures of the raiders and their supply ship. One castaway even gave him a pre-war postcard of the *Kulmerland*, which had been found on board. When the first survivors reached Melbourne Commander Long, Director of Naval Intelligence, personally interviewed them, as did other intelligence officers. The Noumeans and Vietnamese survivors from the *Notou* believed the *Tokyo Maru* (*Kulmerland*) and *Manyo Maru* (*Komet*) were of Japanese origin and stated that supplies on board, such as cigarettes, came from Japan.[17] They also reported that the German crews had high morale, playing music and singing in their spare time.

Commander Long collated all intelligence reports and a general view of the raiders emerged. The *Manyo Maru* (*Komet*) and *Narvik* (*Orion*) were believed to be capable of 22½ knots and armed with 5.9-inch guns, torpedo tubes and 20-mm anti-aircraft cannons.[18] Their weapons had been correctly identified, but their speed had been greatly exaggerated. Some prisoners believed the 'Narvik' had been built in the Baltic due to the shape of her bow, and some survivors noted that her spare anchor came from Hamburg but others believed she was Japanese as some of the welding did not have the finish expected of German workmanship.

The *Tokyo Maru* had correctly been identified as the *Kulmerland* and the survivors described Captain Pschunder as an elderly merchant officer who had been familiar with the waters around New Guinea. Most of her crew wore *Hamburg-Amerika* caps and all the stores came from Japan. A survivor who had been a patient in the hospital had found a book inscribed with the words 'Kobe, April 1940'. Many survivors also believed the *Kulmerland* had laid the *Pinguin*'s Australian minefields, causing Commander Long to incorrectly conclude that 'it therefore appears reasonably certain that KULMERLAND was responsible for the mining of Australian waters'.[19]

The most important information from the castaways concerned Merchant Navy codes, as John Merrylees reported: 'The raiders were well equipped with wireless, were in possession of mercantile codes 8 and 9 and probably others, as their information in the past had been really good: they probably had an expert decoding staff.'[20] Wireless Officer Ward also confirmed that the Germans had captured the *Komata*'s code-books. This information convinced the British to change their codes.[21]

The *B-Dienst* in Germany became outraged as Eyssen's actions compromised their decryption work.[22] The *Seekriegsleitung* reminded all raider captains that prisoners should always be sent to Germany for internment.[23] Eyssen initially rejected all criticism by claiming that his operational areas had already been compromised and the number of prisoners would have been too much of a burden on food supplies. He later changed his tune after it became apparent that the Allies had changed their codes and acknowledged that if he had been able to foresee the repercussions, he would have acted differently.

CHAPTER 13
VON LUCKNER, SPIES AND THE FIFTH COLUMN

A country like Germany, that foresaw this war, that made plans in peacetime on a basis of war, and knew that it was coming, it may be depended upon, has its people in this country and to a greater extent in Britain. They are probably in the least expected quarter. They do not go about with swastikas printed on their foreheads like the brand of Cain, although that may come later.[1]

William 'Billy' Hughes
Australian Navy Minister
4 January 1941

THE WITCH-HUNT

Many Australians suspected that an enemy 'fifth column' in their country had been assisting the raiders. Chief Officer Dravik from the *Tropic Sea*, after being rescued, declared:

The day we left Sydney a German spy had been found who had been

operating a wireless transmitter and receiver from Sydney. . . . I am
sure they were in touch with the Raider as the German Commander
knew about the two warships in Sydney Harbour, and he knew exactly
the route we were to take, the day we were leaving Sydney, in fact all
about us.[2]

After the *Pinguin*'s mines began sinking ships, *The Canberra Times* announced:

Commonwealth authorities are investigating the possibility that the
raider which sowed mines in Bass Strait recently, may have been
assisted by Nazi or Fascist agents in Australia. It is pointed out that
there are hundreds of Italian fishermen along the coast where the
mines were laid.[3]

These rumours reached near hysterical levels after the castaways from
Emirau arrived in Australia, as many of them believed the raiders had been
in contact with spies. This notion originated from a number of statements
made by Eyssen, who often bragged to prisoners about his knowledge of
shipping, wishing to appear all knowing and in control of events. He boasted
to Captain Upton of the *Rangitane*: 'There will be more ships there, but only
one has a gun, the Triadic.'[4] Captain Fish and Chief Engineer MacDonald
from the *Komata* similarly declared:

The Captain [Eyssen] stated that there is definitely an organisation
here in Australia and New Zealand keeping this ship informed. In all
their conversations they mentioned the knowledge of our movements
of ships, which they told me can only be possible by obtaining it from
their sources.[5]

The Australian press widely reported these accusations and the tabloid
Smith's Weekly became obsessed with exposing the 'fifth column' supporting
the raiders.[6] The Navy Minister Billy Hughes planned a security crackdown
at the waterfront to prevent the crews of neutral ships learning information
of value to raiders.[7] The New South Wales Premier Alexander Mair called
for the internment of all enemy aliens as 'it was clear that there was a

leakage from Australia, informing the raiders of the movements of vessels, times and details'.[8]

Some castaways also turned on each other and accused two Polish merchant sailors, Hieronim Nawracala and Roman Nowakoski, from the *Rangitane* of being pro-Nazi, and Thomas Smith accused Nawracala of collaboration:

> The first thing I noticed on boarding the 'Manyo Maru' [*Komet*] was that the Pole was shaking hands with German sailors and conversing in German. Later this man acted as interpreter. . . . During any conversation had with this Pole, it is my opinion that his sentiments were definitely anti-British.[9]

In early 1941 the police interned Nawracala and Nowakoski only to release them almost one year later. They had been on friendly terms with the Germans, like many Anglo-Saxon prisoners, but unfortunately wartime hysteria prevented logic from determining their fate.

THE SEA DEVIL

The spy hunt initially focused on Count Felix von Luckner, who had commanded the raider *Seeadler* in the South Seas during 1917. His exploits and honourable conduct made him a popular figure and the British *Official History* even stated:

> In all the testimonies of his English and French prisoners there is no word of complaint against him; some even go out of their way to say that he treated them kindly; we can therefore conclude, with certainty, that he was a bold, calculating and adventurous leader; and we have every reason to believe that he was a kindly and courteous gentleman as well.[10]

Between the wars Luckner became an international celebrity with fame comparable to Lawrence of Arabia, but the rise of the Third Reich turned him into a controversial figure. When he toured Australia in his yacht

Count Felix Graf von Luckner (left) holding a lifebelt on his yacht *Seeteufel*.
(AUSTRALIAN NATIONAL MARITIME MUSEUM ON THE COMMONS)

Seeteufel in 1938, public opinion polarized between those who remembered his chivalry and those who considered him an emissary of Nazism.

When Luckner visited New Zealand, where he had been held as a prisoner of war, the public treated him as a national hero.[11] In Auckland crowds gave him an enthusiastic reception at the Eden-Roskill Returned Soldiers Club and later at the Wellington Opera House. However, when he arrived in Sydney angry protests organized by the Communist Party of Australia greeted him, but the major newspapers and ABC radio interviewed him and he delivered public lectures at Town Hall. He also visited Brisbane, Melbourne, Adelaide and Canberra. As many Australians feared Luckner was a spy, the police placed him under surveillance and investigated people who associated with him.

As raiders began menacing Australian waters, many believed that Luckner's 'spy ring' had assisted the enemy.[12] In October 1940 an intelligence report concluded:

. . . it is, however, unlikely that raiders rely solely on supply ships, and
it is possible that arrangements were made for such bases and for the
supply of information before the war by agents such as Count Luckner.[13]

Furthermore, the press speculated that Luckner himself commanded a
raider, as *The Argus* reported:

His experience as an able seaman trading to Australia, as commander of
the *Seeadler*, and as the organiser of a spying cruise in the very waters
where an enemy raider has been operating, are strong grounds for the
contention that the 'Sea Devil' is either the organiser behind Germany's
commerce raiding activities or the actual captain of such a raider.[14]

The press campaign against Luckner resulted in his family issuing a rebuttal,
reported in *The Argus* on 6 January 1941:

The Swedish brother-in-law of Count von Luckner denied the
report that the count was commander of the raider in the Pacific.
He said von Luckner spent Christmas hunting wild boar in the Harz
Mountains in Germany.[15]

The press continued to publish rumours about Luckner's involvement with
raiders, as *The Canberra Times* reported on 30 April:

The N.B.C. correspondent at Manila has broadcast that British and
Free Netherlands naval units have been ordered to capture Captain
von Luckner, who is reported to be commanding 12 armed merchant
raiders in the South Pacific, which are believed to be operating from
Japanese bases in the Caroline and Marshall Islands.[16]

Australians forgot the reputation of honour and chivalry Luckner gained
during World War I and now viewed him as a ruthless Nazi raider captain
and spy master. Police investigated people who had been friendly with him
and the government interned many German-Australians who had associated
with him on the suspicion that they were members of his 'spy ring'.[17]

Meanwhile, in Germany Luckner had become an opponent of the Nazis.[18] At times Luckner had praised the achievements of the Third Reich during his 1938 tour, which was partially funded by the German Government, hoping to create a propaganda victory. However, Luckner increasingly became disillusioned with the Nazi regime. He clearly had mixed feelings about Hitler, but as time progressed he became more opposed to the Nazis. When the National Council of the New Zealand Federation of Labour condemned him as a fascist, he declared:

> I can tell you, it is in the working people that the strength of Hitler is placed. I am not a member of the Nazi Party. I am an officer and can belong to no political party. I tell you frankly, at first many of us were not in favour of the Nazi movement, but today we have come to think otherwise. But I do not want to argue with these people. If Wellington does not want me, why, I will go elsewhere. I have come only to spread the gospel of good will. In wartime, for the service of my God, I sank the nitrate carriers whose cargoes would have been converted into munitions to kill thousands of people. I have never deprived a mother of her son. I love the New Zealand people because they were sportsmen when I was imprisoned here, and escaped, captured the *Moa*, and afterwards was caught again. . . . What have I done to deserve this? It hurts me.[19]

After returning to home, the Gestapo concluded that Luckner had failed to conduct himself with a National Socialist attitude as he had made contradictory statements about the regime to the world press. A Court of Honour declared:

> Count Luckner will for the indefinite future be asked under no circumstances to make public appearances, to lead the completely retired life of a private person, and to make sure that in the press and in other public spheres his person is no longer remembered in any way.[20]

The Nazis regarded Luckner as a Freemason and a Jewish sympathizer. He lost his home, fortune and yacht, while his books were banned. He subsequently spent most of the war in Berlin and Hamburg, living in near poverty until an anonymous admirer provided him with money.[21] In 1941 he saved a Jewish woman, Rosalinde Janson, from deportation to Auschwitz by providing her with false documents.[22] After the war Luckner defended himself against the accusations in a letter to a friend:

> On declaration of war I refused a demand of the Ministry of
> Propaganda to renounce my British citizenship of Bermuda and later
> the American one, and thereupon was declared hostile to the State.
> My books were prohibited and removed from all libraries. . . . What
> do Australians think of me today? Hope they believe now that all this
> suspicion was wrong![23]

During the 1950s Luckner organized tours in Germany for American servicemen before dying in Hamburg in 1966.

THE NAURU RADIO

On 7 December 1940 Assistant Harbour Master Captain Town sighted a suspicious vessel off Nauru and recommended informing Sydney but Eric Paul, Secretary to the Administrator, disagreed, believing the ship was the *Triona*. The vessel was either the *Orion* or *Komet*. The next morning the Nauru radio operator Allen Hooper, knowing that a 'Japanese ship' had been sighted earlier, broadcast a general call for nearby Japanese ships to report their positions.[24] Later that morning the *Komet*'s wireless cancelled the *Komata*'s raider warning and the authorities on Nauru did not learn about the raiders until the afternoon.

The Nauru radio's failure to report the possible presence of raiders resulted in accusations of treason after Captain Miller from the *Holmwood*, following his rescue, declared: 'When talking to the Captain of the raider [Eyssen] one remarked that he was very daring to shell so close to the Island. His reply was, "That is alright, the wireless station is fixed".'[25] Lieutenant-Commander Eric Feldt, head of naval intelligence in Port Moresby, reported this accusation to Commander Long, Director of Naval Intelligence.[26] Hughes later stated in Parliament that 'the failure of the authorities at Nauru to notify vessels of the approach of a German raider could only be accounted for by treachery'.[27]

Nauru residents also made allegations against Paul, a man named Barnes, who had been in charge of the radio, and Thomas Hudson, a mechanic with the British Phosphate Commission. The residents believed Paul was a 'spy master' with a mysterious past, including rumours of German nationality, who effectively controlled Nauru due to his ability to manipulate the Administrator, Lieutenant-Colonel Chalmers.

Paul had worked for the British Phosphate Commission until 1935 but left in unpleasant circumstances and his relationship with many employees remained mutually hostile. After the raider attack, many commission employees accused Paul of removing confidential books and keeping them at his house. They also accused a man named Hopper, Hudson and Barnes of disloyalty and having 'sinister' dealings with Paul. Lorna Adams, the wife of a commissioner, accused Hudson of being a secret agent working for a central European country. However, the situation became more complex as others accused Adams of being Hudson's former mistress and Hooper of being 'friends' with a mysterious Kings Cross prostitute Betty Green, a suspected spy protected by influential clients in Sydney.[28]

Mark Ridgway, the Senior Administrative Officer on Nauru, claimed Paul could smuggle out secrets on vessels bound for the Dutch East Indies or Japan, while adding that he had access to the wireless and could secretly communicate with raiders. Furthermore, he declared:

> The whole Island is seething with discomfort and suspicion directed against the Administration. . . . The whole trouble is Paul. . . . For years past (long before the war) rumours here classed Paul as a German agent. . . . German or no German he has unlimited powers and opportunity to betray the Empire.[29]

In Australia an investigation into the Nauru radio confirmed Paul had been born in Auckland and past associates spoke well of him and considered him loyal. While being interviewed by naval intelligence, Hooper stated that Paul was loyal but his arrogance and domineering nature strained his relations with others. Hooper claimed that Paul had overruled the Harbour Master because of his disinclination to act on the suggestion of others.

The investigation concluded that wireless security had been unsatisfactory and the Germans could easily have formed an accurate picture of Nauru shipping by listening to signals, but it found no evidence of espionage:

> There is no substance in the charges levelled at Paul — these originated partly in jealousy, or malice, partly in the desire to find a scapegoat. . . . There is no evidence, beyond the statement of an obviously neurotic woman [Mrs Adams], that Hudson is other than an ordinary citizen, highly efficient in his profession. There is no reason to suspect the loyalty of either Barnes or Hooper.[30]

Paul eventually left Nauru for Sydney, and the NSW Police decided to keep an eye on him, but they never laid charges against him.[31]

JEHOVAH'S WITNESSES

In Australia the government targeted the Jehovah's Witnesses during its security crackdown. Ironically, Nazi Germany had been persecuting this religion and 6000 of its followers were in prison or concentration camps.[32] The 2500 Witnesses in Australia believed the end of the world was near and that Christ would soon return to overthrow all governments. They opposed all forms of participation in government and military service. In Australia many took offence at their claims that sometimes associated the British Empire with 'The Beast' from the Book of Revelation and assertions that Germany would win the war.

The National Security Act enabled the government to ban 'subversive' organizations and Commonwealth police placed the Witnesses under surveillance.[33] Newspapers routinely speculated that they represented a 'fifth column' loyal to Germany. The *Smith's Weekly* launched a sustained scare campaign, even claiming to have uncovered a secret munitions factory run by the Witnesses.[34] Billy Hughes, as Attorney-General, wanted to ban the Witnesses but feared such an act might be illegal as the group constituted a religion.[35] After the raiders began attacking shipping in Australian waters, the government found an excuse to deal with the Witnesses.

The Witnesses had affiliations with four radio stations including 5KA.[36]

On 18 November 1940 Naval Intelligence had been monitoring the station and overheard certain words, songs and noises that could be interpreted as a coded reference to the *Stratheden*'s departure from Port Adelaide.[37] Admiral Ragnar Colvin, Chief of Naval Staff, asked Hughes to close the stations 'as an essential measure of National Security'.[38] He also gave his opinion of the Witnesses:

> Their private lives reveal a lack of education and a vulgarity of outlook on life in general, and especially on sex. They appear to be the type of person who is likely to be really dangerous if he or she should become fanatical, as they have few inhibitions.[39]

On 8 January 1941 Hughes suspended the four radio stations and two days later soldiers and plainclothes police in Adelaide raided the Witnesses' Kingdom Hall, their printing office at Rose Park and private homes. *The Canberra Times* reported these events in an article entitled, 'Gave News to Nazi Raiders':

> The Minister for the Navy (Mr. Hughes) said yesterday that the four stations that had been closed down were either used or owned by 'Jehovah's Witnesses.' They had been closed because, according to naval authorities, information was being supplied to the enemy which imperilled the safety of shipping.[40]

On 17 January Prime Minister Menzies announced that the Jehovah's Witnesses would be declared an illegal organization.[41] The government banned the religion and its members could no longer meet for worship nor could they print, circulate or possess their literature. Across the country police raided homes, farms and businesses, seizing cars, boats, farm machinery and other assets.

The Witnesses went underground and launched a High Court legal appeal in 1943, which lifted the ban. In 1939 the British Government had confirmed that Witnesses in Germany were being persecuted by the Gestapo and given this fact the accusations labelling them Nazi 'fifth columnists' were always bizarre.[42]

COMMISSION OF INQUIRY

While various witch-hunts were taking place in Australia, the authorities in New Zealand became increasingly alarmed by the events taking place across the Tasman, and Prime Minister Peter Fraser expressed concerns to Menzies:

> The New Zealand Government have observed with surprise this morning the publication in the New Zealand press of a matter arriving from Sydney by Tasman airmail on the sensational theories advanced by the survivors landed from the enemy raiders.[43]

Fraser informed Menzies that preliminary enquiries found no evidence to back up the allegations made by the Emirau castaways.[44] The Australian Naval Board's investigation also uncovered no evidence that raiders had received information from spies.[45] Furthermore, the Naval Board determined that shipping movements could have been learned from decoded Merchant Navy signals.[46]

The New Zealand Government appointed a Commission of Inquiry to investigate raider activity and, regarding Eyssen's knowledge of shipping movements, it concluded:

> The statements attributed to him seem to us to be more likely part of an attempt to impress his captives, and, through them, to disseminate uneasiness and distrust in New Zealand, or they may have been manifestations of boastfulness and of a taste for melodrama.[47]

The Commission found no evidence of enemy espionage and the matter was finally resolved after the war when captured German records proved the raiders had not been in contact with spies.[48] The Commission also investigated why the *Holmwood* failed to broadcast a raider warning that would have saved the *Rangitane* and concluded that Captain Miller had failed to perform his duty:

> We are fully aware that any attempt to send the message would have brought about the shelling of the *Holmwood*, and that this might have meant heavy loss of life, including the lives of women and children.

But, having regard to the methods of warfare with which we are faced, that consideration is irrelevant. Loss of civilian lives must be faced in an effort to locate and destroy raiders.[49]

Despite the hysteria about a 'fifth column' in Australia, there is only one instance of information being broadcast to a raider. Billy Hughes accidentally informed Krüder in the *Pinguin* that HMAS *Canberra* had left Fremantle in pursuit of the raider. On 21 November 1940 John Curtin asked Hughes in Parliament for information on the raider reported off Fremantle.[50] Hughes responded, 'An Australian cruiser now in West Australian waters has been detailed for action following reports that an enemy raider has been seen near Fremantle.'[51] After this announcement the editor of the *Sydney Morning Herald* phoned the Director General of Information, Keith Murdoch, to ask if any censorship restrictions would apply to the publication of Hughes' statement. Murdoch replied that official notifications could be published without reference to the censor and the next day ABC radio news announced that a cruiser had left Fremantle to hunt a raider and this information reached Krüder.[52] Hughes knew that statements in Parliament could be published in full and despite his paranoia over the enemy 'fifth column' the only loose lips were his own.[53]

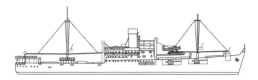

CHAPTER 14
RETURN TO NAURU AND INTRIGUE IN JAPAN

Naval authorities here consider that the activity of the German raiders in the Pacific and Indian Oceans is likely to be intensified as a part of the Axis plan not only to make these places untenable for British shipping but to assist in Japan's southward expansion and Hitler's advance to the Balkans.[1]

The Canberra Times
30 December 1940

BOMBARDMENT

After departing Emirau, the *Komet* headed south-east towards Rabaul. On the night of 24 December 1940 Eyssen planned to mine the approaches to the harbour, but engine failure on the minelaying motorboat *Meteorit* forced him to cancel the operation. After this setback Eyssen decided to return to Nauru to attack the island's facilities.

The *Komet* reappeared off Nauru on 27 December. The crew raised the *Kriegsmarine* flag and draped German ensigns over Japanese markings. Eyssen warned the island by lamp of the impending bombardment:

I will shoot without regards [*sic*] if you use wireless. If you don't use wireless I only destroy your phosphate pier and oil tanks behind and the lighters. Evacuate this area at once diminish casualties. If you don't use wireless your station won't be demolished.[2]

As Nauru was undefended, the authorities complied. Nauru's radio remained silent while the workers evacuated their facilities. At 0640 h the *Komet*'s guns opened fire and shells hit the oil tanks, cantilevers, storage bins, boats, buildings and mooring buoys.[3] The cranes sustained massive damage and flames consumed the oil tanks. Karl Mertens, a sailor on the raider, recalled that 'for an hour we steamed at leisure up and down the coast, pouring shells into the works and cranes near the jetty'.[4]

After ceasing fire the *Komet* disappeared over the horizon, heading northeast. Lieutenant-Colonel Chalmers, the Nauru Administrator, signalled Australia: 'Nauru heavily shelled by one enemy raider. Great Material damage. Oil fuel destroyed. No casualties. Raider had Japanese name and markings.'[5] A short time later he sent a more detailed report:

Raider opened fire at 0640 local time and shelled at close range cantilever loading jetty, all oil storage tanks, cantilever shore storage bin mooring gear store and other Phosphate buildings. Using pompoms [20-mm cannons] destroyed mooring buoys. . . . Raider had marks on sides of hull and flew Nazi flag at Gaff and not as stated in my first message.[6]

The authorities on Nauru organized temporary repairs to the cantilever, and special equipment later arrived from Melbourne, which saved the structure.[7] Nevertheless the attack caused significant long-term economic damage. No phosphate shipments left Nauru for ten weeks and in June 1941 loading proceeded at 20 per cent of normal capacity. In Australia stockpiling of phosphate prevented major shortages.[8] However, in New Zealand shortages resulted in rationing for farmers and the importation of reserve stocks from Britain.[9]

In Australia Prime Minister Menzies falsely claimed the attack took place under Japanese flags:

German raider Komet shells Nauru 27.12.1940

75c

NAURU

A stamp from the Republic of Nauru, remembering the *Komet*'s bombardment of the island on 27 December 1940. (AUTHOR'S COLLECTION)

The raider attacked under a Japanese name and Japanese colours. Nauru was entirely undefended against attack. It had to be under the terms of the League of Nations mandate, by which it was administered. That fact was well known to the enemy, and in itself removed any justification for his action, which was made a greater crime in that it was undertaken under neutral colours.[10]

To counter this acquisition Eyssen signalled Berlin: 'about twenty minutes prior to bombardment of Nauru German ensigns (two) hoisted for brief period'.[11] A German rebuttal quickly followed, which *The Sun* published:

The Berlin correspondent of the Tokio newspaper *Nichi Nichi* says that Germany admits the bombardment of Nauru, but denies that the raider flew Japanese colors, and describes as 'propaganda' the statement by the Australian Prime Minister (Mr. Menzies) that the raider did so.[12]

The Navy Minister Billy Hughes explained to the public why no warships had been near Nauru:

What would people say if, while four or five warships were near Nauru

Plumes of smoke rise over Nauru as a result of the *Komet*'s bombardment.
(AUTHOR'S COLLECTION)

searching for the raiders, Australia was attacked? The warships could
not be everywhere. There should not be any surprise that Nauru had
been shelled. It was surprising that it had not been shelled before.[13]

Following the attack three Hudson bombers arrived in Rabaul to act as a
strike force if the raider headed south and RAN warships began escorting
vessels to Nauru and Ocean Island.[14] To counter the raider threat, the RAN
began concentrating in home waters to protect shipping.[15]

Raider activity in the Australia Station resulted in the VK convoys to protect shipping on the trans-Tasman route. Convoy VK 1 departed Sydney for Auckland with the *Achilles* in escort on 30 December.[16] VK convoys subsequently departed every twenty-two days for the remainder of the war.[17] The RAN also established the ZK convoys between Australia, New Guinea and the Pacific.[18]

Commander Long, Director of Naval Intelligence, believed that the 'Narvik' (*Orion*) and *Manyo Maru* (*Komet*) had most likely returned to Germany since they would require major refits, underestimating the raider crews' ability to keep their engines operational without access to ports.[19] The *Orion*, *Komet* and *Pinguin* remained nearby and had no intention of going home just yet.

THE *OLE JACOB*

The Allies correctly believed that Japan had been assisting raiders, and British residents in Kobe and Yokohama organized round-the-clock surveillance of German freighters. The Allies also believed the raiders had bases in Japanese-controlled Pacific islands and, since this would be a violation of the League of Nations Mandate, they hoped to catch the Japanese in the act.[20] In this tense environment an incident occurred that gave the British an opportunity to apply strong pressure on Japan.

On 4 December the Norwegian tanker *Ole Jacob*, which had been captured by the *Atlantis*, entered Kobe flying the *Kriegsmarine* flag under the command of *Kapitänleutnant* Kamenz with Norwegian prisoners on board. The Japanese and Allies experienced mutual astonishment. The *Seekriegsleitung* had ordered the *Ole Jacob* to proceed to Lamotrek Atoll (Sheltering Place Y) and *Konteradmiral* Wenneker, the naval attaché, incorrectly informed the Japanese Navy that the *Ole Jacob* was heading to Lamotrek.[21] However, Kamenz had headed to Japan on a special mission.

The *Atlantis* had earlier captured the British freighter *Automedon* on 11 November 1940 and the boarding party had found 125 mailbags.[22] The Germans examined the mail, finding British War Cabinet minutes that included a strategic appreciation of the Far East. This summary explained that inadequate British forces in Asia would be incapable of thwarting a Japanese attack and that the Royal Navy, committed to containing the German and Italian navies, was not in a position to send a fleet to the Far

East.[23] The *Automedon* documents also contained a report outlining the defence of Singapore, including a complete order of battle for air, land and sea forces. Rogge immediately realized the importance of the documents. In the hands of the Japanese they were the keys to the fortress of Singapore and, accordingly, Rogge entrusted them to Kamenz to give to Wenneker. The *Ole Jacob* then headed to Japan with the documents and its co-operative Norwegian crew, which Rogge had promised would be released in a neutral port.

Wenneker examined the *Automedon* documents after Kehrmann, the Chief Liaison Office in Kobe, escorted them to Tokyo on a train.[24] Wenneker declared: 'An immediate preliminary search revealed that some of this material was of the very highest significance.'[25] He entrusted the documents to a diplomatic courier who took them to Germany via the Trans-Siberian railway.[26] Wenneker gave the copies to Vice-Admiral Nobutake Kondo who read them with great interest.[27] Many people in Japanese naval circles doubted their authenticity, suspecting them to be forgeries being used in a plot to trick Japan into joining the war.[28] However, initial Japanese scepticism gave way to astonishment and helped propel Japan on her destructive path to Pearl Harbor.[29]

Captain Nakamura meanwhile became furious as he had been assured that the *Ole Jacob* was heading towards Lamotrek. Wenneker attempted to smooth things over by reassuring him that if the *Ole Jacob* went straight to Lamotrek, the Norwegian prisoners would learn the location of 'Sheltering Place Y'.

Wenneker agreed to release the Norwegians in line with Rogge's promise, fearing the *Ole Jacob* would be sabotaged if he refused.[30] The sixty-one Norwegians transferred to the liner *Scharnhorst* before being released. Thirty-seven of them went to Hong Kong after accepting a British offer and the remainder went home to Norway via the Trans-Siberian railway under arrangements made by the German Government. The *Ole Jacob* departed Kobe and proceeded towards Lamotrek to rendezvous with a Japanese tanker that would take her aviation fuel.

The *Ole Jacob* had stayed in Kobe for thirty-six hours, instead of the twenty-four hours allowed under international law. Therefore, Robert Craigie, the British Ambassador, met with Vice Foreign Minister Chuichi Ohashi to protest over the *Ole Jacob* being given twelve extra hours and the presence of Norwegian prisoners.

Eyssen's bombardment of Nauru made the tense diplomatic mood explosive. The attack had been against Japanese interests, as the *Komet* had approached the island disguised as a Japanese vessel and also because Japan imported phosphate from Nauru and Ocean Island. The British accordingly launched a diplomatic offensive to convince Japan to stop covertly supporting the raiders. The British Foreign Office cabled Craigie: 'We are taking line with press that evidently the purpose of the Germans is to embroil Japan in war. You will no doubt find means to bring this home.'[31] Newspaper reports immediately speculated that the Nauru attack had been part of an elaborate German plot, as *The Canberra Times* reported: 'Use of Japanese colors by the Nazi raider which shelled Nauru on Friday is regarded in London as a crude German attempt to create a Pacific incident, involving Japan.'[32]

Craigie met with Ohashi and raised suspicions that Japan had been assisting the raiders. He speculated that the *Elsa Essberger* had left Kobe to rendezvous with raiders in the Marshall Islands and unless he received information to the contrary, his government would have no choice but to resume naval patrols near Japanese waters.[33] Ohashi promised to make enquiries and later informed Craigie that the *Elsa Essberger* had visited a port in Japanese territory. Craigie demanded assurances that she was not supplying raiders, but Ohashi refused to provide any more information since doing so would endanger the vessel.[34] Craigie also mentioned raider use of Japanese flags. Foreign Minister Yosuke Matsuoka agreed that this was contrary to Japan's interests, and Craigie warned that continued use of Japanese disguises would force the Allies to regard all Japanese ships as suspicious.

Australia also joined the diplomatic offensive. John Latham, the Australian Minister in Japan, provided Matsuoka with details on German vessels known to have used Japanese flags and intelligence suggesting that German freighters had resupplied raiders in Japanese waters.[35] Matsuoka, seemingly impressed by this information, replied that he feared phosphate imports would diminish or stop.

The Japanese Government protested to Berlin over the use of Japanese disguises and because it was a customer of the British Phosphate Commission. German–Japanese relations remained strained as Wenneker noted:

Japanese Navy far from pleased about bombardment of Nauru, as its own phosphorus supplies have been damaged, co-operation has been put at risk, and reduction of their support for us will be necessary. Recommend that similar operations in the mandated area be avoided.[36]

The Germans agreed not to repeat these mistakes and the Japanese Government quietly forgot the issue. The Japanese continued to pass on intelligence to the Germans, including copies of all documents concerning raiders that the Allies had given them. The Germans used this information to determine exactly how much the Allies knew about raider operations, and Wenneker remarked that 'the observations made by our enemies are entirely correct'.[37]

The *Komet*'s attack on Nauru caused a major headache for the *Kriegsmarine*, which did not know whether to praise Eyssen for his bold action or punish him for its diplomatic consequences. Eyssen justified the raid in terms of economic damage and disruption to enemy warship movements. Berlin informed Wenneker that the bombardment had been outside the *Komet*'s orders but as a one-off incident it had been a success.[38] The *Kriegsmarine* ultimately gave Eyssen quiet praise while reminding all raider captains that similar attacks were forbidden.

CHAPTER 15
THE RAIDER WAR
IN ANTARCTICA

Not a nice trick? Possibly it was not. But of vital importance to us and
unlike many of the other dirty aspects of war *Pinguin*'s deceit did not
result in a single casualty.[1]

Comment on the *Pinguin*'s Antarctic Operation
Kapitänleutnant Ulrich Mohr

STALKING THE NORWEGIANS

After parting company with the *Storstad*, the *Pinguin* headed towards Antarctica
where Krüder hoped to attack enemy whaling fleets. On 13 December 1940
she passed between Prince Edward and Crozet islands and the crew spotted
their first Antarctic iceberg four days later as the temperature plummeted
and the sea changed colour from blue-green to grey. As the raider navigated
between icebergs, Krüder received a signal from the *Seekriegsleitung*:

Anglo-Norwegian whaling area this year is in a zone of about
200 miles around South Georgia. Those taking part are *Harpon*,
Thorshammer, *Pelagos*, *Vestfiord*, *Ole Wegger* and probably two or
three more. All under English charter.[2]

The *Pinguin* accordingly headed north-west towards Bouvet Island and the wireless detected signals from Norwegian whalers as the raider approached her prey. On Christmas Eve the *Seekriegsleitung* announced that Krüder had been awarded the Knight's Cross, a well-deserved honour. The Heinkel conducted a reconnaissance flight two days later but the seaplane made a forced landing after running out of fuel. After the *Pinguin* retrieved the aircraft, the pilot, *Oberleutnant* Werner, reported that in the freezing climate it consumed fuel 40 per cent faster than normal.

The *Pinguin* manoeuvred north of the whalers so Krüder could cut their access to the open sea. Meanwhile the complacent Norwegians communicated without codes and Krüder learned that a tanker would soon rendezvous with the nearby factory ships *Ole Wegger* and *Pelagos* to deliver fuel and collect whale oil. Armed with this information, he decided to wait for the tanker so he could simultaneously capture all the ships. The crew endured freezing conditions, but their morale remained high as they seemed on the verge of a great triumph. On New Year's Day the weather improved and Krüder outlined his plan:

> It is possible that an attack could be made on one of the catchers from astern, but because of the constant radio contact between ships it is most likely that the alarm would be quickly raised. There are so many of them that an attack on one would alert the others. Nevertheless, I hope that a short, quick attack on one would result in an operation against the second group.[3]

On 3 January Krüder learned the tanker would arrive two weeks late. As the *Pelagos* was almost out of fuel and the *Ole Wegger*'s tanks were almost full of whale oil, they would rendezvous to exchange fuel and whale oil. However, after the Norwegians radioed an American tanker company requesting an update, Krüder decided to attack early as the anticipated tanker seemed likely to be American.

As the *Pinguin* prepared to attack, another signal informed Krüder that the tanker *Solglimt* would rendezvous with the factory ship *Thorshammer* and later with the *Ole Wegger*. As the expected tanker was actually Norwegian, Krüder decided to wait for her arrival and the *Pinguin* patiently remained hidden

The whaler *Ole Wegger*, captured by the *Pinguin*, now a prize ship of the Third Reich as demonstrated by the *Kriegsmarine* flag on her stern. (AUTHOR'S COLLECTION)

among the icebergs while her signallers scanned the airwaves for news.

On 10 January the *Solglimt* rendezvoused with the *Thorshammer* and Krüder planned his attack:

> We have to be careful, for the *Solglimt* may well have been armed for her voyage down the Atlantic. With the ships alongside each other, it would be difficult for the *Solglimt* to use any guns she may have. . . . I will start the approach in the morning and come up under the cover of darkness on the side where there are no catchers so as to gain surprise.[4]

After the *Solglimt* came alongside the *Ole Wegger*, the stationary vessels could not have been more vulnerable.

On 13 January the *Pinguin* proceeded on an intercept course and after sunset a snow squall reduced visibility to almost nothing, but Krüder soon sighted the Norwegian ships:

> White lights in sight 2° to port. A bit later many lights of the two ships lying side by side and several catchers can be made out. Shortly thereafter everything lost in a snow cloud and remained so for about 45 minutes. We can approach unseen.[5]

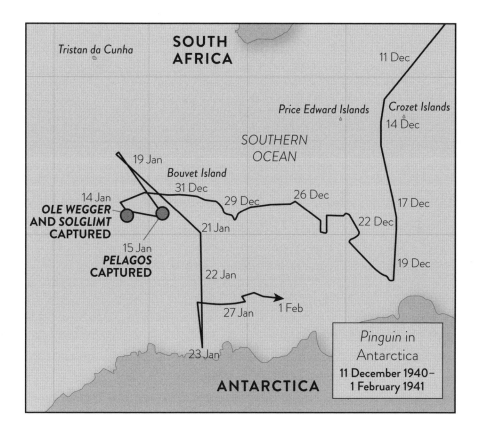

The *Pinguin* approached blacked out while the unsuspecting Norwegians worked using deck lights. The raider's engines suddenly went dead after a cylinder cracked, but she had come within 180 metres (196 yards) of the Norwegians. The boarding parties waited in two boats and the gunners watched the enemy ships while the Norwegians remained oblivious to the danger.

At 0020 h the *Pinguin*'s searchlights lit up the night and Krüder signalled the stunned Norwegians: 'Do not use wireless or telephone, we are sending a boat.'[6] Krüder decided against firing warning shots as he did not want to alarm the whale catchers, which might scatter and flee. One boat headed for the *Ole Wegger* and the other headed towards the *Solglimt*. The boarding parties met no opposition and *Oberleutnant* Warning signalled Krüder: 'Ships in our hands.'[7]

Warning informed Captain Kristian Evensen of the *Ole Wegger* and

Captain Norman Andersen of the *Solglimt* that if they worked, Germany would pay them for their efforts but if they did not, their ships would be sunk. Both captains agreed to co-operate and Warning reported to Krüder: '*Ole Wegger*, Norwegian, 12,201 tons with 7000 tons whale oil . . . *Solglimt*, Norwegian, 12,246 tons, 4000 tons whale oil.'[8]

Krüder despatched *Oberleutnant* Hans-Karl Hemmer in a boat to round up the whale catchers. He hung a sign around his neck with a message: 'I am Ensign Hemmer, Officer of the German Navy. Your boat is captured. Do not offer resistance, let your crew stand to attention.'[9] He recalled what happened next:

> We motored up to the first boat, naturally the slowest one. Rushed on board and up the ladder to the captain's room, pulled my pistol and flashlight, and was met by the sight of a man sleeping in his woolly underwear and snoring in a fug you could cut. I shook the man by the shoulders and rasped out my ditty in a broken voice. The result was staggering. He grunted and turned over. That nearly disarmed me. Just imagine how surprised that captain should have been at suddenly seeing a German officer.[10]

Hemmer rounded up four whale catchers, but three escaped and headed towards the *Thorshammer*, while the *Pinguin*, with its cracked cylinder, could not give chase.[11]

On 15 January Krüder ordered an intercept course towards the *Pelagos*, 220 miles away. A prize crew had been left behind on the captured ships and the Norwegians continued to work. The raider progressed slowly with one working engine, but after the mechanics repaired the second engine she reached full speed. The signallers overheard messages from the whale catchers trying to contact the *Ole Wegger* and *Solglimt*, but after receiving no reply they gave up.

After the lookout spotted a light at 2209 h, Krüder manoeuvred the *Pinguin* around an iceberg and the raider came within 4 miles of the whale catchers without being spotted. The *Pelagos* came into view with five whale catchers alongside her. At midnight the searchlights exposed the Norwegians while boarding parties raced towards the factory ship. The Norwegians offered

In December 1940 the *Pinguin* headed towards Antarctica where *Kapitän* Krüder hoped to attack Anglo–Norwegian whaling fleets. The whaler *Pelagos* (pictured) was one of the whalers captured.
(AUTHOR'S COLLECTION)

no resistance and the boarding party instructed Captain Fritz Gothesen to order the whale catchers to return, and Krüder recalled their capture: 'The master of the *Pelagos* was instructed to recall his boats in a way that would not arouse suspicion. They duly complied and were likewise one by one accounted for.'[12]

The *Pinguin* had captured the 12,083-ton *Pelagos* carrying 9500 tons of whale oil and her seven whale catchers.[13] The other whale catchers successfully escaped and warned the *Thorshammer*, which promptly departed the area. The Royal Navy ordered the armed merchant cruiser *Queen of Bermuda* to search the area and she reached South Georgia six days later but found no trace of the *Pinguin*.[14]

THE GREATEST PRIZE

Krüder's Antarctic operation was the most successful raider action of the war. The prize ships carried 20,500 tons of whale oil worth US$4.1 million and the whale catchers could be converted into auxiliaries.

On 16 January the *Pinguin* rendezvoused with the *Ole Wegger* and *Solglimt* before rendezvousing with the *Pelagos*. As Krüder needed to organize these vessels for their voyages to Europe, the raider and her prizes headed south towards more remote waters and the crew glimpsed the majestic Antarctic continent. Krüder assigned prize crews and the men made preparations while the prisoners worked, as Doctor Werner Hasselmann witnessed:

> Once the Norwegians had got used to the idea, everything went on as though we were not there at all. They carried on their work as usual, and their attitude toward us was, if not friendly, at least not actively hostile.[15]

The Germans transferred the whale oil from *Ole Wegger* to the *Solglimt* since the tanker would arouse less suspicion than a factory ship. Krüder placed *Oberleutnant* Küster in command of the *Pelagos* and *Leutnant* Helmut Bach in command of the *Solglimt*, and both vessels departed for Bordeaux on separate courses on 25 January. The *Ole Wegger* and the whale catchers required more fuel and prize crews before they could depart for Europe, so the *Seekriegsleitung* ordered Krüder to rendezvous with the *Nordmark* at 'Andalusia', 200 miles north-west of Tristan da Cunha. On 1 February the Germans departed Antarctica bound for the secret rendezvous.

CHAPTER 16
THE *KORMORAN* IN THE ATLANTIC

One thing that was firmly embedded in the minds of all the prisoners.
. . . They were all quite certain that we must have been out since the
declaration of war, or had put out from some neutral port since. The
idea that we had sailed out of a German harbour in war time and
through the British blockade just wouldn't go into their heads. For
them the North Sea was British.[1]

Kapitän Theodore Detmers
Commander of the *Kormoran*

THE *ANTONIS*

On 1 January 1941 the *Kormoran*, disguised as the Soviet freighter *Vyatcheslav Molotov*, proceeded south-east through the North Atlantic near the Pan-American Neutrality Zone. Detmers patrolled the Central Atlantic for five days, encountering only American and Spanish vessels, which caused disappointment: 'The whole crew is beaming. We had been in our operational area 14 days without sighting a ship.'[2] The *Kormoran*'s lull ended on 6 January when the lookout spotted a freighter.

Detmers sounded the alarm and the crew ran to their action stations while the raider approached on a converging course. At 2700 metres (2952 yards) Detmers signalled 'what ship?' and the freighter replied 'Antonis'. Detmers hoisted the *Kriegsmarine* flag, uncovered his guns and ordered her to stop.

The small 3729-ton Greek freighter *Antonis* had been proceeding to Argentina from Cardiff carrying coal, with a crew of twenty-eight sailors and one passenger. Although the Greeks had three machine guns, they could not offer meaningful resistance and her captain obeyed the order to stop. A boarding party led by *Oberleutnant* Diebitsch searched the *Antonis* and discovered documents confirming she was operating under British charter.

The boarding party scuttled the *Antonis* and the Greek prisoners boarded the *Kormoran*. Detmers gave the Greek captain the option of quartering with his men in the holds or opting for a cabin. He chose the former, which suited Detmers who believed it best if officers stayed with their men to act as go-betweens, making them easier to control. Other raider captains preferred to keep the officers segregated to discourage rebellion, but Detmers understood that prisoners had their own system of discipline, which worked best with minimal contact with guards. Each prisoner received five cigarettes a day and their presence soon felt normal, as Detmers reflected:

> They lazed in the sun, stood at the ship's rail and looked at the flying fish or at the dolphins swimming along with us and disporting themselves, or they walked around in twos or threes. . . . Just as they got used to their new life so we got used to their presence; and when, as occasionally happened, we had no prisoners on board we felt as though something were missing.[3]

The *Kormoran* headed north-west towards the Azores–Fernando de Noronha route while the lookout scanned the horizon for fresh victims.

THE *BRITISH UNION*

The *Kormoran* patrolled north-west of the Cape Verde Islands and Detmers signalled the *Seekriegsleitung*: 'Have sunk so far 1 vessel. Predominantly neutral shipping in sea area, consider further implementation of task futile, since enemy merchant shipping almost exclusively in convoy.'[4] The raider headed north-west towards the Gibraltar routes, but after having no luck, Detmers decided to head south.

On 18 January the *Kormoran* proceeded west in overcast weather. The lookout spotted smoke just before dusk and Detmers ordered an intercept course, intending to approach hidden in the darkness. After sunset the ship seemingly turned on a night-time zigzag course, the action of an enemy vessel. As the raider approached, the shape of a tanker with a stern gun became clear.

At 5500 metres (6014 yards) the *Kormoran*'s crew hoisted the *Kriegsmarine* flag and Detmers ordered the tanker to stop. The vessel began broadcasting a raider warning so Detmers opened fire. As the searchlights did not sufficiently illuminate the tanker, the gunners fired a star shell, but their first salvo fell short and they adjusted their weapons under the light of the flare.

The 6987-ton tanker *British Union* had been proceeding in ballast from Gibraltar to Trinidad. Captain Atthill, despite his initial surprise, attempted to flee. The 4.7-inch stern gun returned fire but the Royal Navy gunners, disorientated by the searchlight, failed to hit their target. The wireless operator broadcast: 'RRRR British Union Shelled.'[5] The *B-Dienst* in Germany intercepted this signal and the *Seekriegsleitung* correctly assumed the *Kormoran* was responsible. The raider's third salvo hit the freighter, causing fires to erupt. Chief Steward Alexander Bandeen witnessed the attack:

> We were sailing alone quietly in pitch dark when all of a sudden a Star Shell came over the ship. . . . I rushed out on deck then ran back for my Life Jacket and Steel Helmet. I heard our 4.7 gun firing constantly and also our machine guns. I came back to an alley way when a shell hit the forecastle where many men could have been trapped.[6]

Detmers ordered a ceasefire after the *British Union*'s wireless went quiet and her stern gun stopped firing, but as the raider approached closer, the British resumed firing. The raider returned fire and scored more hits while the stern gun fired four more shots before being silenced. Detmers ordered another ceasefire after observing lifeboats being lowered.

Detmers decided to sink the *British Union* and the torpedo officer *Oberleutnant* Greter made his calculations and fired. The first torpedo missed but the second struck the tanker and exploded, although she remained afloat. The lifeboats signalled the raider by lamp 'SOS boats are sinking' after one capsized. The Germans rescued the survivors, as Detmers noted:

Two of my men were at the bottom of the rope ladder and they fished out man after man. When it was the turn of the last man to be hauled in he lost consciousness and released his hold on the oar he had been clinging to. . . . Both my men went in after him, got hold of him and brought him safely to our side. I mention this incident because it was typical of my men: they were ruthless in action, but afterwards there was nothing they wouldn't do to help their victims.[7]

The Germans rescued twenty-eight men, a monkey and a bird in a cage. The *Kormoran* fired several more shells at the *British Union*, but the crippled tanker refused to sink. After a third torpedo struck her amidships and exploded, the tanker listed to starboard and finally sank. Although seventeen British sailors were missing, Detmers knew the *British Union* had successfully broadcast a raider warning so the *Kormoran* fled west.

The armed merchant cruiser *Arawa* had spotted the *Kormoran*'s gun flashes and as she headed towards the battle, her crew believed they were about to engage a pocket battleship, as Commander Irwin Chapman recalled: 'Attacker assumed to be the "ADMIRAL SCHEER" causing those on the bridge to say to one another it was nice knowing you!'[8] The *Arawa*'s lookout spotted the burning tanker and later saw the *Kormoran*'s searchlight. After arriving, her crew found oil, wreckage and a lifeboat containing seven men. She searched the area for three days before resuming her course towards Freetown.[9]

Captain Atthill quartered with his men in the *Kormoran*'s hold in the type of arrangement favoured by Detmers. The bird resided in the Chief Boatswain's cabin and the monkey, renamed Tommy as he came from a British ship, lived in a crate behind the funnel. The crew established a new galley in which a cook from the *Kormoran* and a cook from the *British Union* prepared the food together.

THE *AFRIC STAR*

The *Seekriegsleitung* ordered Detmers to proceed to 'Andalusia', 200 miles north-west of Tristan da Cunha, where the *Kormoran* would rendezvous with the *Nordmark*, as the supply ship needed the raider's U-boat supplies to replenish *U-A*. Before the rendezvous Detmers would continue operations north of the equator as the *Thor* remained active in the South Atlantic.

As the *Kormoran* proceeded south-east between the Cape Verde Islands and the equator, the engineering officer *Kapitänleutnant* Stehr informed Detmers that poor quality white metal in the bearings was causing engine problems. Detmers could return to port where the bearings could be recast but he decided to continue the voyage and requested additional white metal from the *Seekriegsleitung*.

On 29 January the *Kormoran* passed south of the Cape Verde Islands while haze blanketed the sea. The lookout had spotted a freighter emerging from mist, which suddenly changed course. Detmers did not react, hoping she would resume her original course, and after she did, the distance between the two ships slowly reduced.

The 11,900-ton Blue Star Line freighter *Afric Star* had been bound for Britain from Buenos Aires carrying frozen meat and butter. Captain Clement Cooper, responsible for seventy-two sailors, two naval gunners and two female passengers, stood on the bridge observing a 'Soviet' freighter. The female passengers happily sunbathed on the deck in their bathing suits drinking coffee, unaware that Detmers would soon interrupt their leisure time.

After Detmers spotted a stern gun, the freighter suddenly turned away so Detmers ordered her to stop and fired a warning shot. Captain Cooper ordered full speed and the *Afric Star*'s wireless broadcast a raider warning. The *Kormoran*'s gunners opened fire and their third salvo struck the freighter, convincing Captain Cooper that resistance would be pointless. The *Afric Star* ceased broadcasting, stopped and her crew lowered their lifeboats. Her 4.7-inch stern gun never returned fire.

A boarding party led by *Leutnant* Johannes Diebitsch seized the *Afric Star* and captured her Merchant Navy codes, which later enabled the signals officer *Kapitänleutnant* Reinhold von Malapert to read merchant ship traffic. Diebitsch informed Detmers that the *Afric Star* had suffered too much damage to become a prize. The boarding party escorted the prisoners to

On 29 January 1941 the *Kormoran* captured the 11,900-ton Blue Star Line freighter *Afric Star*, which had been bound for Britain from Buenos Aires carrying frozen meat and butter.
(AUTHOR'S COLLECTION)

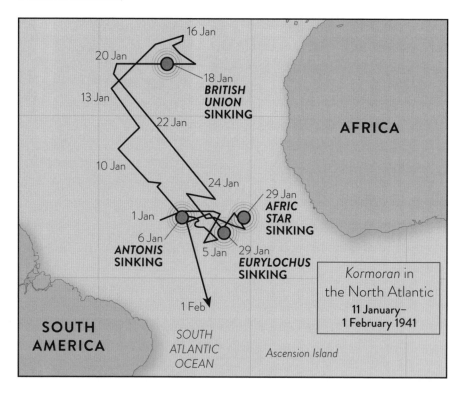

the raider but, as the women were still wearing bathing suits, Detmers ordered Diebitsch to bring back their clothes and Greter remarked, 'We noticed that the vaunted German efficiency had broken down. We had forgotten to take along clothes for the captured ladies.'[10] The guards escorted the women to a cabin near the hospital. One lady had been returning to England with her husband while the other, a young typist, had also been heading home.

The explosives placed by the boarding party failed to sink the *Afric Star* so Greter fired a torpedo that exploded under her bridge and she disappeared beneath the waves. As the *Kormoran* fled south-west, the wireless room confirmed that the enemy had received the *Afric Star*'s warning. The officers gathered in the wardroom to celebrate their latest success and they painted the names of their victims on the wardroom wall. The watch officer who had spotted the *Afric Star* received a bottle of champagne and the boarding party presented Detmers with a brass bell from the *Afric Star* which he placed in his cabin.

THE *EURYLOCHUS*

Two hours after the sinking of the *Afric Star*, the *Kormoran*'s lookout spotted another ship in the evening darkness. Detmers rushed to the bridge and saw a British Blue Funnel Line freighter proceeding without lights. He ordered an intercept course.

The 5723-ton freighter *Eurylochus* had left Glasgow in Convoy WS 5B bound for Takoradi in Ghana with a cargo of sixteen heavy bombers but had recently separated from the convoy. Her crew of seventy-one men included many Chinese sailors. Captain Caird had avoided coastal waters, fearing U-boats, but headed straight towards the *Kormoran*.

On the *Eurylochus*' bridge, Fourth Officer Sparks raised the alarm after spotting another vessel approaching. Captain Caird rushed to the bridge and saw a ship signalling 'what ship?' and he replied, 'Eurylochus'. The unknown vessel increased speed, came alongside and at 3200 metres (3500 yards) ordered the *Eurylochus* to stop. Captain Caird ordered full speed and his wireless broadcast a raider warning.

Detmers ordered his gunners to shell the *Eurylochus*. A star shell lit up the night but the *Kormoran*'s first salvo went over the freighter. The stern gunner Frank Laskier returned fire with his 4.7-inch cannon, but the raider's searchlight disorientated him. As German shells struck the *Eurylochus*, Third Officer Povey tried to organize fire-fighting teams, but the Chinese firemen deserted their posts.[11] Many Chinese sailors also emerged from their accommodation and vanished.[12]

The *Eurylochus* received more hits, but her wireless kept broadcasting. After a shell exploded near the stern gun, putting it out of action, and the fires destroyed her steering, Captain Caird decided to abandon ship. Sparks signalled the raider requesting a ceasefire. Detmers agreed and his guns went silent. The freighter's crew began lowering their lifeboats, but shortly afterwards the *Kormoran*'s radio room reported that the *Eurylochus* had resumed broadcasting. The raider's 20-mm anti-aircraft guns pounded her wireless room with rapid tracer shells, as Detmers remembered: 'The steamer suddenly transmits a radio message in numbers, permission to fire to main battery and 2 cm guns, until the opponent stops transmitting. The superstructure of the ship is completely shot up.'[13] After the transmissions stopped, Detmers ordered another ceasefire.

As Captain Caird had been wounded with a shattered leg and broken shoulder, Chief Officer McGregor carried him to a lifeboat before returning to the bridge to make sure the code-books had been destroyed. Captain Caird later described the engagement:

> They were concentrating on the bridge with their devilish machine gun fire, so I fear Mr Baker [a writer in the wheelhouse] must have been killed. The whole affair was ghastly and it is evident that none of us were intended to get out alive. It was a murderous attack and I now marvel how any one of us really did get away.[14]

Detmers sank the *Eurylochus* with a torpedo while her crew watched from two lifeboats and two rafts. Laskier witnessed the end of his ship: 'She mounted high in the air, she bowed to the sky. Then with a roar, as of hatred and vengeance, she slipped under. The huge wave of her sinking rose and engulfed the survivors.'[15]

The *Kormoran* rescued four English and thirty-nine Chinese survivors and the guards escorted three badly wounded men to the hospital, but one man died that night.[16] Detmers searched for the twenty-eight missing men, including Captain Caird, but after failing to find them the raider fled at full speed. When the crew discovered the *Eurylochus* had been carrying sixteen heavy bombers intended for Egypt, they felt a strong sense of pride, and Detmers remarked, 'We were lending direct assistance to Rommel's Afrika Korps, a circumstance which gave us a good deal of pleasure.'[17]

As the cruisers *Norfolk* and *Devonshire* as well as the armed merchant cruiser *Bulolo* converged on the area, the *Kormoran* headed south-east towards her rendezvous with the *Nordmark*, while the officers added a fourth name to their wardroom wall.

When morning came Captain Caird counted twenty-eight survivors on the two rafts that had escaped the raider. Sharks circled but the crew kept them at bay with oars. The Spanish ship *Monte Teide* rescued them and later encountered the *Bulolo*, which took the wounded and eight others but Captain Caird, Chief Engineer Creech and the others remained on board, eventually disembarking at Buenos Aires.

The new prisoners on the *Kormoran* adjusted to captivity and Seaman Gustav Heinz observed their routine: 'The prisoners were permitted to see a picture once a week — had their own galley and were issued with smokes. They were permitted to listen to the Radio and were kept up to date with news.'[18] The Chinese prisoners had been given their own quarters on the second deck. The supply officer *Oberleutnant* Herbert Breitschneider suggested employing Chinese volunteers as laundrymen and, after Detmers agreed, he found four willing men. They would work for the duration of the cruise and be paid on arrival in Germany.

The two English women could exercise on deck each day and talk with the other English prisoners and the married woman could even see her husband. During action stations the guards escorted them to the hospital where Doctor Friedrich Lienhoop kept an eye on them. Detmers observed the impact of their presence:

> Our two ladies were as cheerful as their situation would allow. They never missed the exercise hours and it was not long before I noticed that as many of my own men who could manage it used to appear as

onlookers to 'get an eye-full' of the girls, who were, as it happened, both young and attractive.[19]

On 1 February the *Kormoran* crossed the equator, entering the South Atlantic, and the *Seekriegsleitung* ordered Detmers to transfer his prisoners to the *Nordmark* at 'Andalusia'. On 5 February the crew conducted a crossing of the line ceremony as Detmers had postponed this event, wanting it to occur in more remote waters. Neptune appeared dressed in a blue admiral's uniform with a blond beard, robes and a large telescope. Sailors who had not crossed the equator before came forward and Neptune's guards placed them on a board over the swimming pool and tossed them into the water as the raider headed south towards the *Nordmark*.

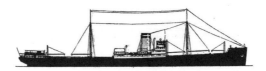

CHAPTER 17
REMOTE ENCOUNTERS AND THE ISLANDS OF DESPAIR

In a heavy sea but exceptionally good visibility we saw a wild and
forbidding coastline, topped by a range of snow-clad hills and with
long narrow promontories flanked by scores of little islands and reefs.
It was the first land we had seen for many a day.[1]

Description of the Kerguelen Islands
Vizeadmiral Bernhard Rogge
Commander of the *Atlantis*

PACIFIC RESPITE

After departing Emirau, the *Orion* proceeded north-west towards Lamotrek
Atoll (Sheltering Place Y), where Weyher planned to overhaul her engines
and transfer his prisoners to the blockade runner *Ermland*.

On Christmas Day 1940 the *Orion* reached Lamotrek and rendezvoused
with the *Ole Jacob*. As Weyher approached the tanker in a motorboat, he
received a great surprise as her master was his friend Captain 'Allright'
Steinkrauss. Weyher had not seen him since he had departed on the *Tropic Sea*.
Weyher knew the prize ship had been intercepted by the British submarine

Truant. Steinkrauss explained that after he scuttled the *Tropic Sea*, the Royal Navy placed him in a lifeboat with his men before departing. The Germans and Norwegians in the lifeboats sailed towards France and the next day a Sunderland flying boat rescued the Norwegians. The Germans decided to row to Spain after bad weather destroyed their sails and, after arriving, they travelled to France. Steinkrauss flew to Berlin where the *Kriegsmarine* offered him command of the *Ole Jacob* and he departed for Japan on the Trans-Siberian railway.

After the *Ole Jacob* replenished the *Orion*, the raider proceeded south-west towards the Panama–Honolulu route to hunt new victims, while the tanker remained behind to wait for the *Regensburg* and *Ermland*. Weyher patrolled the route for four days without success and the crew's morale plummeted as rumours circulated that they would soon head home.

The *Orion* returned to Lamotrek on New Year's Eve and rendezvoused with the *Ole Jacob* and *Regensburg*, which had recently arrived with stores, including Japanese beer just in time for New Year's celebrations. On New Year's Day the engine overhaul work commenced; however, as the *Munsterland* had left Japan headed for Maug Island in the Marianas with additional supplies for the raider, Weyher decided this would be a safer location to complete the overhaul, as the Emirau castaways might have compromised 'Sheltering Place Y', and the work stopped.

On 4 January the *Regensburg* left for Japan and the next day the *Ermland* arrived.[2] Weyher inspected the blockade runner and ordered Captain Kragge to clean her cockroach-infested holds and, after this had been done, 183 prisoners boarded the vessel. Three days later the German ships left Lamotrek. The *Ermland* later took additional prisoners from the *Scheer* and *Nordmark* before arriving at Bordeaux on 4 April.[3] Edward Sweeney, a prisoner from the *Turakina*, later escaped by jumping from the train taking him to Germany:

> I crossed the Pyranees [*sic*] into Spain, and was arrested and jailed by the Civil Guard for not having papers to prove my identity. After a spell in filthy jails, I was imprrisoned [*sic*] in a labour concentration camp at Miranda de Ebro, in Northern Spain, carrying a large basket of stones on my back, helping to build a new major road. Fifteen months after

my leaving England, I was eventually released, reaching Glasgow, via Gibraltar, none the worse for my adventures.[4]

On 12 January the *Orion* and *Ole Jacob* arrived at Maug, a small island on the edge of an extinct black rock volcano. Weyher found an uncharted entrance into the volcano and the two ships entered a natural harbour. The volcano's inner walls, green with vegetation, sheltered the vessels from the outside world, making it the perfect place to finish the engine overhaul work.

Weyher expected the island to be uninhabited but scouts spotted a small jetty, three wooden buildings and a Japanese flag on a beach. The Germans made contact with nine Japanese men and forty Filipino labourers who were constructing a weather station. The Japanese permitted the Germans to stay and allowed them to set up a lookout on top of the volcano.

The Japanese Government boat *Marana Maru* arrived from Saipan as the weather station had presumably reported the German presence. Weyher met the Japanese officials on the *Ole Jacob* and Steinkrauss gave them ice cold beer. Weyher explained that the ships were blockade runners that had stopped temporarily due to engine problems. The Japanese seemingly accepted this story and all present toasted the Tripartite Pact, but one official asked why a Japanese flag had been painted on the *Ole Jacob*'s funnel. Steinkrauss replied that it would be removed.

On 18 January the *Regensburg* arrived with fresh food and water. Doctor Raffler, who had been suffering from an incurable tumour pressing against his spine, transferred to the *Regensburg*. He had won the admiration of the crew and prisoners by performing his medical duties through sheer willpower, despite being in intense pain. The *Regensburg* departed for Japan, arriving on 2 March, as *Konteradmiral* Wenneker, the naval attaché, noted:

> Raffler's descriptions of the conditions on board the auxiliary cruiser, on the other hand, were particularly valuable for me so far as the future supply of the vessel is concerned. It was particularly encouraging to hear from his own lips that morale on board has not been affected in the slightest despite the lengthy absence from home.[5]

Doctor Raffler returned to Germany only to die under surgery. The *Regensburg*

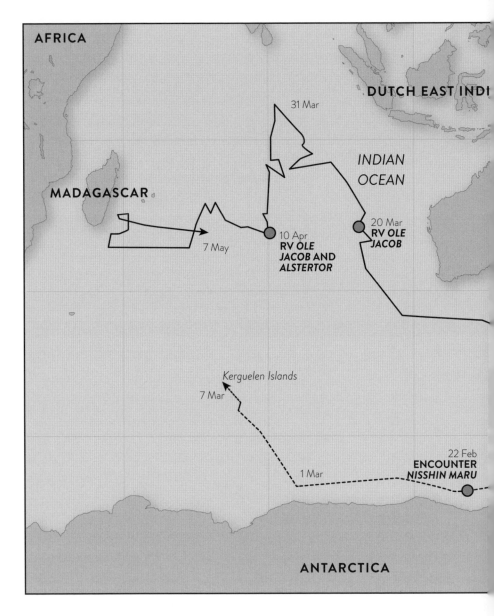

became a blockade runner and later arrived in Bordeaux on 27 June.

On 1 February the *Munsterland* arrived at Maug with more supplies and a Japanese Nakajima seaplane, which Wenneker had purchased for the *Orion*. The *Orion*'s engines became ready for testing four days later and the engineering officer *Kapitänleutnant* Kolsch reported that three boilers functioned

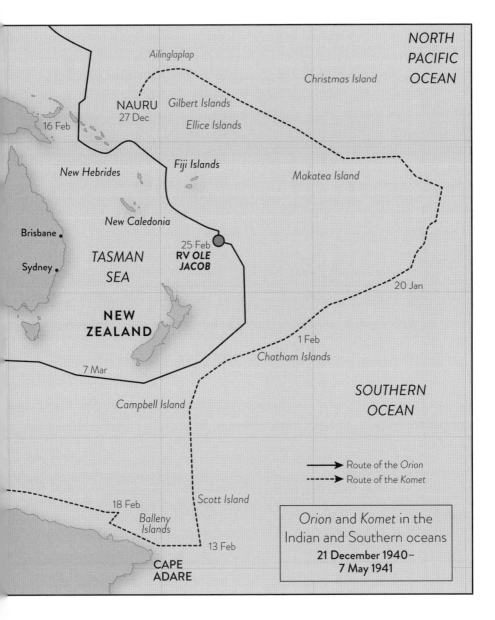

well, while the fourth was leaking, but this problem could be fixed. Overall, the raider made an impressive 13 knots. Weyher planned to head towards his new operational area in the eastern Indian Ocean via the Great Australian Bight. The *Orion* and *Ole Jacob* left Maug the next day and Weyher became hopeful of finding fresh victims on the Australian shipping routes.

The *Orion*, disguised as an anonymous vessel, and the *Ole Jacob* continued through the Central Pacific on a south-easterly course, sighting only a steamer, which soon vanished. On 15 February the German ships crossed the equator and the next day they passed between Bougainville and the Choiseul Islands, entering the Coral Sea, and eleven Catalina flying boats on their way to Australia from America appeared overhead.

At noon Steinkrauss spotted an RAAF Sunderland flying boat, which circled the *Ole Jacob* and crossed the *Orion*'s bow before disappearing. The wireless room overheard coded signals, presumably from the flying boat to Port Moresby. The radio waves became alive with transmissions from nearby air bases and it seemed certain the Germans had aroused enemy suspicion. Therefore, Weyher decided to leave the Coral Sea.[6] The Australians did suspect a raider as a signal noted: 'Aircraft sighted two vessels. . . . Description somewhat similar to Narvik [*Orion*] and Tanker Olde Jacob.'[7]

The *Orion* and *Ole Jacob* separated but Weyher and Steinkrauss planned to rendezvous three days later between New Hebrides and New Caledonia. The lookout spotted another flying boat the next morning, which did not notice the raider, and at midday the radio detection unit identified five patrolling aircraft, but Weyher kept the raider out of sight by plotting a course between their flight paths. A signal from the *Ole Jacob* stating that she had spotted another aircraft convinced Weyher to postpone the rendezvous.

The *Orion* rounded the Solomon Islands and Weyher avoided a ship as investigating might attract nearby planes and warships. The crew saw the Santa Cruz Islands and, after sunset, they saw the red glow of lava from a volcano pouring into the sea as the raider continued south towards New Zealand.

On 25 February the *Orion* rendezvoused with the *Ole Jacob* north-east of the Kermadec Islands. After the tanker refuelled the raider, both ships headed south-west towards the Chatham Islands and the men experienced the fierce storms and mountainous waves of the Roaring Forties. On 3 March the lookout spotted the Bounty Islands and the vessels entered Antarctic waters. Storms rocked the *Orion* as Doctor Müller-Osten conducted an operation on a sailor to remove his appendix. After two long hours of surgery, while the helmsman struggled to keep the ship as stable as possible, he saved the sailor's life.

The *Orion* rounded New Zealand the next day and the crew sighted Auckland Island. After proceeding through the Great Australian Bight, Weyher reached his new operational area in the eastern Indian Ocean, south-west of Cape Leeuwin, and the crew hoped that fresh victories would come their way before the raider headed home.

KORMORAN AT 'ANDALUSIA'

On 7 February 1941 the *Kormoran* rendezvoused with the *Nordmark* and the *Duquesa* at 'Andalusia', 200 miles north-west of Tristan da Cunha. Detmers boarded the *Nordmark* and *Korvettenkapitän* Peter Grau informed him that only American ships had been seen in these waters. The *Kormoran* received beef, eggs, fuel and fifteen torpedoes, but Grau had no white metal for her bearings. The raider's 172 prisoners transferred to the *Nordmark* after Detmers thanked the Allied captains for the good behaviour of their men and shared beer with them. Second Officer King from the *Afric Star* recalled: 'Drinks and games didn't enter into the game of war but we were glad we had been decently treated.'[8]

The *Seekriegsleitung* offered Detmers a whale catcher captured by the *Pinguin*, which had been heading towards 'Andalusia', to use as an auxiliary minelayer, but he declined because he felt his *Leichte Schnellboot* better suited to the task.[9] On 9 February the *Kormoran* left 'Andalusia' on a north-easterly course towards South Africa.[10]

The prisoners on the *Nordmark* experienced worse conditions compared with the *Kormoran* but the guards allowed them on deck during the day except during meals. They later transferred to the blockade runner *Portland* and, as she approached France, a small group of prisoners led by Able Seaman Arthur Fry from the *Afric Star* broke into an adjacent hold and started a fire. While the Germans extinguished the flames, the guards kept a tense watch on the prisoners and during the standoff the lights went out and, in the confusion, one guard fired three shots, killing two prisoners, including the husband of the English woman from the *Afric Star*. Able Seaman Appleby from the *Port Brisbane* remembered the aftermath of the mutiny: 'Strong punitive measures were taken by the Germans in the form of lashings, rifle buttings, etc.'[11] The blockade runner arrived in Bordeaux on 16 March.[12]

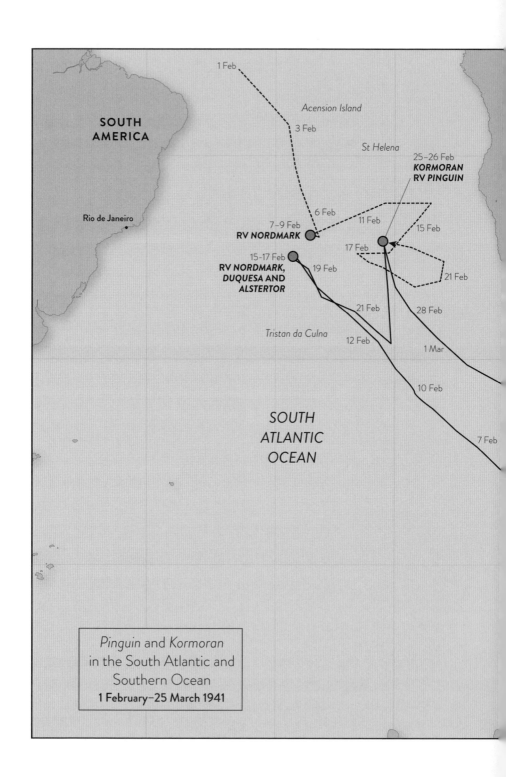

1 Feb

SOUTH
AMERICA

Acension Island

3 Feb

St Helena

25–26 Feb
KORMORAN
RV PINGUIN

Rio de Janeiro

6 Feb

7–9 Feb
RV NORDMARK

11 Feb

15 Feb

17 Feb

15-17 Feb
RV NORDMARK,
DUQUESA AND
ALSTERTOR

19 Feb

21 Feb

21 Feb

28 Feb

Tristan da Culna

12 Feb

1 Mar

10 Feb

SOUTH
ATLANTIC
OCEAN

7 Feb

Pinguin and *Kormoran*
in the South Atlantic and
Southern Ocean
1 February–25 March 1941

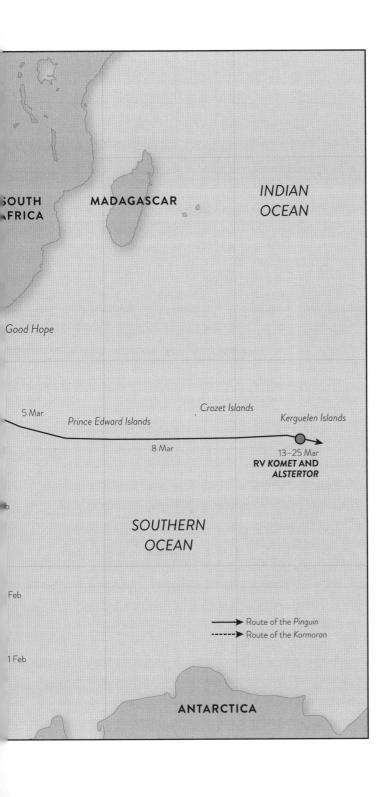

The Germans sentenced Fry to death but later reprieved his sentence after Swiss intervention. He was awarded the British Empire Medal and his citation read: 'Fry was the chief ringleader and displayed courage and determination in pursuing the project of liberation by forceful measures.'[13]

PINGUIN AT 'ANDALUSIA'

On 15 February the *Pinguin*, *Ole Wegger* and the whale catchers rendezvoused with the *Nordmark* and *Duquesa* at 'Andalusia'. As Krüder needed additional sailors for his prize vessels before they could proceed to Europe, the *Seekriegsleitung* arranged prize crews from the *Scheer*, which boarded the *Duquesa*.[14] The raider received meat and eggs from the *Duquesa*, but she had been reduced to a shell because her crew had been forced to burn her materiel to feed the furnaces, and the Germans scuttled her on 18 February.

The supply ship *Alstertor* commanded by Captain Wilhelm Nielsen arrived that day with additional supplies for the raiders, including shells, torpedoes, mines and two Arado seaplanes.[15] Krüder gave Captain Nielsen a copy of his war diary and the crew received mail from home, but the transfer of supplies did not take place immediately as Krüder decided to conduct this work at the Kerguelen Islands. He also retained the whale catcher *Pol IX* as a reconnaissance vessel, renaming her *Adjutant*, and *Oberleutnant* Hemmer took command.

The *Ole Wegger* commanded by *Oberleutnant* Blaue and ten whale catchers departed for Bordeaux on 20 February while the *Pinguin*, *Adjutant* and *Alstertor* headed towards the Cape of Good Hope. The tanker *Spichern* refuelled the whale catchers in the North Atlantic and their voyages continued without incident until 13 March, when the sloop *Scarborough* intercepted *Star XIX* and *Star XXIV* near Gibraltar. The British boarded *Star XXIV* and allowed her to pass, but when the sloop approached *Star XIX* the prize crew scuttled their ship, forcing the crew of *Star XXIV* to do the same. The *Pelagos*, *Solglimt* and *Ole Wegger* arrived safely in Bordeaux and the eight surviving whale catchers reached France and subsequently became auxiliary anti-submarine vessels and minesweepers.[16]

KORMORAN AND PINGUIN

Detmers planned to patrol the waters between St Helena and Cape Town before mining the approaches to Walvis Bay, but anticipated little success, believing the area to be quiet given the recent operations of the *Thor* and *Scheer*. On 14 February he cancelled the mining operation due to heavy seas and the *Kormoran* proceeded south-west to patrol the Cape Town–Freetown route. The raider's engine bearings again broke down as the stock of white metal was simply too weak. Two groups of technicians worked alternate shifts to mould new bearings and Detmers requested fresh stocks, and the *Seekriegsleitung* ordered him to rendezvous with the *Pinguin*, where Krüder would supply him with white metal. The raider meanwhile stayed in the South Atlantic and Detmers expressed frustration: 'The order means that our real task is postponed for an extra month, since it will hardly be possible to do anything in the allotted operational area.'[17]

On 25 February the *Kormoran* and *Pinguin* rendezvoused south-east of St Helena. After receiving orders to rendezvous with the *Kormoran*, Krüder had headed north while the *Adjutant* and *Alstertor* remained behind. Detmers' men lined the deck and gave the *Pinguin* three cheers, which Krüder's men duly returned, and both crews lowered boats to socialize and trade popular items, such as films. To Detmers' delight Krüder provided him with 210 kilograms (462 pounds) of white metal.

Detmers and Krüder met on the *Pinguin* to discuss tactics, as Detmers recorded:

> He told me that at first the hunting in the Indian Ocean had been exhilarating, but then game had become much scarcer because the depredations of our auxiliary cruisers had compelled the enemy wherever possible to re-route his ships along the shore. The only hopeful areas left were the Arabian Sea and the Bay of Bengal.[18]

Detmers informed Krüder that he expected to enter the Indian Ocean in May, and both captains agreed to a future rendezvous. The raiders departed the next day and both crews assembled on deck to wave goodbye.

THE *KOMET* IN ANTARCTICA

After the bombardment of Nauru, the *Komet* headed north-east towards the Gilbert Islands and chased a Norwegian ship without success, and on New Year's Day the *Kriegsmarine* promoted Eyssen to *Konteradmiral*. The *Seekriegsleitung* refused permission for him to operate near the Panama Canal and ordered him to Antarctic waters to hunt enemy whaling fleets before proceeding to the Indian Ocean. Eyssen reflected:

> In view of the disturbances caused by our successes in Australian and New Zealand waters, it is wiser to make a large sweep to reach the Indian Ocean, rather than to take the shortest route (Tasman Sea).[19]

On 19 January the *Komet* approached Pitcairn Island, home of the HMS *Bounty* mutineers, but after sighting no ships she headed south-west towards the Chatham Islands along the Panama–New Zealand route without encountering any vessels. During this quiet time Eyssen gave his crew two weeks' leave in which they could organize their own time, except during action stations. Leisure activities included films in the cinema, an orchestra and a jazz band. Eyssen also began inviting men on their birthdays to join him and his executive officer *Korvettenkapitän* Josef Huschenbeth for a social chat followed by a party with the crew with wine, beer and punch.[20]

After rounding the Chatham Islands on 6 February, the *Komet* proceeded south towards Scott Island, arriving six days later. Eyssen planned to repeat the *Pinguin*'s success by attacking enemy whalers in Antarctic waters. After the raider entered the Ross Sea, the icy water had the unexpected benefit of removing barnacles from her hull.

The *Komet* passed Cape Adare and the crew sighted the Antarctic continent, but Eyssen had no success and his signallers only heard radio broadcasts from Japanese whalers. The raider continued east, hugging the Antarctic coast, and on 22 February she encountered the Japanese whale factory ship *Nisshin Maru*. The Germans found the Japanese crew to be friendly and they obtained whale meat in exchange for wine. The raider's wireless room heard no trace of enemy vessels, but it intercepted a signal from the American Antarctica Expedition led by Admiral Richard Byrd.

In February–March 1941 the *Komet* was in Antarctic waters, hunting for enemy whalers. Note the Japanese flags on her hull, as she was disguised as a Japanese freighter.
(AUTHOR'S COLLECTION)

On 28 February Eyssen abandoned the hunt and the *Komet* headed towards the Kerguelens to rendezvous with the *Pinguin* and *Alstertor*.

THE KERGUELEN ISLANDS

On 7 March the *Komet* arrived at the Kerguelens and anchored in Royal Sound off Grave Island. The islands, an extremely remote volcanic group in the southern Indian Ocean, are a bleak, treeless and mountainous landscape of black and white rock, ravines, marshes and bogs. The group had been discovered by the French explorer Yves-Joseph de Kerguelen in 1772, and Captain Cook, who charted the islands in 1776, wanted to name them the Islands of Despair. The French-owned islands had once been a whaler base but had long since been abandoned. The *Atlantis* had visited the Kerguelens in December 1940 and Rogge found them to be an ideal location to overhaul his raider in isolation, finding a safe anchorage in remote bays and a plentiful supply of fresh water from glaciers.

A shore party from the *Komet* landed and found the empty settlement Jeanne d'Arc. The crew spent three days on the island, taking all the abandoned stores, including coal, wood and pipes, and explored the island, hunting rabbits and collecting Kerguelen cabbage, which prevented scurvy.

On 12 March the *Komet* rendezvoused with the *Pinguin* and *Alstertor*, 120 miles east of the Kerguelens. Krüder wanted to use a harbour in the Kerguelens to transfer the stores from the supply ship, so Eyssen and Krüder headed towards Port Couvreux. The *Komet*, after receiving ammunition from the *Alstertor*, departed on 14 March to rendezvous with the *Ole Jacob* at 'Siberia' in the central Indian Ocean, midway between Australia and Madagascar.

The *Pinguin* stayed in Gazelle Bay for eleven days where she received stores, ammunition, 100 mines and an Arado seaplane from the *Alstertor*. The mechanics overhauled the engines and repaired the rudder while the crew cleaned the holds to remove coal dust and rotten vegetables. Off duty sailors explored the remains of Port Couvreux, finding a broken wooden jetty, dilapidated wooden buildings and a small French cemetery with a few graves. Some men hunted rabbits and others found some penguins, which they kept as pets.

Krüder decided to disguise the *Pinguin* as the Norwegian freighter *Tamerlane*. The crew converted the *Adjutant* into a minelayer and she received forty mines, leaving the raider 130.[21] Krüder learned the *Ketty Brovig*, a Norwegian tanker captured by the *Atlantis*, would replenish his raider off the Saya de Malha Bank near Mauritius. He planned to use the *Ketty Brovig* and *Adjutant* as auxiliary minelayers to simultaneously mine the approaches to Karachi and Bombay. On 25 March the *Pinguin* and *Adjutant* departed on a northerly course towards the rendezvous with the *Ketty Brovig*, while the *Alstertor* headed towards 'Siberia' to supply the *Orion*.

'SIBERIA'

The *Orion*, after exiting the Great Australian Bight, proceeded north-west through the Indian Ocean. On 20 March the *Ole Jacob* refuelled the raider and the tanker departed the next day to rendezvous with the *Komet*. The *Orion* resumed her course towards India while the Nakajima seaplane flew reconnaissance missions without spotting any ships. On 26 March the wireless room intercepted a QQQQ signal from the *Rajula*, originating from the north, but after Weyher failed to find the British ship, the raider headed north-west towards the Colombo–Cape Leeuwin route. The Nakajima spotted a ship three days later and the raider set an intercept course, but she turned out to be the Vichy French freighter *Pierre Louis Dreyfus*, and morale declined.

On 10 April the *Orion* rendezvoused with the *Ole Jacob* at 'Siberia' and the *Alstertor* soon arrived. The tanker refuelled the raider and provided her with food, medicine, radio parts, engine spares, ammunition and a new Arado seaplane. She also delivered sacks of mail, the first news the crew had received from home during their voyage, including patriotic letters from Hitler Youth Girls, an unexpected gift that renewed optimism.[22]

The *Ketty Brovig* had not yet arrived and Weyher searched for her without success before heading west towards Mauritius. As most merchant vessels leaving Australia and New Zealand took the longer Panama Canal route to avoid the raider-infested Indian Ocean, Weyher's operational area seemed empty.[23] On 23 April he ordered a southerly course towards Madagascar, and rumours spread among the crew that they had started their homeward journey. After the raider reached her new patrol area south of Madagascar, the wireless room detected only neutral traffic and Weyher shared the boredom of his crew, visiting areas of the ship where captains normally did not venture to cheer up his men.

After the Nakajima spotted a ship 120 miles south-west of Madagascar on 3 May, the *Orion* rushed towards her, but by midday she had not been sighted. The seaplane again found her and the lookout soon sighted the vessel. Weyher signalled 'what ship?' and she replied, 'Illinois'. As the *Illinois* was an American freighter, he let her go and she broadcast: 'Calling everybody. Nothing new here.'[24] Weyher knew this was a coded suspicious ship sighting but saw a positive side as 'the presence of a merchant raider in the Southern Madagascar area will be known. This may lead to a small strategical compensation for the lack of tonnage success.'[25] On 7 May the *Ole Jacob* replenished the *Orion*, giving her enough fuel to last until August and the crew hoped for the restoration of their fortune.

CHAPTER 18
TANKER HUNT IN THE ARABIAN SEA

Pinguin inflicted heavy damage, nearly rivalling our own record of
tonnage sunk, and being the only raider to approach it.[1]

Kapitänleutnant Ulrich Mohr
Adjutant, German Raider *Atlantis*

THE *KETTY BROVIG* IS MISSING

On 2 April 1941 the *Pinguin* and whale catcher *Adjutant* rendezvoused with
the tanker *Ole Jacob* at 'Siberia' in the central Indian Ocean, midway between
Australia and Madagascar. Captain 'Allright' Steinkrauss informed Krüder
that the prize tanker *Ketty Brovig* had vanished. The Germans had no idea
that she had recently been sunk by HMAS *Canberra*.[2] After the *Ole Jacob*
refuelled the *Pinguin*, the raider headed north towards the Arabian Sea and
the tanker departed for her rendezvous with the *Orion*.

The *Pinguin* and *Adjutant* reached the rendezvous location south-east of the
Saya de Malha Bank five days later, but there was no sign of the *Ketty Brovig*.
As Krüder had planned to use her as a minelayer, he needed a replacement
tanker and requested the *Ole Jacob*, but the *Seekriegsleitung* refused as she had

The *Ketty Brovig*, after attack by HMAS *Canberra*. The *Ketty Brovig*, a Norwegian tanker captured by the *Atlantis*, was to replenish the *Pinguin* near Mauritius. (AUTHOR'S COLLECTION)

been assigned to the *Orion*. Krüder could either capture a tanker or scale down his minelaying plans, which envisaged the *Pinguin*, *Adjutant* and a third vessel simultaneously mining the approaches to Karachi and Bombay. Wanting to repeat the success of the Australian operation, made possible by the prize tanker *Passat*, he decided to hunt a tanker on the Abadan–Cape route. As this would be dangerous given the area's closeness to enemy bases, he planned a quick sortie followed by an immediate withdrawal.

The *Pinguin*, disguised as the Norwegian freighter *Tamerlane*, commenced the tanker hunt. *Oberleutnant* Hans-Karl Hemmer in the *Adjutant* and *Oberleutnant* Werner in the seaplane searched for a suitable victim. On the morning of 24 April the *Adjutant* sighted a large ship 360 miles north-east of the Seychelles and Hemmer reported her course, speed and position to Krüder before shadowing her, keeping his prey just in sight.

The 6828-ton British India Steam Navigation Company freighter *Empire Light* had been carrying hides and ore from Madras to Durban. The lookout spotted the *Adjutant* but her captain believed she was a small British auxiliary and expressed little concern when she vanished over the horizon.

The *Pinguin* proceeded on an intercept course. After sunset Hemmer approached closer and placed a small light on the *Adjutant*'s stern as a beacon

North of the Seychelles, Indian Ocean, 25 April 1941. The British cargo vessel *Empire Light* showing battle damage sustained in action with the *Pinguin*.
(AWM: NAVAL HISTORICAL COLLECTION)

Burial at sea in April 1941 in the Indian Ocean of men killed when the *Empire Light* was attacked by the *Pinguin*.
(AWM: NAVAL HISTORICAL COLLECTION)

for the raider. The raider appeared in the morning as a shadow in the pre-dawn darkness and Hemmer heard the quiet hum of her engines as she overtook his whale catcher. Krüder would have preferred a tanker, which would attract less suspicion, but would settle for a freighter.

The *Empire Light* became clearly visible at dawn and Krüder opened fire without warning with a salvo that destroyed her radio mast and damaged her steering. The helpless freighter, taken completely by surprise, slowed to a halt and after the third salvo the crew began abandoning ship. A boarding party inspected the freighter to find her steering had been badly damaged, making her an unsuitable prize. Seventy crewmen became prisoners on the raider and two sailors had been killed. The boarding party scuttled the *Empire Light* and, as no raider warning had been broadcast, the outside world knew nothing about the encounter.

The *Pinguin* and *Adjutant* proceeded north-east towards the Maldives after Krüder signalled Hemmer: 'Adjutant has carried out its job superbly.'[3] Krüder now hoped to find a tanker in the Arabian Sea near the entrance to the Persian Gulf. On 27 April the raider's lookout sighted three freighters west of the Maldives: two southbound and one northbound. Krüder decided to capture the northbound freighter and the raider shadowed her and after sunset increased speed. At midnight Krüder adopted a converging course, planning to strike at first light.

The 7266-ton British Cayzer Line freighter *Clan Buchanan* had left Liverpool carrying military equipment for the British Army in India with a crew of twenty-five British officers and ninety-six Lascars, while two Royal Navy gunners oversaw the 4.7-inch stern gun and an anti-aircraft gun. Captain Devenport-Jones had been warned about two raiders in the Indian Ocean but hoped his ship's excellent top speed of 17½ knots would see him safely to port. Chief Officer Stanley Davidson, on watch in the bridge, suddenly realized that shells had struck his vessel before seeing gun flashes 3 miles away. Captain Devenport-Jones rushed to the bridge, while the wireless broadcast a raider warning. After a shell destroyed the stern gun, Captain Devenport-Jones decided to abandon ship.

The *Clan Buchanan*'s crew lowered lifeboats while Second Radio Officer Walter Clarke kept broadcasting despite a signal from raider: 'Cease using your wireless or we will continue shelling.'[4] Krüder ordered a ceasefire after her radio went dead. Nobody had been killed but two Lascars were wounded. A boarding party led by *Oberleutnant* Warning arrived as Davidson witnessed:

> The raider ceased shelling us about 0525, after ten minutes continuous firing, and sent her motor boat alongside our ship with a boarding party, consisting of Commander Warning and six heavily-armed ratings, who came on board and took charge of the bridge.[5]

The *Clan Buchanan*'s steering had been too badly damaged for her to become a minelayer. After the crew transferred to the raider, the boarding party scuttled the freighter.

Krüder expressed concern about the *Clan Buchanan*'s raider warnings, but his signals officer *Oberleutnant* Karl Heinz Brunke did not believe they had been received, so Krüder resumed the hunt for a prize ship.[6] However, Allied shore stations had received the warning and the news quickly spread, as an intelligence report noted: 'An "R" Distress message was read by Colombo, Karachi and Seychelles radios. . . . Ship was probably *Clan Buchanan*.'[7] The Royal Navy now had actionable intelligence about a raider in waters close to their bases and Admiral Ralph Leatham, Commander-in-Chief of the East Indies Station, ordered warships to converge on the area while Krüder remained unaware of his change in fortune.

HMS CORNWALL

On 28 April the County-class heavy cruiser HMS *Cornwall*, armed with eight powerful 8-inch guns, departed Mombasa with Captain Percival Manwaring in command. The *Cornwall* would search north of the Seychelles while the aircraft carrier HMS *Eagle* and the cruiser HMS *Hawkins* would patrol to the west. The New Zealand cruiser *Leander* left Colombo the next day to join the hunt.

The *Pinguin* headed north-west and the *Adjutant* proceeded towards 'Violet', north-east of Mauritius, to see if there were any enemy warships nearby just in case the *Clan Buchanan*'s signal had been heard. Krüder also requested a rendezvous with the supply ship *Alstertor* at 'Violet' to transfer his prisoners. The captives adjusted to life on the raider and Davidson recalled: 'We were all kept in excellent health and spirits during our sojourn on Raider and her Commander expressed to Captain Jones his satisfaction and pleasure on our behaviour and conduct.'[8]

On 6 May the *Pinguin* approached the Persian Gulf while the Allied warships searched further south. After the lookout spotted a tanker 375 miles east-south-east of Cape Guardafui, Somalia, Krüder felt satisfied that his search would soon be over.

The 3663-ton tanker *British Emperor* had been proceeding in ballast from Durban to Abadan with a crew of nine British officers and thirty-six Lascars. Krüder ordered a parallel course to shadow her, intending to strike at night. After sunset Krüder increased speed and closed the distance in the darkness before dawn, then fired a warning shot. Captain Henderson decided to flee and the wireless officer John Thomas began transmitting a raider warning. Krüder abandoned hope of capturing the *British Emperor* intact and salvos struck the tanker, causing fires. After her steering failed, the crew began abandoning ship and the radio went dead. Krüder sent boats to rescue the survivors, but Thomas began transmitting again. Krüder could do nothing with his boats close to the tanker, but once they retreated his gunners resumed fire and the radio went silent for a second time and he sank her with a torpedo.

The *British Emperor*'s signals had been received and the Admiralty noted: 'British Emperor (bound for Barry) reported being shelled. . . . She was probably attacked by same raider which attacked "Clan Buchanan".'[9] The cruisers *Liverpool* and *Glasgow* now joined the hunt. Krüder's signallers confirmed the raider warnings had been received so he abandoned his tanker hunt and the *Pinguin* fled south-east towards her rendezvous with the *Alstertor*.

The *Cornwall* had been heading to the Seychelles to refuel when Manwaring intercepted the *British Emperor*'s signal. The cruiser, only 500 miles to the south, altered course to north-north-west at cruising speed of 25 knots. The *Leander*, *Liverpool* and *Hector* changed course to close the trap. At night the *Cornwall* altered course to east-south-east, directly towards the *Pinguin*.

At 0330 h on 8 May the *Pinguin*'s lookout spotted a shadow. Krüder rushed to the bridge and saw the silhouette of a British cruiser against the moon and immediately ordered evasive action. The *Cornwall* soon disappeared and sunrise revealed a calm sea with nothing on the horizon.

At dawn the *Cornwall* launched two Walrus seaplanes. The plane flown by Lieutenant Wilfred Waller flew north and the observer, Lieutenant Paul Wormell, soon sighted a suspicious ship heading south-west at 13 knots, 65 miles west of the *Cornwall*. Krüder spotted the seaplane, but took no action to avoid appearing suspicious. Waller returned to the *Cornwall* and reported the sighting. Manwaring waited for his second seaplane to return before ordering an intercept course.

Chief Officer Davidson witnessed tensions building up among the German crew:

> On this day we gathered from the amount of activity around the decks that something unusual was happening. At lunch-time this became so obvious, as our famous soup had no salt in it, also the prison guard outside our cell was dressed in his best and had his lifebelt and gas mask handy.[10]

At 1015 h the *Cornwall*'s second Walrus took off with Lieutenant Frank Fox in the pilot's seat, and he soon spotted the *Pinguin*. The seaplane circled from a distance and again Krüder believed his best chance would be to act like a Norwegian. The crew remained below deck except for key personnel posing as merchant sailors wearing ragged uniforms. The seaplane flew closer and signalled 'what ship?' and Krüder replied, 'Tamerlane'. The signaller had responded in a slow and awkward manner as Krüder expected merchant sailors to be unprofessional, but this ruse instantly made Fox suspicious because the genuine *Tamerlane* belonged to the *Wilhelmsen* Line, which had very high standards. The seaplane returned to the *Cornwall* and as the *Tamerlane* was not expected in the area, the evidence suggested that Manwaring had found a raider. The cruiser increased speed to 28 knots and Waller's seaplane took off with orders to observe the suspected raider's course and speed.

Krüder, believing a British cruiser was just over the horizon, grimly decided that if his bluff failed the *Pinguin* would engage the enemy, even though his guns would be outmatched and one lucky hit could ignite the 130 mines on board. After the lookout spotted smoke astern, the unmistakable shape of a British cruiser became visible.

The *Cornwall*'s lookout sighted the 'Tamerlane' and although Manwaring remained confident that he had found the raider, he still had to identify her beyond doubt before opening fire. Furthermore, he feared making a horrible mistake as only a few days earlier he had challenged a genuine British freighter that refused to stop and he had almost opened fire.[11] As the distance closed to 17,300 metres (18,919 yards), the *Cornwall* signalled 'heave to or I open fire', which Krüder ignored. Manwaring repeated the signal and fired a warning shot. Krüder broadcast a QQQQ raider warning, indicating the *Tamerlane* was being challenged by an unknown ship and the *Cornwall*'s radio room informed Manwaring that the message seemed genuine. Manwaring experienced creeping doubt and ordered Waller by radio to inform the '*Tamerlane*' that she was being approached by a British warship and must stop. Krüder ignored the order, reasoning that at the very least the cruiser would have to come closer to investigate and would be in better range of his guns. Manwaring feared approaching a suspected raider but needed to confirm her identity and he also worried that Allied prisoners might be on board.

At 1714 h the distance between the two vessels decreased to 7300 metres (7983 yards) and Krüder anticipated the cruiser would soon begin firing salvos.[12] The *Pinguin* turned sharply to port as Krüder had decided to fight. The crew raised the *Kriegsmarine* flag and Brunke signalled the *Seekriegsleitung*: 'After sinking 136,550 gross register tons and obtaining excellent mine results am now engaged with British heavy cruiser Cornwall.'[13] After repeating this message three times Brunke received an acknowledgement from Berlin.

The *Pinguin* fired a series of broadside salvos at the *Cornwall* under the direction of the gunnery officer *Oberleutnant* Karl Helmut Rieche. Even though the range was too great for accurate fire, a few shells struck the cruiser and one landed in the Chief Petty Officers' pantry, starting a small fire, but she only sustained slight damage, although splinters wounded three sailors.

The *Cornwall* turned to port to fire her broadsides, but a fuse in an electrical circuit blew, preventing the movement of her 8-inch gun turrets. Increasingly frequent and accurate German shells hit the cruiser for the next two minutes while she remained unable to fire. With luck on her side, the *Pinguin* seemed to be defying the odds, as Manwaring reflected:

I had the annoying experience of being at effective gun range of an enemy ship and with His Majesty's Ship under my command under rapid and fairly accurate fire, frequently being straddled and the main armament pointing anywhere but at the enemy.[14]

Manwaring made a tactical retreat and the *Cornwall* turned away to get beyond range of the German guns. By the time the forward turrets had been brought under manual control, a shell disabled the fore steering gear. Manwaring required time to make repairs and seven minutes later the *Cornwall's* guns became ready for action. The *Pinguin's* torpedo officer *Oberleutnant* Gabe fired two torpedoes, but these missed after the seaplane spotted their tracks, allowing Manwaring to take evasive action. The *Cornwall's* 8-inch guns opened fire as the two ships proceeded on near parallel courses.

After a shell broke the *Pinguin's* foremast and rigging, Krüder decided to cease fire as further resistance would be pointless because the *Cornwall* had found her range and his fire was no longer accurate. Krüder ordered his men to scuttle their raider and release the prisoners.[15] At 1725 h the *Cornwall* fired a four-gun salvo while Manwaring remained unaware of Krüder's ceasefire. The salvo struck the raider, hitting her foredeck, bridge and engine room. The last shell penetrated her hull through the No. 5 Hold and exploded inside the mine storage area. The mines instantly detonated, creating an explosion which tore the *Pinguin* apart, causing flames to jump hundreds of feet into the air. Manwaring remembered the spectacle: 'The whole ship disappeared in a thick white cloud which also rose vertically at least 2000 feet and hung as a cloud for many minutes afterwards.'[16]

The explosion propelled the lookout in the crow's nest into the sky and the sailor landed alive in the water, while debris from the *Pinguin* scattered across the ocean. When the shell hit the bridge, the explosion threw Chief Quartermaster Ernst Neumeister backwards and after coming to he saw that the port half of the bridge, where the officers had been standing, had vanished. Krüder and his navigator *Kapitänleutnant* Michaelson had both died instantly. Neumeister jumped overboard and swam away and, after turning around, saw the *Pinguin*, vertical in the water, going down fast with several sailors on her deck holding onto the rail. Before the raider submerged under the waves, an officer unlocked the door to the prison quarters and this noble action saved many lives. Chief Officer Stanley Davidson described emerging from the hold:

. . . a terrific blast shook the ship, throwing us from one side of the cell to the other. When I picked myself up, I found that I was beside the prison door, which was open. (I later discovered that a minute before the blast a German had opened the door of the cell.) . . . I went to the ship's side to ascertain what was happening, and found that the after end of the ship had been completely blown away and the ship was sinking rapidly by the stern. . . . On reaching the water I turned on my back and swam away from the ship. By this time the raider's bow was vertical in the air, and she sank almost immediately.[17]

The damage to the *Cornwall*'s electrical system meanwhile caused her extractor fans to stop, increasing the heat in the engine room to over 90°C. The engine and boiler room men evacuated their stations, but Lieutenant George Winslade later died of heat stroke. As the cruiser could not reduce speed, her crew threw Carley floats overboard and the survivors held on to whatever debris they could find. After the mechanics repaired the damage, the cruiser stopped and rescued nine British, fifteen Lascars and sixty Germans.[18] The German survivors included Doctor Werner Hasselmann, the meteorologist Doctor Ulrich Roll, prize officer *Leutnant* Oskar Boettcher and fifty-seven sailors. The Allied survivors included Second Officer Wilfred Wright from the *British Emperor*, Chief Officer Stanley Davidson from the *Clan Buchanan*, seven other officers and fifteen Lascars. The *Pinguin*'s dead included 341 crewmen and 203 prisoners, including Captain Devenport-Jones. Davidson had witnessed the captain's death:

I saw half the ship under water and the rest going quickly and immediately shouted to Captain Jones who was near me, that she was sinking fast and to jump quickly. He waved his hand and those around me jumped with me as ship heeled over to starboard and started to sink quickly by the stern. On reaching water I turned round to look at the ship and found her with her bows right in the air — she was gone in five seconds. Captain Jones was last seen with his foot on ship's side smoking his pipe.[19]

The *Cornwall*'s crew helped the exhausted survivors to the quarterdeck

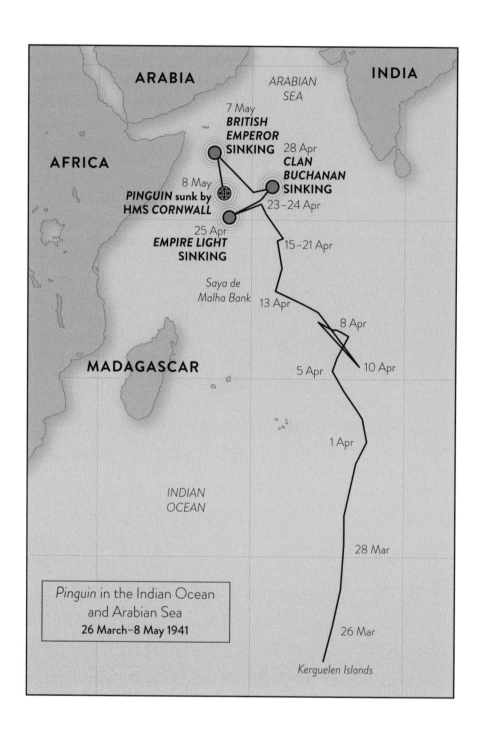

ARABIA

ARABIAN
SEA

INDIA

7 May
**BRITISH
EMPEROR
SINKING**

28 Apr
**CLAN
BUCHANAN
SINKING**

AFRICA

8 May
**PINGUIN sunk by
HMS CORNWALL**

23–24 Apr

25 Apr
**EMPIRE LIGHT
SINKING**

15–21 Apr

Saya de
Malha Bank

13 Apr

8 Apr

10 Apr

MADAGASCAR

5 Apr

1 Apr

INDIAN
OCEAN

28 Mar

Pinguin in the Indian Ocean
and Arabian Sea
26 March–8 May 1941

26 Mar

Kerguelen Islands

The German raider *Pinguin* operated successfully in the Indian Ocean, sinking a number of Allied merchant ships after minelaying operations off the Australian coast. (AWM)

where they gave them hot tea and cigarettes as well as hot water and soap for the men covered in oil. Guards escorted the German sailors to a large compartment and accommodated the three surviving officers in an aft cabin. Doctor Hasselmann helped the wounded in the hospital, treating German and Allied survivors. The British survivors told the *Cornwall*'s surgeon how much they respected Doctor Hasselmann.

The *Pinguin–Cornwall* action had resulted in the first German auxiliary cruiser casualty of the war. Manwaring's behaviour reflected caution and demonstrated the unique difficulties faced by Allied captains trying to identify a suspected raider, and this experience provided valuable lessons for Allied warship captains as Admiral Leatham expressed: 'Definite identification of a suspicious ship without risk to one's own ship must always be a very difficult matter especially with an enemy so well versed in the art of deceit as the Germans.'[20]

Grossadmiral Raeder informed Hitler about the *Pinguin*'s demise:

> The Commanding Officer's character is a sufficient guarantee that
> the auxiliary cruiser fought a gallant battle after vainly attempting to

escape from the enemy cruiser through use of deception. Ship '33'
[*Pinguin*] was the most successful German auxiliary cruiser, which
carried out extremely well all the tactical and operational demands
made of her. . . . The total success achieved by ship '33' exceeds that
of cruiser *Emden* or auxiliary cruiser *Wolf* in the World War.[21]

Krüder was posthumously awarded the Knight's Cross with Oak Leaves.
The *Pinguin* was the most successful raider of the war, sinking or capturing
thirty-two vessels totalling 154,619 tons. She had spent 328 days at sea and
had covered 59,188 miles of ocean. Krüder, a bold raider captain, used
his seaplanes imaginatively to capture ships and knock down radio aerials.
The triumph of his Australian minefields and the capture of the Norwegian
whaling fleet off Antarctica would remain feats without equal in the raider
war. Krüder had been a risk taker, always driven to achieve greater success.
However, this characteristic ultimately led to his demise as it caused him to
relentlessly pursue his tanker hunt in the Arabian Sea, resulting in his fatal
encounter with HMS *Cornwall*.

The *Pinguin*'s destruction had only been made possible by the courageous
wireless operators on the *Clan Buchanan* and *British Emperor*, who continued
signalling under intense fire. Without these signals the *Cornwall* would not
have had sufficient intelligence to intercept the raider.

On 11 May the *Cornwall* arrived in the Seychelles and, after the prisoners
landed, the British asked them to sign an oath declaring they would not
attempt to escape, but Doctor Hasselmann on behalf of his countrymen
refused.[22] The British transferred the prisoners to South Africa where they
were held at a transit camp at Clairwood, outside Durban, before being
shipped to the United Kingdom.[23] The British interrogators found the
Pinguin prisoners to be highly difficult:

Interrogating Officers were of the opinion that, for the purpose of
extracting information, they were among the worst prisoners yet
captured in this war. This is explained by the fact that, during the
eleven months they had been at sea, they had been subjected to
intensive training in security-mindedness.[24]

The interrogation resulted in 'Section 19' correcting many past mistakes. Previously the Allies had not known of the *Pinguin*'s existence and she posthumously became 'Raider F' and her exploits were no longer incorrectly attributed to other raiders.[25] The *Pinguin* prisoners remained in POW camps in Britain until the end of the war.

CHAPTER 19
A NEW
OPERATIONAL AREA

Captain Rogge told me about his experiences in the Indian Ocean,
where he had made a fine bag earlier on, about a year previously;
but then the enemy shipping lanes had been shifted closer and closer
inshore and it had been made more and more difficult to find anything.[1]

Kapitän Theodore Detmers
Commander of the *Kormoran*

RENDEZVOUS AT 'RED'

In March 1941 the *Kormoran* headed north-west through the South Atlantic towards the equator and, as she entered the Natal Straits, Detmers anticipated new victories: 'In the area which I am entering now, it is my opinion that there will be quite lively traffic, because the vessels bound for Freetown must leave the Neutrality Zone here.'[2] On 10 March the raider entered the North Atlantic and Detmers encountered a steamer without lights, but he lacked the speed to give chase. He received new orders to rendezvous with the *Scheer* as the *Kormoran* had radar quartz that the pocket battleship required.

On 15 March the *Kormoran* rendezvoused with *U-124* at 'Red', north-east of St Peter and St Paul Rocks. *Kapitänleutnant* Schultz boarded the *Kormoran* and asked for torpedoes and supplies. Detmers invited the U-boat crew on board so they could experience some comfort away from their cramped quarters. The raider's crew gave them a tour of their vessel before providing a meal made from their best food. The submariners also watched a movie in the cinema and in return some *Kormoran* crewmen visited the U-boat.[3]

The *Scheer* arrived the next day and the *Kormoran*'s crew lined the deck to greet the pocket battleship. Detmers boarded the *Scheer* and *Kapitän* Krancke confirmed that enemy shipping had become harder to find in the Indian Ocean and advised that the Arabian Sea and Bay of Bengal would be the most promising hunting grounds.[4] Krancke obtained the *Kormoran*'s radar quartz, but the *Scheer* had no white metal for the raider. The *Scheer* departed and both crews lined the decks to bid each other farewell, and the pocket battleship arrived at Kiel on 1 April.[5]

Schultz provided Detmers with 350 kilograms (770 pounds) of white metal, but as rough weather prevented the transfer of torpedoes, the *Kormoran* and *U-124* headed south-west in search of calmer seas, and the transfer commenced on 17 March. The U-boat received seven torpedoes, and mechanics from the *Kormoran* repaired a leak on the submarine. After *U-124* departed, Schultz sank seven freighters before returning to Lorient.[6]

Detmers decided to patrol south of the U-boat operational area close to the equator before rendezvousing with *U-105* and *U-106*. The *Kormoran* headed south-east and avoided a steamer as she was still inside the Pan-American Neutrality Zone. On 22 March she reached the Freetown–South America route and the lookout spotted a tanker on a converging course. The lookout could not identify her nationality in the morning haze but a stern gun soon became visible. Detmers signalled 'what ship?' and she replied, 'Agnita'.

The small 3561-ton tanker *Agnita* owned by the Anglo-Saxon Petroleum Company had departed Freetown in ballast bound for Venezuela, armed with one 4-inch stern gun and two 76-mm anti-aircraft guns. The *Agnita* turned, increased speed and broadcast a raider warning, which the *Kormoran*'s signallers jammed. The raider's gunners prepared for action, while *Agnita*'s First Mate Hill-Willis watched:

. . . the forecastle head folded down, the deckhouses of the fore and
after decks vanished, No 3 hatch rolled back, and a large platform
mounting a rangefinder shot up the foremast, whilst the German flag
appeared at the mainmast head. This whole transformation had only
taken seconds, and what seemed to be a harmless merchant ship was
now a very lethal looking warship.[7]

Detmers ordered the *Agnita* to stop, before opening fire. A shell hit the tanker's
engine room and after the second salvo she stopped, her wireless went dead
and the crew lowered lifeboats. Detmers scuttled the *Agnita* and her crew of
thirteen English and twenty-five Chinese sailors became prisoners on the
raider. Detmers decided to stay close to where the *Agnita* had been sunk,
contrary to the usual practice of getting as far away as possible, as it would
be unexpected, believing such risks could be taken on rare occasions.

On 25 March the lookout spotted a ship that disappeared into thick mist.
Detmers ordered a gradual intercept course to avoid suspicion, fearing she
might be a warship on account of her light grey colour, but a break in the
mist revealed a tanker with a stern gun. The *Kormoran* fired two warning
shots, but the tanker increased speed and broadcast a raider warning, which
the raider's wireless room jammed. Detmers ordered his gunners to open
fire, but since he wanted to capture the vessel, he instructed them to avoid
causing serious damage. After the second salvo almost hit the tanker, she
stopped, ceased transmitting and her crew lowered lifeboats.

The 11,309-ton Canadian tanker *Canadolite* had been proceeding to
Venezuela from Freetown. A boarding party captured her without incident
and as she had not been damaged, Detmers decided to send her to France as
a prize. The boarding party found a monkey they hoped would make a good
companion for Tommy, and the crew built a new hutch on the deck with a
line to Tommy's hutch and both creatures bonded well.

Detmers organized a prize crew of sixteen sailors under *Leutnant* Bloh to
take the *Canadolite* to France. Bloh had developed sciatica and some of the
prize crew had tropical sicknesses so Detmers wanted to send them home.
The tanker's captain, chief engineer, wireless operator and a senior Royal
Navy gunner transferred to the *Kormoran*, but forty-four prisoners remained
on the tanker. The *Canadolite* departed and reached France on 13 April.[8]

The *Kormoran* proceeded west towards the Pan-American Neutrality Zone and rendezvoused with the *Nordmark* north of St Peter and St Paul Rocks on 27 March. As the naval supply ship had inadequate fuel stocks, the tanker *Rudolf Albrecht* would later refuel the *Kormoran*, but the *Nordmark* transferred supplies to the raider, including seven U-boat torpedoes. *U-105* and *U-106* arrived two days later and the *Kormoran* transferred supplies to the U-boats then the *Nordmark* departed. Off duty U-boat men boarded the raider and *U-105* provided Detmers with white metal, of good quality but small in quantity. After the U-boats departed, *U-105* sank another six freighters before returning to Lorient, while *U-106* sank three merchant ships before reaching the port.[9]

The *Kormoran* proceeded towards her rendezvous with the *Rudolf Albrecht*, which had recently departed Spain, and the two ships rendezvoused north-west of St Peter and St Paul Rocks on 3 April. Captain Engellandt provided Detmers with fuel, food, magazines and English cigarettes, and Detmers expressed gratitude: 'It must be specially mentioned that the crew and especially the captain of *Rudolf Albrecht* gave up everything for the auxiliary cruiser. We found here a cooperation which came from the heart.'[10]

The *Nordmark* arrived two days later to take the raider's U-boat supplies and her forty-two prisoners, but tensions erupted after *Korvettenkapitän* Peter Grau refused to embark the raider's prisoners, instead suggesting they be transferred to the *Rudolf Albrecht*. As the tanker did not have a military guard, such a transfer would be illegal under international law.[11] Therefore, Detmers commissioned Engellandt as a *Leutnant* and formed a naval guard with one sailor from the *Kormoran* and three from the *Nordmark*. With the requirements of international law satisfied, the prisoners boarded the *Rudolf Albrecht*, which later reached France.[12]

The *Kormoran* headed south-east towards the equator, as Detmers wanted to return to the waters where he had intercepted the *Agnita* and *Canadolite*. On 9 April the lookout spotted a freighter and Detmers estimated she would overtake the raider so he reduced speed to 8 knots to allow the distance to gradually close. As she gave no indication of being suspicious, most bridge officers believed her to be American until they spotted a stern gun. When the two ships became parallel at 4500 metres (4921 yards), Detmers fired a warning shot. The freighter turned away and broadcast a raider warning. When Detmers saw the stern gunners running towards their weapon, he ordered his guns to open fire and their first salvo destroyed the gun, but the freighter increased speed. After three minutes of shelling she stopped and her radio went silent. Detmers ordered a ceasefire but two minutes later she started to move and her radio resumed transmitting. The raider's guns opened fire and several more shells struck the freighter, causing fires to erupt amidships, and after stopping for a second time, her crew began lowering lifeboats. Detmers sent across a boarding party to the brightly burning freighter.

The 8022-ton British freighter *Craftsman* had been voyaging from Rosyth, Scotland, to Cape Town, carrying a large anti-submarine net. Five sailors had been killed and forty-six survivors became prisoners. Detmers sank the freighter with a torpedo and the *Kormoran* fled south-east and entered the South Atlantic. The next day the *Kriegsmarine* promoted Detmers to *Fregattenkapitän*.

On 12 April the lookout spotted a freighter near the Pan-American Neutrality Zone. Detmers manoeuvred the *Kormoran* between the ship and the zone, to prevent her escape. The freighter turned to starboard, but Detmers did not give chase and, after she resumed her original course, the distance gradually decreased. After Detmers ordered her to stop, she attempted to flee and broadcast a raider warning. After a shell struck the freighter, she stopped and her radio went dead and her crew lowered lifeboats.

The small 5486-ton Greek vessel *Nicolas de L* had been transporting timber from Vancouver to Durban. As her bridge had been damaged, Detmers decided to sink her. The boarding party placed demolition charges in the engine room and her crew of thirty-eight sailors became prisoners. The explosion failed to sink her so Detmers ordered his 20-mm guns to shoot the timber on the deck, hoping to start a fire. When this failed the 5.9-inch guns reduced the *Nicolas de L* to a burning hulk and the *Kormoran* fled southwards. The Greek wireless operator had succeeded in broadcasting a raider warning but had in error given the position as 20°S instead of 02°S, good news for Detmers as enemy warships would be converging on the wrong location.

The *Seekriegsleitung* ordered Detmers to rendezvous with the *Atlantis* and the supply ship *Alsterufer* at 'Andalusia', 200 miles north-west of Tristan da

Cunha, and the meeting took place on 19 April. Rogge had recently captured the *Speybank* and sunk the *Mandatory* and *Zamzam*.[13] Detmers boarded the *Atlantis* to learn about Rogge's experiences in the Indian Ocean as it would become his new operational area. Rogge explained that he had achieved less success there compared with the previous year because few enemy merchant ships voyaged alone.

The supply ship *Alsterufer* had left Hamburg with supplies for Rogge and Detmers. The *Kormoran* received ammunition and seventy-seven prisoners transferred to the supply ship. Detmers also gained two new officers from the *Alsterufer*: *Leutnant* Rudolf Jansen and *Leutnant* Bruno Kube.

The *Nordmark* arrived the next day with fresh provisions and fuel for both raiders. As it was Hitler's birthday, Detmers awarded the Iron Crosses that had been allocated to his ship. The *Nordmark* supplied the *Kormoran* with fuel and food, while three wounded men and an orderly from the *Craftsman* transferred to the *Nordmark* as she possessed better medical facilities. However, one of the wounded men, Chief Engineer Carruthers, later died on board.[14] Detmers also entrusted mail from his men to the *Nordmark* and she took the U-boat supplies.

After the German ships parted company, the *Nordmark* arrived in Hamburg on 20 May and the *Alsterufer* arrived in Bordeaux four days later.[15] Detmers decided to disguise the *Kormoran* as the Dutch freighter *Straat Malakka* and she headed towards the Cape of Good Hope.

THE BIG ROUND UP

As 1941 continued *Grossadmiral* Raeder anticipated great victories. The *Thor* had recently sunk two freighters in the South Atlantic as well as the armed merchant cruiser *Voltaire*. The raider reached Hamburg on 30 April, having sunk twelve ships during her highly successful voyage.[16]

The battlecruisers *Scharnhorst* and *Gneisenau* had terrorized the Atlantic, claiming twenty-two ships and creating massive disruption to the Allied convoy system, before safely arriving in Brest. Patrick Beesly reflected upon this time: 'The battlecruisers had cruised for two whole months without once being brought to action. . . . In conjunction with the armed merchant raiders and *Scheer* and *Hipper*, they had forced on us an enormous dispersal of effort.'[17]

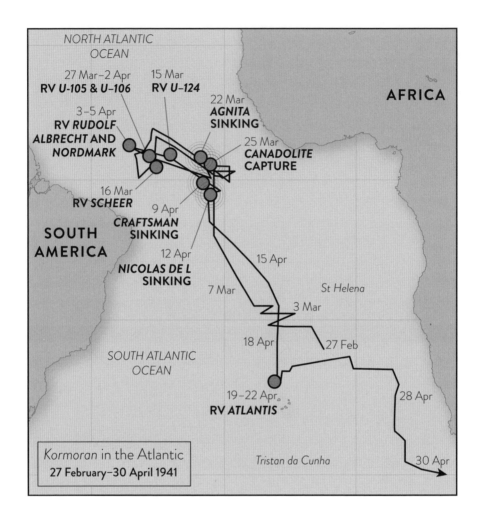

In May 1941 the battleship *Bismarck* and the heavy cruiser *Prinz Eugen* departed on a commerce raiding mission on the high seas.[18] After sinking the battlecruiser HMS *Hood* in the Denmark Strait, the *Prinz Eugen* continued the mission and the *Bismarck* headed towards St Nazaire, France, for repairs. However, Swordfish planes from the aircraft carrier HMS *Ark Royal* attacked and a torpedo explosion jammed the *Bismarck*'s rudder, forcing her to circle towards pursuing British warships, which destroyed the battleship. Germany had lost her finest warship, but Raeder's fortunes would soon become much worse.

On 8 May three destroyers damaged *U-110* and a boarding party captured the U-boat, her secret papers and an Enigma code machine. The Royal Navy quickly despatched this material to Bletchley Park, where codebreakers used it to crack the U-boat Hydra cipher. The auxiliary cruisers and their supply ships communicated with Special Cipher 100, Tibet or with other ciphers allocated to specific ships, which the British never cracked.[19] However, the compromised U-boat signals could be used against auxiliary cruisers and supply ships when replenishing U-boats at sea. As the *Seekriegsleitung* organized these meetings and signalled the rendezvous details to U-boats using the compromised Hydra cipher, the Royal Navy now could learn where and when U-boats would rendezvous with auxiliary cruisers and supply ships. As it was far more common for supply ships to rendezvous with U-boats, they would receive the full force of the coming offensive.

The Admiralty's counter-attack against the *Kriegsmarine*'s supply ships became known as the 'Big Round Up'. The loss of the *Bismarck* has made this possible because warships, which only days earlier had been committed to containing the battleship, were now free to conduct other operations. In June the Royal Navy sank four supply ships and six tankers using the new intelligence.[20] The casualties included the tankers *Egerland* and *Lothringen*, which had been assigned to the *Orion*, as well as the *Alstertor*, which had previously replenished the raiders. The 'Great Round Up' turned the tide of the war against the raiders as Captain Stephen Roskill explained:

> These successes were the more important because some of the intercepted ships had been sent out to supply U-boats and disguised raiders . . . and seriously dislocated all the enemy's plans for the prosecution of the *guerre de course* against our merchant shipping.[21]

Raeder's grand vision of waging war at sea on a global scale had received a death blow and the *Kriegsmarine*'s decline became irreversible.

THE INDIAN OCEAN

On 3 May 1941 the *Kormoran* rounded the Cape of Good Hope, entering the Indian Ocean where a flock of albatrosses greeted her. As the raider headed north-east towards the Cape Town–Fremantle route, Detmers decided against mining South African ports.[22] After encountering no ships, he concluded that all shipping must be hugging the coast. On 9 May the *Kormoran* passed Madagascar and the wireless room discovered that a raider had been sunk by HMS *Cornwall*. Detmers knew this must have been the *Pinguin*. As the *Pinguin* had been expected to rendezvous with the *Alstertor* at 'Violet', north-east of Mauritius, the *Seekriegsleitung* ordered Detmers to proceed there to refuel and determine the fate of the whale catcher *Adjutant*.

The *Adjutant* had been at 'Violet' when *Oberleutnant* Hemmer overheard Krüder's final signal. Hemmer, deeply upset, called together the crew for three hurrahs and played the record 'Good-Bye Johnny'.

Detmers ordered a special parade and informed the crew of the *Pinguin*'s destruction:

> Captain Krüder and most of his men were at the bottom of the sea now. Only about thirty men had survived. I now called my own men together and informed them of what had happened. They listened to me in silence.[23]

Detmers decided to disguise the *Kormoran* as the Japanese freighter *Sakito Maru* and the raider arrived at 'Violet' on 14 May. After rendezvousing with the *Alstertor* and *Adjutant*, Hemmer informed Detmers that Krüder had ventured into the Arabian Sea, where he sank two ships. Detmers considered retaining the *Adjutant* as a scout ship but felt a whale catcher would be out of place in these waters so he agreed to assign her to the *Komet*, as Eyssen had requested the vessel. Detmers wished Hemmer good luck and the *Adjutant* departed towards the rendezvous.

Detmers decided to patrol the Mauritius–Sabang route hoping to repeat the success of the *Atlantis* and *Pinguin*. On 20 May the *Kormoran* reached her operational area, but Detmers postponed his plan to mine the Indian coast, not wishing to risk his raider by approaching close to enemy bases.[24] The *Kormoran* headed north-east and Detmers remarked: 'For a reasonable space of time, we shall be the only German warship in the Indian Ocean. I now have the freedom of action that I've always wanted.'[25] On 3 June the Arado seaplane conducted a reconnaissance flight, but the pilot *Oberleutnant* Ahl spotted nothing. Detmers decided to disguise the *Kormoran* as the Japanese *Kokusai Kisen*

Kaisha Line freighter *Kinka Maru* and gave up on the Mauritius–Sabang route in favour of patrolling between the Chagos Islands and the Maldives.

On 15 June the lookout spotted a liner heading south. Detmers would normally avoid liners due to their superior speed, but as their courses would converge at 9100 metres (9951 yards), he decided to make an exception. The *Kormoran* decreased speed to avoid suspicion, but the smoke apparatus malfunctioned and laid a smoke screen. The liner turned away while smoke prevented the gunners from firing, and the crew expressed bitter disappointment after weeks of inactivity.

After finding no enemy ships on the Colombo–Sabang route, Detmers ordered a northerly course, intending to mine the approaches to Madras. On 21 June the *Kormoran* entered the Bay of Bengal where the crew experienced hot weather with humid monsoon rains.

On 24 June the *Kormoran* approached the Indian coast and Detmers planned to commence minelaying that night. However, in the afternoon the lookout sighted a ship that appeared to be a Madura class vessel of the East India Company. Detmers did not wish to intercept her as a raider warning would compromise the minelaying operation. The ship increased speed and turned towards the raider and Detmers, believing he had encountered an armed merchant cruiser, decided to flee. The vessel gave chase but gave up after making no progress and resumed her original course towards Madras. Detmers feared local patrols would be warned so he cancelled the mining operation.[26]

The *Kormoran* headed south-east towards the Colombo–Sabang route and the lookout spotted a faint light at 0224 h on 26 June. Detmers raced to the bridge and at first saw nothing as thick clouds obscured the moonlight but then the outline of a freighter became visible. He signalled 'what ship?' followed by 'stop', but the ship continued without responding.

The unarmed 4153-ton Yugoslav steamer *Velebit* had been proceeding in ballast from Bombay to Mombasa. After Detmers ordered his guns to open fire, a star shell lit up the night and the first salvo struck her bridge while the second struck her bows and caught fire. After she stopped Detmers ceased fire:

She was in a terrible condition by this time. Her whole upper deck was a mass of flames, her deck planks were bursting and her ironwork bending in the intense heat. Her masts stood up bare against the night sky and what was left of her bent and battered funnel looked like a sieve. We searched the decks through our glasses but we could see no sign of life.[27]

The *Velebit*'s crew had lowered lifeboats and Detmers did not send across a boarding party, leaving the freighter to sink in her own time. The *Kormoran* circled the burning wreck, but the crew only found one lifeboat containing nine men. Many sailors had died on the *Velebit*, but some of her crew remained on board and extinguished the flames. She drifted and eventually ran aground on a beach in the Andaman Islands, and several weeks later a passing ship rescued the castaways.

The *Kormoran* resumed her south-east course but in the afternoon the lookout sighted another freighter, and she adopted a reciprocal course without being seen and at 5500 metres (6014 yards) Detmers ordered her to stop.

The small 3472-ton Australian steamer *Mareeba*, owned by the Australian United Steam Navigation Company, had been transporting sugar from Batavia to Colombo. After being challenged, Captain Skinner ordered his radio to broadcast a raider warning. The *Mareeba* turned to port and her wireless broadcast a QQQQ message, while the *Kormoran*'s wireless attempted to jam the signal. The raider opened fire and her first salvo struck the wireless room, the second hit the foreship and the third landed on the waterline. After the crew lowered lifeboats, a boarding party lead by *Oberleutnant* Diebitsch searched the freighter, but she had been too badly damaged for use as an auxiliary minelayer. Her entire crew of forty-eight men transferred to the raider. Detmers remembered their arrival:

> The captain of the *Mareeba* was an old sea-dog named Skinner, who was not in the least bit intimidated. He immediately agreed to his being quartered with his men and being responsible for their good behaviour, and the whole time we had no trouble. In return we made things as easy for them as we could.[28]

The boarding party scuttled the *Mareeba* and the *Kormoran* headed south-east and reached the Dondra Head–Sabang route, but Detmers cancelled

In June 1941 in the Indian Ocean the *Kormoran* captured the small Australian steamer *Mareeba* and her entire crew of forty-eight men transferred to the raider.
(AUTHOR'S COLLECTION)

operations on 28 June: 'Supply ships cannot be counted on in the immediate future. That forces me as well to be particularly careful with my engines.'[29] The 'Great Round Up' of supply ships in the Atlantic had even restricted the *Kormoran*'s operations in the Indian Ocean, testimony to the effectiveness of the Allied counter-offensive. The raider headed south to find an isolated location in which to make repairs.

TRACKING RAIDER G

The *Kormoran*'s exploits in the Atlantic had alerted the Allies to the existence of a new auxiliary cruiser labelled 'Raider G'.[30] The *Mareeba*'s garbled raider warning had been received and the Allies suspected the presence of a raider in the Indian Ocean, but they had no certainty as Admiral Ralph Leatham, Commander-in-Chief of the East Indies Station, expressed:

> . . . a report was received of a possible distress message on the 26th about half way between Ceylon and Achin Head, but to date there has been no confirmation that a Raider is actually operating there, though one possible victim (S.S. 'MAREEBA') is overdue off Colombo.[31]

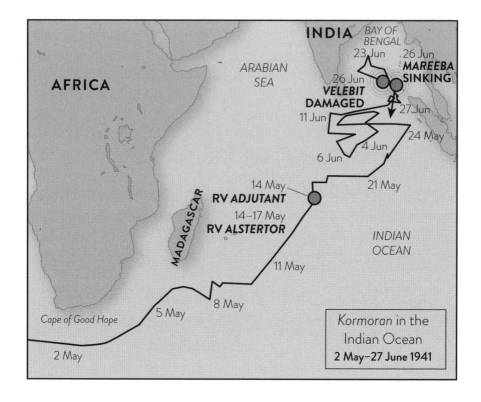

On 23 June a possible direction-finding bearing of a German warship in the
Indian Ocean suggested the presence of a raider, but 'Section 19' considered
it more likely to have originated from the South Atlantic.[32] However, by mid-
July more evidence indicated a raider had been in the Bay of Bengal after the
Velebit became overdue, but 'Section 19' remained uncertain as bad weather
might have been responsible.[33] On 28 July the Allies re-evaluated the earlier
direction-finding report and concluded that it had originated from a raider
in the Indian Ocean that had sunk the *Mareeba* and *Velebit*.[34] By the time
the Allies confirmed the *Kormoran*'s presence in the Indian Ocean it was too
late to do anything about it. 'Raider G' had disappeared and nobody knew
where she had gone.

CHAPTER 20
THE VOYAGE OF
THE *ADJUTANT*

Several converted whale catchers are operating as Auxiliary anti-
Submarine and mine sweeping ships off South African coast.
. . . Masters of British Allied Merchant Ships are to be informed
confidentially of above and instructed to treat all whale catchers
sighted on ocean route with suspicion.[1]

Admiral Ralph Leatham
Commander-in-Chief of the East Indies Station
10 May 1941

THE *ADJUTANT'S* NEW MASTER

After departing the Kerguelen Islands the *Komet* rendezvoused with the *Ole Jacob* at 'Siberia' in the central Indian Ocean on 24 March 1941. After the tanker refuelled the raider, Eyssen ordered a south-east course towards Fremantle. The men experienced a quiet time as most Allied shipping either hugged coastal waters or had been re-routed across the Pacific via the Panama Canal. The raider continued across a seemingly empty Indian Ocean.

On 22 April the *Komet* headed north-east towards Western Australia before patrolling the Australia–Dutch East Indies routes. On 7 May the raider approached Onslow in Western Australia, but Eyssen had no success and two days later radio news informed him that HMS *Cornwall* had sunk a raider. Knowing this must have been the *Pinguin*, he held a memorial service and the crew honoured their fallen comrades. Eyssen requested the *Pinguin*'s auxiliary whale catcher *Adjutant* and, after the *Seekriegsleitung* agreed, the *Komet* headed west to rendezvous with her new scout ship.

On 21 May the *Komet* and *Adjutant* rendezvoused in remote waters east of 'Siberia'. *Oberleutnant* Hemmer signalled 'K to K' (commander to commander) but Eyssen replied, 'Your report to read "K to A" (commander to admiral). Where have you been so long? Come alongside immediately.'[2] After this bad start Hemmer, who had enjoyed much independence under Krüder, found himself subordinated to an extremely rigid captain. Eyssen and his executive officer *Korvettenkapitän* Josef Huschenbeth, extremely formal men, reinstated navy protocol, causing Hemmer to become depressed and his men grumbled. Eyssen gave them bad quarters on the *Komet* and they resented Huschenbeth's discipline. The *Adjutant*'s crew, as men from the *Pinguin*, looked down upon the *Komet*, which had only sunk five ships, a small tally compared with Krüder's accomplishments.[3]

The *Komet* headed south-west towards the Great Australian Bight with the *Adjutant* in tow to conserve fuel. Eyssen upgraded the whale catcher with a 60-mm gun, two 20-mm cannons, a range finder, magnetic mines and smoke screen equipment while the raider's mechanics overhauled her engines.

THE NEW ZEALAND OPERATION

After the *Komet* and *Adjutant* passed south of Cape Leeuwin on 8 June, Eyssen announced that the whale catcher would mine New Zealand waters. *Oberleutnant* Wilfried Karsten, the raider's mining officer, would command the whale catcher and Hemmer had been demoted to navigator. However, to ease the situation, Karsten allowed Hemmer to remain in the captain's cabin and elected instead to sleep in the radio room. Hemmer, however, remained bitter about his loss of command and tension among the two crews remained high.

The two vessels parted company and the *Adjutant* proceeded towards New Zealand while the *Komet* headed for the Chatham Islands, where she would wait for the whale catcher. Eyssen outlined his plan: 'Ship 45 [*Komet*] sent Adjutant, as planned, to lay ten T.M.B. [*magnetic*] mines in the approaches to the New Zealand harbours of Port Lyttelton and Port Nicholson (Wellington) during the next new moon period.'[4] On 13 June the *Adjutant* rounded Tasmania, entering the Tasman Sea, and the crew spotted Auckland Island seven days later. The whale catcher experienced engine trouble but Karsten, determined to continue, set a north-east course towards New Zealand's South Island.

On 24 June the *Adjutant* headed west directly towards Lyttelton and, after sunset, Karsten noted that the darkness would be ideal for minelaying. The crew spotted lights from Lyttelton and the whale catcher turned north towards Cook Strait between the North and South Islands. At 2100 h Hemmer spotted the Baring Head Lighthouse near Wellington, and the peacetime navigation lights greatly assisted his progress, especially the Godley Head Lighthouse and the aircraft beacons at Christchurch.

At midnight the *Adjutant* laid ten mines in the approaches to Lyttelton, 3 miles off Godley Head. The Germans saw no sign of the New Zealand Navy. In the morning the whale catcher departed on a north-easterly course at 10 knots. Shortly afterwards the crew spotted the lights of a steamer, which Karsten avoided, and after sunset the men saw snow-capped mountains, reminding them of home. Karsten focused on the next phase of his mission:

> I want to lay the mines at Wellington tonight before the harbour
> is warned — and, so far, Lyttelton has not reported anything. If,
> however, I proceed at a safe distance of 150 to 200 miles off the coast,
> I shall not get there today. The same arrangements hold for Wellington
> as for Lyttelton, except that it will be more difficult, as Wellington is
> better defended.[5]

The *Adjutant* headed north towards Wellington at 7 knots during a dark night with calm seas and a light north-westerly breeze. At 2100 h the men spotted the Baring Head Lighthouse and one hour later they saw the Pencarrow Lighthouse, and the whale catcher turned north-west directly towards it. Two large searchlights between Palmer Head and Pencarrow Head guarded the entrance to Wellington Harbour, and the lookout spotted three patrol

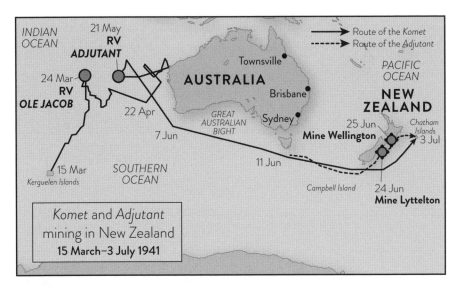

Komet and Adjutant
mining in New Zealand
15 March–3 July 1941

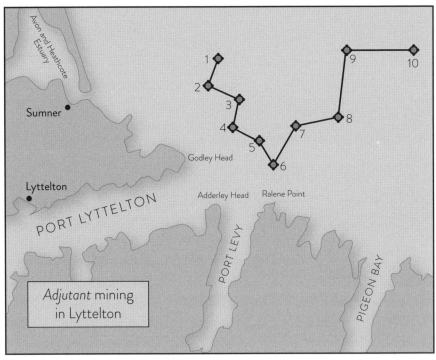

Adjutant mining
in Lyttelton

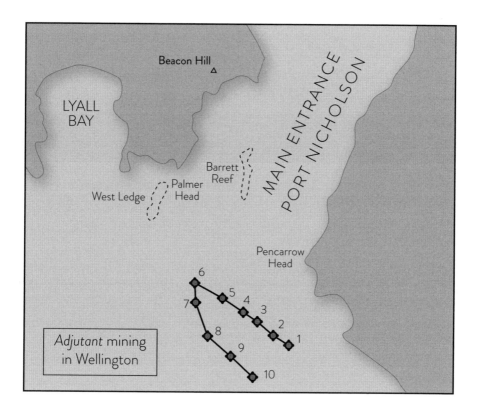

boats with masthead lights but Karsten kept his distance. He decided to lay ten mines off Pencarrow Head across the entrance to the harbour at full speed before making a quick exit under the cover of a smokescreen.

The shore station at Baring Head challenged the *Adjutant*, but Karsten did not reply. The station signalled the searchlight, which exposed the whale catcher, but Karsten held his nerve and continued his mission. At 2316 h the *Adjutant* began laying her minefield and a searchlight illuminated the ship as the fourth mine dropped into the sea. Karsten ordered a smokescreen and the men laid the final mine at 2328 h. The *Adjutant* had laid twenty mines in New Zealand waters. As the whale catcher made her escape, the searchlight swept the area and Karsten recalled the commotion:

> There are three M.T.B.'s [motor torpedo boats] and one minesweeper between the searchlight and Pencarrow Head and one M.T.B. between the searchlight and Palmer Head. One small M.T.B. type of vessel was

making black smoke. All the ships were burning navigation lights. The patrol vessels had moved into the beam of the centre searchlight and lay burning masthead lights; they maintained Morse communication with the signal station on Beacon Hill.[6]

Karsten had been prepared to fight, but the patrol boats never challenged him. After the *Adjutant* rounded Baring Head, she headed east towards the Chatham Islands and the rendezvous with the *Komet*. No pursuing patrol boats had followed her, although the wireless detected signals between New Zealand airfields and naval bases, causing Karsten to believe that a search operation had commenced. The *Adjutant* briefly stopped to make engine repairs before continuing at 9 knots with the assistance of an emergency sail.

The New Zealand authorities knew nothing about the operation. The *Adjutant* did resemble minesweepers that operated between Lyttelton and Wellington, and it is likely the searchlight personnel mistook her for one of them.

On 1 July the *Adjutant* rendezvoused with the *Komet* north-east of the Chatham Islands and Eyssen gave a positive assessment of her operation: 'I do not think the *Adjutant* was seen during the operation, in spite of the searchlight activity.'[7] The *Komet*'s wireless room scanned the airwaves for news about the mines and, after hearing nothing, Eyssen commented, 'No news of any sort was ever obtained about losses of shipping brought about by the *Adjutant* minefields.'[8] Unfortunately for the Germans, none of these mines claimed any victims and were most likely defective. In New Zealand nobody knew anything about the operation until after the war when the Allies captured German records.

As the *Adjutant*'s engines completely broke down, Eyssen decided to scuttle her, which he regretted as the *Komet* would lose a scout ship. Hemmer removed the whale catcher's wheel and bell and, after witnessing the *Adjutant*'s demise, he reported to Eyssen and Huschenbeth for a dressing down over his 'superior' attitude. Eyssen made his dislike of Hemmer clear:

Ensign Hemmer had unfortunately become rather self-assured by the fine success of *Pinguin* and his independence as commander of *Adjutant* and both he and the whole crew of *Adjutant* believed that they could look down condescendingly and with exaggerated pride on *Komet*![9]

Eyssen confined Hemmer to quarters for five days and he took his punishment but quietly reminded himself that as navigator he had been responsible for the success of the minelaying operation.

On 3 July the *Komet* had been at sea for one year and the *Seekriegsleitung* gave the raider Iron Crosses for Eyssen to award at his discretion. Huschenbeth, Karsten and the engineering officer *Kapitänleutnant* Alms received the Iron Cross, as did Hemmer for his service on the *Pinguin* and for commanding the *Adjutant*.

Eyssen decided to operate off the east coast of Australia but, three days later, due to changes in Australian shipping routes, he decided instead to patrol the New Zealand–Panama route. He also planned to attack shipping near the Panama Canal and would soon take the war inside the Pan-American Neutrality Zone.

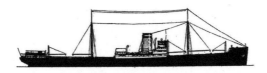

CHAPTER 21
DESTINATION BORDEAUX

Thus, untiring, the extraordinary cruise of our untouchable ship
went on, the enemy thinking he saw us everywhere at once. . . . But
everything has an end.[1]

War Correspondent
German Raider Orion

THE SEAPLANE SIGHTING

On 7 May 1941 the *Orion* and *Ole Jacob* headed east through waters near
Madagascar when the wireless intercepted a QQQQ warning from the
British Emperor. Weyher correctly guessed that the *Pinguin* was attacking
another victim. After receiving a QQQQ signal from the *Tamerlane* the next
day, Weyher once again believed that Krüder had intercepted a ship and had
no idea the 'Tamerlane' was in fact the *Pinguin*. Weyher discovered Krüder's
fate after a signal informed him that a raider had been sunk. This news
was a double blow as the *Pinguin* had been sunk close to his position and,
with a strong Royal Navy presence in the area, he abandoned his planned
northern thrust towards the Seychelles. However, the *Seekriegsleitung* argued

that a northern thrust made sense as the British now felt secure and Weyher ordered a northerly course.

The *Ole Jacob* departed and the *Orion*, disguised as a French freighter, headed north-west towards the Arabian Sea. After rounding the Seychelles, the lookout kept a watch for the *Ketty Brovig*, unaware that she had been sunk. The Arado conducted two reconnaissance flights each day without sighting anything. On the morning of 18 May *Oberleutnant* Winterfeldt took off on another reconnaissance flight, but the raider's crew watched his seaplane suddenly climb into cloud cover. Weyher assumed he had spotted a ship, but the Arado unexpectedly returned and launched two red flares, signalling danger.

After the seaplane landed Winterfeldt informed Weyher that a heavy cruiser with three funnels was 45 miles away.[2] Winterfeldt had sighted either HMS *Cornwall* or *Glasgow*.[3] As the raider and the cruiser were converging, Weyher ordered a south-east course at full speed. He expected to see the cruiser astern by 1000 h, but by then the raider should be under the horizon and out of sight. The *Orion*'s fate depended upon the skill of the men in the boiler rooms who had to prevent black smoke emitting from the funnel while keeping the engines at full speed. As expected, the lookout spotted smoke shortly after 1000 h. The cruiser had maintained her original course and, as the distance increased, the crew started to relax and the smoke disappeared.

The *Seekriegsleitung* ordered the *Orion* to proceed to a new operational area in the South Atlantic and the raider headed south. On 26 May the Nakajima seaplane capsized in rough seas while attempting to take off and, although the crew rescued the aircrew, the plane sank into the ocean.

The *Orion* headed south-east to rendezvous with the tanker *Ole Jacob*. Weyher realized his voyage would soon come to an end because the raider's engines and propeller shaft were deteriorating. He addressed the crew, telling them that their final destination would be France, which resulted in wild cheering.[4]

On 3 June the *Orion* rendezvoused with the *Ole Jacob* at 'Siberia' in the central Indian Ocean. Captain 'Allright' Steinkrauss boarded the raider to collect despatches for the *Seekriegsleitung* and letters from the crew. This had been the first time Weyher had allowed his men to write home. After the tanker refuelled the raider, Weyher wished Steinkrauss a safe voyage and the *Ole Jacob* departed, arriving in Bordeaux on 19 July.

RETURN TO THE ATLANTIC

The *Orion* headed south-east towards the Cape of Good Hope and entered the South Atlantic on 20 June as the crew struggled against hurricane force winds and the rough seas of the Roaring Forties. The propeller's white metal had completely worn away, resulting in steel grinding against steel, and it could only be repaired in a dry dock. After the bolts holding down the tail shaft bearings broke, the raider stopped. Although the mechanics got the propeller spinning again, to reduce the probability of the shaft snapping they placed timber over the bearings to reduce vibrations, and the *Orion*'s voyage continued.

On 27 June the *Seekriegsleitung* informed Weyher that the tanker *Egerland*, assigned to him, had been sunk. The 'Big Round Up' had also claimed the supply ship *Alstertor*, which had been allocated to the *Orion*, further diminishing the raider's ability to patrol.[5]

The *Seekriegsleitung* ordered the *Atlantis* to refuel the *Orion* in remote waters 300 miles north of Tristan da Cunha, and both raiders rendezvoused on 1 July, with loud cheering erupting as the ships came together.

On the *Atlantis*, Rogge told Weyher that the *Alstertor*'s sinking may have resulted in rescued prisoners compromising his presence in the South Atlantic. Therefore, he needed enough fuel to reach a new operational area in the Pacific and could not provide the *Orion* with 900 tons of fuel. Weyher disagreed and assured Rogge that he would be compensated with fuel from the *Anneliese Essberger*. Rogge, however, reminded Weyher that the *Atlantis* could better serve the war effort given the *Orion*'s inefficient fuel consumption.[6] Weyher insisted that without 900 tons he would have to wait six weeks for the *Anneliese Essberger* to arrive, but with it he could operate without restrictions until arriving home in September. However, the *Seekriegsleitung* sided with Rogge.[7] The *Orion* received 581 tons of fuel from the *Atlantis*, enough to reach France but not enough to allow Weyher to conduct extensive patrols on his homeward voyage. Rogge recalled how envious Weyher had been of his modern ship:

> Weyher — like myself, a former captain of a sailing training ship — was a very angry man. . . . His ship was an oil-burning one with a high rate of consumption and as a result he was never free from anxiety

The German raider *Atlantis* (pictured) refuelled the *Orion* in the Atlantic on 1 July 1941. Note her 5.9-inch guns, which would normally be hidden from sight.
(AUTHOR'S COLLECTION)

> about his endurance. He had never felt the same freedom as I had in the diesel-driven *Atlantis*.[8]

Although Weyher and Rogge haggled over fuel, the two captains discussed strategy and compared charts. Weyher gave Rogge food supplies and his surplus ammunition. On 6 July both raiders departed; the *Atlantis* headed towards the Pacific and the *Orion* proceeded west towards South America disguised as the Japanese freighter *Uyo Maru*.

Weyher decided to delay his homeward voyage because several German and Italian ships in Brazilian ports would soon be attempting a breakout. The *Kriegsmarine*, fearing that Brazil would soon join the Allies, had ordered them to return home, so Weyher waited for this breakout to commence as it would divert the Royal Navy's attention.

The Arado flew reconnaissance missions three times a day and Winterfeldt spotted the Brazilian steamer *Joazeiro*, which the *Orion* avoided. The raider uneventfully patrolled the La Plata–Freetown route for four days before heading north-east. On 19 July the Arado capsized after being hit by a wave and, although the aircrew escaped, the damaged plane would not fly again.

On 21 July the *Orion* began her northward voyage home and three days later entered the North Atlantic. Anxiety on board increased as she neared the North Atlantic war zone. Weyher ignored two steamers as they were on the route used by Axis blockade runners and might be friendly.

The lookout spotted a freighter south-west of the Cape Verde Islands on 29 July. Weyher ordered a parallel course and after sunset the absence of lights indicated she was an enemy vessel. Weyher, worried she might broadcast a raider warning, decided to shell her wireless room without warning, but as the *Orion* closed the distance, he instead decided to attack with torpedoes. The raider fired three torpedoes and shortly afterwards the wireless room overheard: 'SSS Chaucer.'[9]

The 5792-ton British vessel *Chaucer* had been proceeding to Buenos Aires in ballast from Middlesbrough. Captain Charles Bradley saw the torpedoes narrowly miss and, assuming a U-boat was responsible, the wireless room broadcast an SSSS submarine warning, but the operator gave the wrong location, 235 miles north of the true position.

The *Orion*'s gunners opened fire, but their first salvos fell short and the *Chaucer* signalled: 'SSS Chaucer gunned.'[10] The wireless operator, upon realising he had encountered a raider, sent an RRRR warning. The freighter turned away and returned fire with her 4-inch cannon and 40-mm Bofors gun, which poured a stream of tracer fire aimed at the *Orion*'s forward searchlight. Shells struck the raider's foredeck and bridge, causing slight damage but no causalities.

The *Orion*'s 5.9-inch guns continued firing and her 37-mm and 20-mm guns opened fire, causing tracer rounds to illuminate the night sky. The weight of fire caused the *Chaucer* to stop and flames erupted from her bridge and deck. Another ship eventually acknowledged her original SSSS message, good news for Weyher as a U-boat warning would cover his presence.

Weyher fired three more torpedoes and one struck the *Chaucer* but failed to explode. After her crew began lowering boats, he ordered a ceasefire and rescued forty-eight survivors, including thirteen wounded. The *Orion*'s guns shelled the doomed freighter, which soon vanished beneath the waves, and British radio news announced that the *Chaucer* had likely been sunk by a U-boat.

The *Orion* could no longer patrol as the gun vibrations had damaged her electrical system and also because of her deteriorating propeller shaft and diminishing fuel supply. As the raider continued towards the Central Atlantic, Weyher and his men knew they would soon be crossing dangerous waters frequented by the Royal Navy.

RUNNING THE GAUNTLET

On 6 August the *Orion*'s lookout spotted a ship in the pre-dawn darkness, but Weyher ignored her. The *Seekriegsleitung* ordered Weyher to rendezvous with two U-boats near the Azores, which would escort the raider until destroyers took over this duty in the Bay of Biscay. Minesweepers would eventually guide the raider through the Gironde minefields to Bordeaux. As the raider headed north-east towards France, Weyher received some good news. The Spanish Navy had been holding exercises off the Azores and the Spanish Government collier *Contramaestre Casado* had been participating. The *Orion* assumed her identity after the crew painted her hull grey with yellow and red Spanish markings.

The crew feared a last minute disaster as the *Orion* approached France since British warships, submarines and aircraft had a strong presence in the Bay of Biscay. On 16 August the raider reached the rendezvous location off the Azores and *U-75* and *U-205* surfaced and made contact. Convoy OG 71 had recently been attacked by U-boats nearby, which added to Weyher's concerns as the Royal Navy would no doubt be close.

The *Orion* turned east towards Spain, but *U-75* had to be detached due to engine trouble. After the raider entered the Bay of Biscay, the lookout spotted a Spanish fishing trawler with no lights and an unusual number of radio aerials, which quickly vanished in the darkness, causing Weyher to fear that she might be a British spy ship. The raider passed numerous Spanish fishing boats and the sight of another suspicious trawler increased anxiety on board as the raider continued east towards the Iberian Peninsula.

On 21 August the lookout spotted a plane, but the bridge officers relaxed after they identified it as a Focke-Wulf Condor. A short time later more Condors appeared overhead followed by two Heinkel 115s. One Heinkel exchanged recognition signals with the raider and added: 'Bravo Tommy from Tommy.'[11] The pilot was the brother of the raider's torpedo officer *Oberleutnant* Thomsen. In the evening the *Orion* rendezvoused with her destroyer escorts and the ships headed towards Bordeaux. The next day four minesweepers appeared and the flotilla commander signalled 'Where are you from?' and Weyher replied, 'Directly from Kiel.'[12] The escorts surrounded the raider and the crew removed the Spanish disguise and raised the *Kriegsmarine* flag. Weyher, not yet out of danger, feared British submarines, which often attacked ships just before they reached port.

The *Orion* continued towards Bordeaux and in the evening more Condors appeared overhead. After midnight the minesweepers led the raider through the minefields. On the morning of 23 August the lookout spotted land, and the raider anchored off Royan to wait for the tide to change. A tugboat gave the men fresh food and mail. In the early afternoon a pilot vessel and two minesweepers escorted the raider up the Gironde River while the crew, some with tears in their eyes, gazed upon the unfamiliar sight of dark green woods, hills and villages. At 1800 h the men assembled on deck in their best uniforms as the raider passed German and Italian ships, including the *Regensburg*, which had supplied the raider in the Pacific, causing much delight among the men.[13] As the sun began to set, the men saw the *Ermland* and *Ole Jacob* under the evening sky.[14] Steinkrauss stood on the deck of his tanker to greet them and with intense joy sounded his siren and the other ships in the harbour joined in. The raider arrived inside the port of Bordeaux and her voyage came to an end.

The *Orion*, a successful raider, accounted for fifteen ships totalling 71,200 tons during her cruise of 510 days, which covered 112,337 miles, five times the circumference of the earth, the longest raider voyage in history. The *Orion*'s remarkable achievements were made despite her poor engines and high fuel consumption. She never should have become a raider but Weyher's leadership and the skill of his men kept her operational well beyond the expectations of the *Seekriegsleitung*, a tremendous example of seamanship.

Weyher was awarded the Knight's Cross and the *Seekriegsleitung*, extremely happy with the *Orion*'s voyage, declared:

> That this unsuitable ship which bore no relation to an auxiliary cruiser, could account for 80,000 tons of enemy shipping, shows the excellent

direction of the vessel, and the commendable conduct, perseverance and eagerness of the crew.[15]

Weyher, an informal and flexible leader, formed a strong bond with his men and won the admiration of the enemy. Most prisoners spoke well of Weyher and after the war Captain Parker from the *Ringwood* presented him with a fine-quality camphor chest in gratitude for his humane imprisonment. After the voyage Weyher stated: 'I led my ship with common sense and luck, my men with my heart . . . we did our duty.'[16] After the war he said:

> Our operation could never have succeeded, nor could I have dreamed of bringing my ship back home, had it not been for the never-stinted support of my crew, and their trustfulness — and my good fortune; the men played their part with all their hearts. The honour was mine, but the merit for any success was the men's.[17]

Weyher later worked in the *Seekriegsleitung* before becoming First Admiralty Staff Officer to the Admiral Commanding the Aegean Region. He was promoted to *Kapitän* in June 1942 and later commanded the 10th Local Escort Division in the Black Sea. Weyher next served as the Senior Naval Officer on Crete and in November 1944 became the commandant of East Frisia. He was promoted to *Konteradmiral* in January 1945.

When the war ended Weyher reflected: 'I had the distinction of surrendering in one war as the Kaiser's youngest Cadet, and in another as Hitler's youngest Admiral.'[18] In West Germany Weyher became a *Konteradmiral* in the *Bundesmarine* (Federal Navy) and served as the Commander of First Defence Area, Kiel. He also worked on the British Admiralty's study of the naval war in the Black Sea and wrote an account of the *Orion* entitled *The Black Raider*. After leaving the Navy he became a writer and lecturer. He lived with his wife Margaret in Wilhelmshaven and his son also became an officer in the *Bundesmarine*. When reflecting upon his time on the *Orion*, Weyher remarked: 'It was the most independent and thus the finest command of all for a naval officer.'[19] Weyher died in Wilhelmshaven on 17 December 1991.

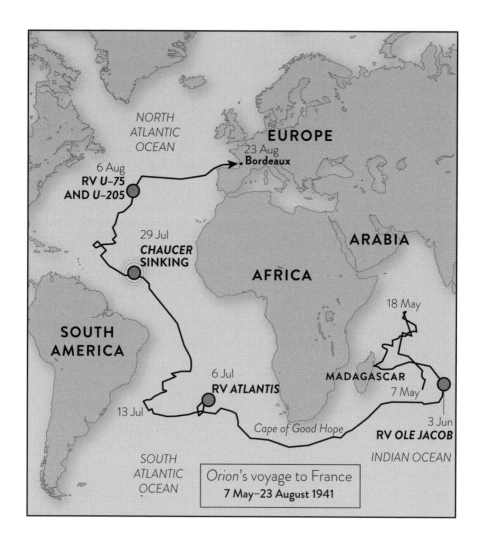

NORTH
ATLANTIC
OCEAN

EUROPE

23 Aug
Bordeaux

6 Aug
RV U–75
AND U–205

29 Jul
CHAUCER
SINKING

ARABIA

AFRICA

18 May

SOUTH
AMERICA

6 Jul
RV ATLANTIS

MADAGASCAR

7 May

13 Jul

Cape of Good Hope

3 Jun
RV OLE JACOB

INDIAN OCEAN

SOUTH
ATLANTIC
OCEAN

Orion's voyage to France
7 May–23 August 1941

BALTIC EVACUATION

In 1945 Germany faced total defeat as the Red Army advanced through East Prussia, causing a flood of refugees. With limited land transport and the Soviets surrounding several coastal cities, many refugees fled to Baltic ports, where their only hope of escape would be by sea. To evacuate the populations trapped in the ports, the *Kriegsmarine* initiated Operation Hannibal — the largest seaborne evacuation in history — which evacuated 2,360,000 people on 1080 ships, a scale far exceeding Dunkirk.[20]

The *Orion*, renamed *Hektor* and converted into a gunnery training ship, evacuated 20,000 troops and refugees during Operation Hannibal under the command of *Kapitän* Joachim Asmus.[21] On 4 May the former raider proceeded through waters near Swinemünde in Germany loaded with refugees when Russian bombers attacked and, after sustaining heavy damage, she beached on the Baltic Prussian coast, four days before the war ended. The beach later became part of Poland and in 1952 Polish labourers salvaged her wreck and broke up the once proud *Orion*.[22]

CHAPTER 22
THE GALÁPAGOS
ISLANDS RAIDER

When you see a rattlesnake poised to strike, you do not wait until he
has struck before you crush him. These Nazi submarines and raiders
are the rattlesnakes of the Atlantic. They are a menace to the free
pathways of the high seas; they are a challenge to our sovereignty.[1]

President Franklin Roosevelt
13 September 1941

THE GALÁPAGOS ISLANDS

The *Komet*, after departing the Chatham Islands, rendezvoused with the
blockade runner *Anneliese Essberger*, which had departed Manchuria bound
for France carrying rubber, at 'Balbo' between Pitcairn Island and New
Zealand on 14 July 1941. She replenished the *Komet* and Otto Giese, an
officer onboard, remembered Eyssen:

Often during this time we could hear across the water the bully
voice of Admiral Eyssen, who had a personal interest in everything
happening aboard his vessel. He kept his ship in fine shape and his

men in the best trim. In spite of the long time they had been away from home, the discipline and spirit of the crew were impressive.[2]

After the two ships parted company, the *Komet* headed north-east towards the Galápagos Islands disguised as the Japanese freighter *Ryoku Maru* and the *Anneliese Essberger* continued her voyage, arriving in Bordeaux on 10 September.[3]

The *Seekriegsleitung* ordered Eyssen to return home by October, but he first wanted to operate on the Panama–Australia route until the end of August, and the *Seekriegsleitung* gave him permission to attack shipping near the Panama Canal.

On 14 August the lookout spotted a ship 20 miles south of the Galápagos Islands. The 5020-ton New Zealand freighter *Australind* had been proceeding to Britain from Adelaide with a cargo of dried fruit, honey and zinc. Captain Stevens observed the raider and, believing her Japanese disguise, decided to let her pass.

The *Komet* raised the *Kriegsmarine* flag at 4500 metres (4921 yards) and fired two warning shots. Captain Stevens ordered full speed and instructed his wireless room to broadcast a raider warning while the RAN gunner McStavick and his men ran towards their 4-inch stern gun. The *Komet*'s gunners opened fire and McStavick fought back until a shell landed near him, knocking his weapon out of action. The second salvo hit the bridge, killing Captain Stevens and two officers. Third Officer Bird witnessed the destruction:

> I was about to go on the lower bridge when a further shell struck the master's accommodation. I ran onto the bridge, and saw the captain lying face down at the foot of the lower bridge ladder, covered by a heap of debris. I turned him over, saw that he had been shot through the head and neck, and was dead.[4]

The *Australind*'s radio went silent and the crew lowered lifeboats. A boarding party led by *Oberleutnant* Wilfried Karsten captured the freighter and escorted the forty-three survivors to the *Komet* before scuttling their ship. An injured British officer later died of his wounds and Eyssen gave him a burial at sea.

The *Komet* remained near the Galápagos Islands and chased a suspected

Dutch freighter next day without success. At night the wireless room intercepted a signal from the British freighter *Lochmonar* giving her position and expected time of arrival at the Panama Canal. Eyssen calculated she would be nearby the next day, but the *Lochmonar* failed to appear, leaving the crew disappointed.

The *Komet*'s luck changed after the lookout spotted a freighter on 17 August. The 7322-ton Dutchman *Kota Nopan* had departed New York bound for Makassar (Sulawesi), carrying rubber, tin, manganese, coffee, tea and spices with a crew of thirty-five Dutch and sixteen Javanese sailors. Captain Hatenboer was about to conduct a morning church service when the watch officer called him to the bridge. After seeing a ship dead ahead, he increased speed and headed towards the safety of Galápagos Harbour, 40 miles away.

After the *Kota Nopan* began broadcasting a raider warning, Eyssen fired a warning shot. The freighter's 4-inch stern gun opened fire but missed, and after a salvo from the *Komet* landed close to the freighter, Captain Hatenboer decided to abandon ship. Eyssen ceased fire and the *Kota Nopan*'s crew became prisoners on the raider. A boarding party captured the freighter and Eyssen decided to send her home with a prize crew of twenty-four Germans with the assistance of willing Dutch and Javanese sailors, who would receive a wage. The crew transferred some of her cargo to the *Komet* to increase the odds that some of the booty would reach Germany and to make room they threw overboard the minelaying motorboat *Meteorit*, empty barrels and other items.

The *Komet*'s lookout spotted another ship two days later south-south-west of the Galápagos Islands. The 9036-ton British India Steam Navigation Company steamer *Devon* had been on passage from Liverpool to New Zealand with a crew of 144 men. Captain Redwood attempted to flee and broadcast a raider warning, but after a pursuit of twenty-five minutes, the raider opened fire at 7300 metres (7983 yards). After a near miss the *Devon* stopped and her radio went silent. A boarding party scuttled the freighter and the *Komet* and *Kota Nopan* fled on a south-west course.

Eyssen had in quick succession claimed three ships in remote waters that had previously been untouched by the war but, as these attacks occurred within the Pan-American Neutrality Zone, he made a powerful new enemy.

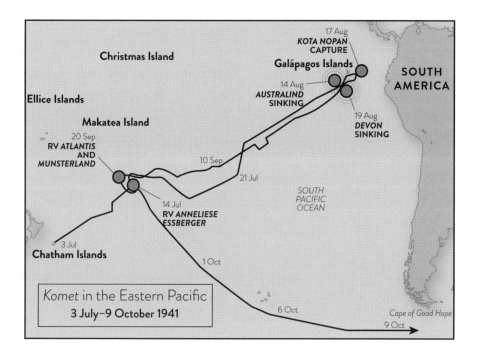

Komet in the Eastern Pacific
3 July–9 October 1941

RAIDER HUNT IN THE NEUTRALITY ZONE

The Royal Navy suspected the presence of a raider near the Galápagos Islands when the *Australind* became overdue and the *Kota Nopan*'s raider warning confirmed this suspicion.[5] The Admiralty ordered shipping to avoid the area and the cruiser HMS *Orion*, the only nearby Allied warship, commenced a raider hunt. The cruiser's captain did not have charts of the area, forcing the navigator to rely on a freehand map and an atlas.

The *Komet* had also come to the attention of the United States. The American Government, deeply angered over the violation of their Neutrality Zone, ordered its navy to sink the intruder. At this time the US Navy was in an undeclared state of war with the *Kriegsmarine*.[6] On 17 October *U-568* torpedoed the destroyer USS *Kearny* near Iceland after she attacked a U-boat wolf pack. The destroyer survived, but eleven sailors lost their lives. Two weeks later *U-552* sank the destroyer USS *Reuben James*, which had been escorting a convoy, and only forty-five of her 160 crew survived.[7] Eyssen's attack within 'American waters' had heightened an already tense state of undeclared war.

The US Navy unsuccessfully hunted for the *Komet* off the Galápagos Islands during late August and early September.[8] In mid-September the Americans extended their search across a wider area south-west of the Panama Canal, and the US Navy declared:

> Whether the sea raider reported to have been active in the Pacific in the vicinity of Galápagos Islands is a submarine, surface warship, or armed merchantman is not known. . . . It is understood that under President Roosevelt's recent declaration any US warship would be authorized to fight such a raider on sight.[9]

Rear-Admiral Sadler, the commander of the 15th US Naval District, announced that 'if the raider is operating within 600 miles of the Panama Canal it will not operate there for long'.[10] Despite this boast the Americans failed to find any trace of the *Komet* and the British search also achieved nothing, although at one stage HMS *Orion* came within 100 miles of the raider.[11] Eyssen had once again created international headlines before vanishing.

THE *KOMET* AND *ATLANTIS*

As Eyssen needed fuel for the *Kota Nopan*'s voyage to France, the *Seekriegsleitung* arranged a rendezvous at 'Balbo' with the *Atlantis* and the blockade runner *Munsterland*, which had left Yokohama. The *Komet* and *Kota Nopan* adopted a south-west course and rendezvoused with the *Atlantis* on 20 September. As the *Atlantis* approached, *Kapitänleutnant* Mohr reminded Rogge that Eyssen was now an admiral, so the *Atlantis* fired a salute to honour Eyssen's promotion, as Mohr noted:

> Rogge, in spotless white, and heavy with gold braid, went across to pay a courtesy call, just as though he was a cruiser Captain calling; upon *Bismarck*. But alas for our sense of fun. Eyssen took it all at face value and received us with the dignified formality of the C-in-C [Commander-in-Chief] himself.[12]

Eyssen and Rogge had positive initial discussions, but on the second day

A U-boat rendezvous with the *Pinguin* in the Atlantic.
(AUTHOR'S COLLECTION)

the *Munsterland* arrived and both men squabbled over her supplies. Eyssen demanded stores allocated to the *Atlantis* and Rogge argued that his raider had greater needs as she would be continuing operations while the *Komet* would soon head home.[13] Eyssen backed down and only took a portion of the beer and food in exchange for ammunition, aircraft fuel, an x-ray machine, nails and clothing. The *Komet* and *Kota Nopan* both received enough fuel from the *Munsterland* to reach home. The *Atlantis* transferred her prisoners; the officers went to the *Komet* and the sailors to the *Kota Nopan*.

On 24 September the German ships departed and the *Munsterland* later arrived in Japan.[14] The *Komet* and *Kota Nopan* approached southern Chile and rounded Cape Horn on 10 October, entering the South Atlantic, and seven days later they parted company. The *Kota Nopan* arrived safely at Bordeaux on 16 November.[15]

The *Atlantis* rounded Cape Horn and entered the South Atlantic. Rogge planned to reach France in December but had orders to first resupply U-boats. On 15 November he refuelled *U-68* south of St Helena, but the British knew about this encounter because Bletchley Park had decrypted compromised U-boat signals. The codebreakers next read a signal to *U-126* informing the submarine to rendezvous with the *Atlantis* north-east of Ascension Island, and Captain Oliver on the nearby cruiser HMS *Devonshire* received orders to sink the raider.[16] The *Atlantis* rendezvoused with *U-126* on 22 November and shortly afterwards the *Devonshire* appeared. Rogge unsuccessfully claimed his vessel was the *Polyphemus* and the cruiser opened fire.[17] Shells struck the *Atlantis* and, as her guns lacked sufficient range to return fire, Rogge scuttled his raider and the crew abandoned ship. The *Atlantis*, one of the greatest raiders in history, had claimed twenty-two ships totalling 145,697 tons.[18]

HOMEWARD VOYAGE

The *Komet* headed east towards Tristan da Cunha before turning north and Eyssen hoped to attack shipping in South Atlantic waters. After spotting an unknown freighter on the night of 1 November, Eyssen abandoned his pursuit due to the raider's slow speed. The lookout spotted smoke four days later, but Eyssen decided against investigating.

On 6 November the *Komet* entered the North Atlantic and Eyssen received orders to cease commerce warfare and proceed to Hamburg via the English Channel. On 17 November the raider, disguised as the Portuguese freighter *S. Thome*, rendezvoused with *U-516* and *U-652* near the Azores, which would escort her to Cape Finisterre, Spain. Morale soared after the men sighted German aircraft and the raider entered the Bay of Biscay. Although an escorting aircraft appeared overhead the crew still had to transit dangerous waters frequented by British submarines. After rendezvousing with a minesweeper the men felt a greater sense of security.

The *Komet*, disguised as a *Sperrbrecher* pathfinder, neared Bordeaux and headed north, hugging the French coast, while the Bletchley Park codebreakers tracked her movements as, upon entering home waters, her wireless had switched to a compromised Enigma key.[19] The Royal Navy's Dover Coastal Force planned to sink the raider in the English Channel.

On 26 November the raider's lookout sighted the French coast and she anchored at Cherbourg before reaching Le Havre. After the raider departed with an escort of eleven minesweepers and three torpedo boats, British torpedo boats attacked in the pre-dawn darkness on 28 November. The opposing vessels fought an inconclusive action. Three men died on the escort ships, one sailor on the *Komet* received minor injuries and several British boats sustained damage. Three additional torpedo boats reinforced the escort and the German force continued through the channel.

The *Komet* sheltered in Dunkirk before continuing north and, as she neared Holland, the Dutch prisoners listened to radio programmes from home. A low-flying Bristol Blenheim aircraft attacked the raider and three bombs fell harmlessly into sea but the fourth hit the bridge 3 metres (9 feet) from *Oberleutnant* Hemmer. The explosion caused only minor damage and no casualties.

On 30 November the *Komet* anchored off Cuxhaven and disembarked the prisoners and later that day she anchored off Brunsbüttel so Eyssen could meet *Kapitän* Gumprich, who would command the *Thor*'s second cruise.[20] The raider continued north and at 1800 h she anchored in Hamburg and her voyage came to an end. The gunnery officer, *Kapitänleutnant* Karl Balser, experienced one of the most moving nights of his life. While on watch, before anybody had permission to disembark, he walked down the gangplank in the night rain and touched land.[21] The crew enjoyed forty-five days of well-deserved leave and Eyssen received the Knight's Cross.

The *Komet* had spent 515 days at sea crossing 86,988 miles of ocean. She had claimed ten ships totalling 42,959 tons, a modest score given the length of the cruise, but Eyssen did get his raider and men safely home.[22] The *Komet*'s voyage through the Siberian Ice Passage had been a remarkable feat of seamanship. Eyssen, a formal and anachronistic officer, lacked the aggressive spirit of the other raider captains and had a tendency to blunder. His release of prisoners on Emirau resulted in the Allies discovering their Merchant Navy codes had been broken and his attacks on Nauru strained German–Japanese relations. However, he treated his prisoners exceptionally well, and the *Komet*'s cruise was a success.

Eyssen later became the naval liaison officer to Airfleet IV on the Eastern Front before becoming the Chief of the Naval Depot in Oslo, responsible for the movement of shipping. Afterwards he became the commander of the Military District in Vienna before retiring on 30 April 1945, eight days before the war ended. Eyssen died on 31 March 1960. Balser delivered his eulogy and remembered him with the words, 'You spared lives . . . you will live . . . as a beaming good friend', while his adjutant Wilfried Karsten wrote in a dedication, 'Remembered with gratitude.'[23]

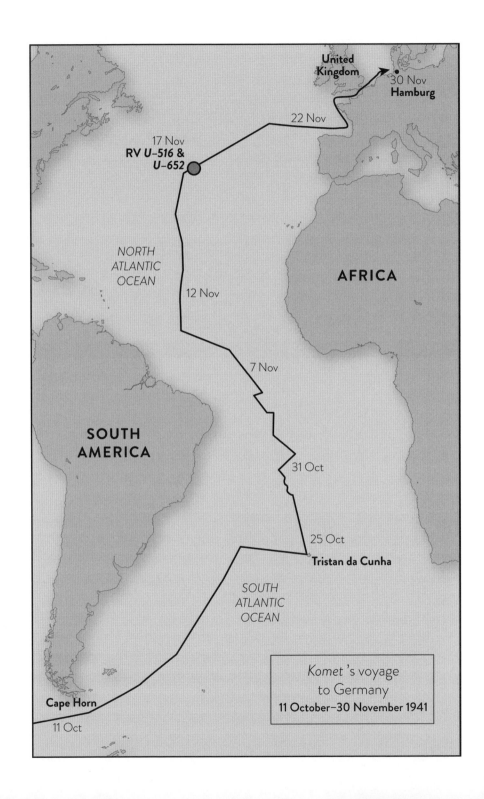

Komet's voyage
to Germany
11 October–30 November 1941

SECOND CRUISE

In October 1942 the *Komet* departed Germany on her second cruise disguised as *Sperrbrecher 22*. *Kapitän* Ulrich Brocksien planned to break out into the Atlantic via the English Channel. *Korvettenkapitän* Huschenbeth and the signals officer *Oberleutnant* Wilhelm Dobberstein were the only two officers remaining from the raider's previous voyage. Bletchley Park learned of the raider's departure as she had been using the compromised Hydra cipher.[24] The codebreakers tracked her from Kiel to Swinemünde and correctly concluded she would soon enter the English Channel.[25] However, they lost track of her after she changed Enigma keys.[26] On 7 October Bletchley Park rediscovered the *Komet*'s whereabouts after decrypting a signal stating that *Sperrbrecher 22* would arrive in Flushing (Holland) that day. As the British knew the genuine *Sperrbrecher 22* had been sunk, they correctly guessed this was a reference to the raider. The Royal Navy waited for the *Komet* in the English Channel but, as it took thirty-six hours for an Enigma signal to be deciphered and read, the British could not be certain of the raider's exact location. On 10 October a force of destroyers failed to find her and air patrols had no success.

On 13 October the *Komet* arrived at Le Havre and departed that evening to run the gauntlet of the English Channel with four torpedo boats. 'Section 19' tracked her movements, as Patrick Beesly recalled:

> *Komet*'s next move round Cape Barfleur to Cherbourg was almost certainly planned for the night of the thirteenth, so that afternoon the Commander-in-Chief Portsmouth gave orders for Operation Bowery, involving nine destroyers and twelve M.T.B.s [motor torpedo boats], to be put into effect.[27]

As the *Komet* headed towards Cap de la Hague, the four torpedo boats formed a defensive circle around her. At 2100 h British radar near Barfleur detected the raider, and a Swordfish plane dropped flares nearby. The commander of *T-14* suggested sheltering in Cherbourg, but Brocksien overruled him and the flotilla held its course.

At 0205 h the *Komet* signalled that she was under attack. British destroyers opened fire and the motorboats launched torpedoes. All the escorts sustained damage and fifteen German sailors died, including the flotilla leader *Kapitänleutnant* Hans Wilke. The commander of *T-14* later claimed that the panic-stricken crew of a 20-mm gun on the *Komet* had fired on three torpedo boats despite good visibility.[28] Sub-Lieutenant Drayson in *MTB 236* fired a torpedo at the raider. At 0215 h the *Komet* exploded, sending a stream of flames high into the night sky, and soon only burning oil and debris remained. *T-14* returned to St Malo and reported: 'Definitely no survivors.'[29] Brocksien and his entire crew of 350 men perished, while the British only suffered two wounded and slight damage to one destroyer.

According to the surviving German torpedo boat officers, the explosion most likely resulted from gunfire igniting the aviation fuel, which detonated the forward magazines. They did not see a fountain of water consistent with a torpedo strike and no torpedo denotation was heard.[30] The British, however, attributed the sinking to Drayson. Beesly reflected: 'It had been an extremely successful operation made possible by accurate intelligence and sound appreciations based on thorough knowledge of German procedures.'[31]

CHAPTER 23
ENCOUNTER OFF SHARK BAY

Representing any particular ship is not at all necessary. The times of
a *Wolf* or *Seeadler* are over. The opponent is on the watch and stops
everything. However, if one is stopped at all, there is only one way
out: battle.[1]

Kapitän Theodore Detmers
Commander of the *Kormoran*
8 July 1941

THE *KORMORAN* RESTS

On 2 July 1941 the *Kormoran* arrived in isolated waters south of Sri Lanka,
where work commenced on the engine overhaul. Seaman Kurt Hoffmann
had been repairing the floats of an Arado seaplane with a drill when he
received an electric shock and, after being taken to the hospital, attempts
to revive him failed. Detmers gave Hoffmann a burial at sea and a court of
inquiry concluded that three sailors had been negligent.

Detmers decided to again disguise the *Kormoran* as the Dutch freighter
Straat Malakka, because only older Japanese ships operated in this area. The
men painted the hull dark grey, the superstructure light brown, the funnels

black and the masts yellow. Detmers described how the men became restless:

> Life on board an auxiliary cruiser is very monotonous. For weeks on end,
> months on end in fact, the men have to do the same routine duties with
> never a word from home, never a card or letter, and certainly never a
> parcel — and no shore leave. Only through the wireless did the men
> have a vague idea of what was going on at home.[2]

The prisoners swam in the swimming pool and some started their own boxing competition in a ring built on the deck. William Jones from the *Mareeba* recalled captivity:

> We were well treated during our five months aboard the raider. . . . He
> [Detmers] was most fond of Australia, he told us and he was anxious
> to treat us well in appreciation of the hospitality he had received at our
> countrymen's hands. Indeed, on his birthday, he arranged a sing-song,
> and he would have got us drunk with great pleasure. Other members
> of the crew used to drop cigarettes and other gifts at the bottom of
> the stairway so we would find them 'accidentally'.[3]

After the crew finished the overhaul on 16 July, Detmers planned to return to the Bay of Bengal to conduct his long-anticipated minelaying operation.[4] The *Kormoran* headed north-west towards the Chagos Islands, but Detmers abandoned his plan due to increased Royal Navy presence in the Bay of Bengal. He instead planned to operate off Sumatra and Java before heading towards Western Australia, and the *Kormoran* accordingly proceeded east towards the Dutch East Indies. On 25 July the raider crossed the Siberoet Strait without sighting any ships, and Detmers decided to patrol the Fremantle–Sunda route and the Lombok Straits.

The *Kormoran* spent over a week zigzagging the waters between Java and Australia without any success, but on 13 August the lookout spotted a ship in the early evening twilight, 200 miles west of Carnarvon. Detmers took no action as their courses were converging, then the vessel suddenly turned towards the raider. He found this action strange as merchant vessels would normally maintain their course or flee. The vessel began broadcasting

QQQQ signals every five to ten minutes without giving a position, which suggested she must be a decoy ship for a convoy. Detmers ordered an intercept course, but gave up after making no progress.[5]

Detmers considered mining the approaches to Carnarvon and Geraldton but decided against the idea: 'It would be quite possible at both places. On account of the sparse traffic in them even in peace-time, however, my mines are still too valuable for that.'[6]

The *Kormoran* headed north-east towards the Dutch East Indies and rounded Christmas Island on 22 August. The crew spotted the Boca Boca mountain peak on the Isle of Enggano (off Sumatra) three days later, the first land they had seen since the beginning of their voyage, which to Detmers appeared 'in front of us like a South Sea fairy story in wonderful illumination'.[7] The *Seekriegsleitung* informed Detmers that the *Kulmerland* would soon leave Japan to resupply the *Kormoran*. He decided to patrol the waters near Sri Lanka before the rendezvous.

On 1 September the lookout spotted a Waigani class ship south of Sri Lanka and, as she had a flag on her stern, Detmers feared she might be an armed merchant cruiser. As she maintained her course, though, he became convinced she was not a warship. Detmers decided to keep his distance before striking at night. After the ship disappeared over the horizon, he changed course and ordered full speed. The ship appeared again only to disappear in a rain squall, and Detmers relented due to the *Kormoran*'s slow speed. He felt disappointment but nevertheless considered his presence to be worthwhile: 'The task of the auxiliary cruiser in the Indian Ocean at present is police work, in that by his presence he prevents the use of shorter routes.'[8]

The *Kormoran* headed east towards the Saya de Malha Bank before heading north-west towards the Red Sea. After the raider reached the Eight Degree Channel–Seychelles route, the Arado conducted a reconnaissance flight without sighting anything.

On the night of 23 September the lookout spotted the green light of a ship between the Maldives and the Seychelles. Detmers signalled 'what ship?' and she replied, 'Greek ship Stamatios G Embiricos'. He ordered her to stop. Captain Michael Palaeograssas obeyed, believing the raider was a British ship, and only when the boarding party led by *Oberleutnant* Diebitsch arrived with drawn pistols did he learn otherwise.

The small unarmed 3941-ton freighter *Stamatios G Embiricos* had been proceeding to Colombo from Mombasa, Kenya in ballast. The boarding party scuttled the freighter after transferring Captain Palaeograssas and five sailors to the raider, but two lifeboats carrying twenty-four men evaded the Germans, hoping to reach the Seychelles. The next day the seaplane found the missing lifeboats and the raider captured the fugitives.

The *Kormoran* continued south-east and rendezvoused with the *Kulmerland* at 'Marius' in the mid-Indian Ocean on 16 October. The supply ship had left Kobe with fuel and provisions for the raider. She would also transfer Detmers' prisoners to the blockade runner *Spreewald* at 'Balbo', between Pitcairn Island and New Zealand. Carl Gunderson, a prisoner from the *Mareeba*, aged fifty-two, suffered a fatal heart attack. Detmers gave him a burial at sea, and Jones recalled that 'the Germans gave him a most impressive funeral ceremony, for which all were assembled on the deck'.[9]

The two ships proceeded north-west to look for fairer weather to transfer the supplies and the next day work began in calm seas. The *Kulmerland* refuelled the *Kormoran* and Detmers finally obtained a sufficient supply of white metal for the bearings. The raider also received fresh food and beer as well as intelligence reports on shipping from *Konteradmiral* Wenneker, the naval attaché in Japan.[10] The prisoners transferred to the *Kulmerland* except for the four Chinese laundrymen who had joined the raider's crew. As the prisoners would be transferred to the *Spreewald*, Detmers provided a five-man naval guard to accompany them, including his navigation officer *Oberleutnant* Oetzel, who was suffering from a tropical rash, Petty Officer Heckhoff and three sailors with signs of vitamin deficiencies. Detmers wrote a final entry in his war diary before providing a copy for Pschunder to give to Wenneker:

> I intend to proceed immediately with carrying out alterations to adapt Engine I as reserve ship's network engine. Thanks to the speedy completion of the provisioning, I hope to be back in my operational area by the next new moon period.[11]

On 26 October the *Kulmerland* departed and headed towards her rendezvous with the *Spreewald*. Jones later complained about the poor conditions on the supply ship: 'Treatment on this ship was the worst . . . we lived like pigs on rice thrice daily, and slept on Chinese matting.'[12] The prisoners transferred to the *Spreewald* at 'Balbo' and the *Kulmerland* returned to Japan on 16 December.[13] The *Spreewald* continued her voyage to Europe but Alec Matheson, a crewman from the *Mareeba*, died of natural causes on the blockade runner.

As the *Spreewald*'s voyage neared its end, *U-333* unintentionally torpedoed her in the Bay of Biscay on 31 January 1942. The blockade runner had been in the wrong position and ahead of schedule. *U-333*, under the command of *Kapitänleutnant* Peter-Erich Cremer, had spotted the ship zigzagging, which appeared to be an enemy vessel heading to Britain. Vic Tessy from the *Mareeba* witnessed the panic:

> There was a wild scramble as soon as she was hit. Many were killed by the explosion, and every boat on the port side was blown to hell and in the panic the Germans were the worst of the lot. Everyone tried to get into a big steel boat on the starboard side. . . . In the panic and confusion three Germans, a steward, a guard and the second mate, lost their nerve and shot themselves.[14]

U-105 rescued twenty-five Germans and fifty-five prisoners from three lifeboats. The *Spreewald*'s master Captain Bull, Captain Skinner from the *Mareeba* and twenty-three others, including seven sailors from the *Mareeba*, in the fourth lifeboat were never seen again.[15] When *U-105* reached France all the surviving prisoners landed. Cremer stood trial in a court-martial, but it acquitted him as the *Spreewald* had disregarded procedures for passing through the Bay of Biscay.

THE INDIAN OCEAN RAIDER

During September Allied intelligence suspected the presence of a raider in the Indian Ocean. Their attention had incorrectly been drawn towards the southern Indian Ocean as a direction-finding report suggested a raider was between the Kerguelens and Amsterdam Island.[16] This gave weight to a statement made by a prisoner from the *Pinguin* who claimed his raider had rendezvoused with the *Alstertor* in the Kerguelens.[17] HMAS *Australia* reached the

In November 1941 the Allies suspected a raider in the Indian Ocean might be heading towards Australia, but nobody foresaw the disastrous result of the *Kormoran's* appearance off Western Australia.
(AUTHOR'S COLLECTION)

islands on 1 November where the crew found evidence of German presence, namely scrubbing brushes, bottles and tins of aviation fuel, all with German labels.[18] The cruiser mined the key channels and anchorages before departing.

Allied intelligence had not accurately reconstructed the *Kormoran's* voyage. They suspected the *Orion* had been responsible for Detmers' actions in the Bay of Bengal.[19] They made a further error two weeks later when Australian naval intelligence attributed the Galápagos sinkings to 'Raider G' (*Kormoran*).[20] However, one week later they correctly concluded that the *Kormoran* had been responsible for the Bay of Bengal sinkings as 'all the positive evidence points to Raider G (No.46) being both the Indian Ocean and the Pacific Ocean Raider'.[21] Although the Allies had finally figured out the *Kormoran* had been in the Bay of Bengal, they now believed she was in the Pacific, and at the end of September the Indian Ocean appeared to be free of raiders.[22]

In October the Australians still believed the *Kormoran* was in the Pacific as the Area Combined Headquarters reported: 'Raider "G" [*Kormoran*] repeat "G" which may be Pacific raider is probably German "Steermark" 9800

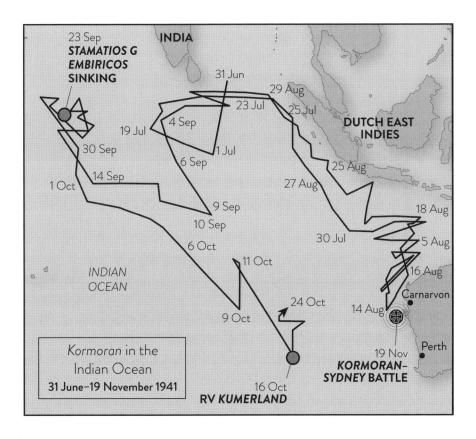

tons.'[23] At the same time the Australians received an indication that a raider might be active in the Indian Ocean after all when the *Stamatios G Embiricos* became overdue. The RAN concluded: 'Such a raider could now be on the Australia Station.'[24] This suspicion became stronger in late October:

> The fact that the 'S.G.EMBIRICOS' has failed to arrive and a further unit is overdue strengthens the view that a raider is operating in the Indian Ocean and was possibly in the Arabian Sea area early this month. Such a raider could now have reached the western section of the Australia Station.[25]

The Allies suspected the presence of a raider in the Indian Ocean that might be heading towards Australia, but nobody predicted how tragic the *Kormoran*'s appearance off Western Australia would be.

A FATEFUL DECISION

Detmers needed to rewire the *Kormoran*'s engines and the navigator *Oberleutnant* Henry Meyer suggested this work could be done in remote waters to the west. Detmers agreed and, after the raider reached this location, work on the engines commenced.

Detmers intended to mine the approaches to Fremantle but on 14 November the *Seekriegsleitung* signalled: 'A cruiser, presumably "Cornwall", left an Australian port on 6 November, to meet a convoy west of Australia at 41 South on 11 November.'[26] The cruiser in question was actually HMAS *Canberra*, but the report convinced Detmers to avoid Fremantle and he instead decided to investigate the waters off Shark Bay on the Western Australian coast:

> I proposed to sail up the western coast of Australia, perhaps laying mines in Shark's Bay if opportunity afforded; and then moving northward again, leaving Java and Sumatra to starboard and penetrating into the Bay of Bengal once more, perhaps laying mines off Calcutta and other harbours.[27]

This would only be a small operation given the low amount of shipping passing through these waters and also because Detmers wanted to conserve his mines for eventual use in more important waters. He had previously decided against mining the approaches to Carnarvon and Geraldton because of their minimal importance but changed his mind because he wanted to make his presence felt. A small operation would create disruption by reminding the enemy that his raider was active, and with this goal in mind a minelaying mission of Shark Bay made sense.

On 19 November the *Kormoran* disguised as the *Straat Malakka* headed towards Shark Bay.[28] As the raider continued through a moderate sea with medium swell, the lookout scanned the horizon in the perfect visibility of a clear hot day. Detmers planned to maintain his current course before turning east towards Shark Bay at night. As the day was the German holiday of *Buss-und Bettag* (Day of Repentance and Prayer), many crewmen did not have normal duties and most of the men rested in their hammocks, read or talked among themselves.

In the afternoon Detmers left the bridge to join his officers in the wardroom for coffee. At 1555 h a messenger informed him that a ship had been sighted by *Leutnant* Jansen from the crow's nest and that it might be a sailing ship. Detmers immediately proceeded to the bridge while the watch officer *Oberleutnant* Joachim von Gosseln gulped his remaining coffee before running to his cabin to get his cap. Once on the bridge Detmers saw the vessel about 20 to 25 miles away, appearing only as a speck on the horizon in the shimmering light. Gosseln retrieved his cap and raced for the bridge: 'I hurried to the bridge, obtained data on course and speed, hung up my binoculars, and reported to the commanding officer as the battle watch officer.'[29] The sighting reports quickly changed with the foretop lookout calling out 'two sail', 'several ships' and then 'smoke'.[30] Detmers and the bridge officers could now see two sailing ships while several other ships and two columns of smoke appeared to be further away. The sight looked like a convoy with escorts.[31]

At 1600 h Detmers ordered action stations, hard to port and full speed before proceeding to the signal deck to get a better look through the sighting telescope used for gunnery control. The hot air obscured his vision but soon an image came into focus and his heart sank. The impression of sailing ships and other vessels had been optical illusions and the clear shape of a single grey vessel became apparent with a bridge, tall masts and funnels. Detmers recognized the shape of an Australian Perth class cruiser. He had just encountered HMAS *Sydney*.

CHAPTER 24
THE *KORMORAN–SYDNEY* BATTLE

In a mock battle off the coast tonight an Australian cruiser showed how ships of the RAN would deal with an enemy raider caught off our shores. This cruiser was practicing an action that has already been a reality for other Australian units. The speed with which the ship went into action and the accuracy of the gunnery made it easy to understand why units of the Australian fleet serving in waters overseas have had such an excellent record in the war.[1]

The Argus
7 June 1941

HMAS *SYDNEY*

After the outbreak of war Captain John Collins assumed command of the 6830-ton Perth Class light cruiser *Sydney* and, after arriving in the Mediterranean in 1940, she sank the Italian destroyer *Espero* and the cruiser *Bartolomeo Colleoni*, becoming the pride of the RAN. The cruiser returned to Australia in February 1941 and an enthusiastic public gave her a hero's welcome.

On 15 May Captain Joseph Burnett assumed command of the *Sydney*.

The cruiser HMAS *Sydney* in 1940.
(AWM: NAVAL HISTORICAL COLLECTION)

During World War I he served on the *Australia* in the North Sea and after the conflict he served on the *Adelaide* and *Canberra*. He later worked at the Navy Office and became the executive officer on the *Canberra* and the battleship HMS *Royal Oak*. After the outbreak of war, Burnett became the Deputy Chief of Naval Staff working to Admiral Ragnar Colvin, who declared:

> He had much service in ships of the Royal Navy and came to me from them as my Vice-Chief of the Naval Staff a few months after the outbreak of war with high recommendations. These were not belied, for his capacity to grasp a situation rapidly and to formulate decisions was quite remarkable.[2]

Although the *Sydney* was Burnett's first command, he had considerable experience at sea. In his first mission he escorted the troopship *Zealandia* carrying the 8th Division to Singapore, before carrying out escort duties and local patrols. On 11 October the cruiser escorted convoy US 12B from Melbourne to the Sunda Strait before returning to Fremantle. During this time Lieutenant-Commander Ravenscroft served under Burnett:

Officers and crew of the HMAS *Sydney* after its successful action against the Italian cruiser *Bartolomeo Colleoni* on 19 July 1940.
(AWM)

> My impressions were that Captain Burnett was a capable ship handler. He was aware that he commanded a highly skilled and well trained ship's company and was backed up by highly trained, experienced and battle hardened senior officers. He struck me as a man who would listen and take advice.[3]

On 11 November the *Sydney* departed Fremantle bound for the Sunda Strait to escort the *Zealandia* headed for Singapore. HMS *Durban* took over the escort duty six days later and the *Sydney* set a course for Fremantle.[4] The crew probably expected an uneventful voyage home, but the lookout spotted a freighter on the afternoon of 19 November, and soon all 645 men on board the *Sydney* would be dead.

A STRANGE ENCOUNTER

The battle ready *Sydney* had complete superiority over the *Kormoran*.[5] Her eight 6-inch guns, twin-mounted inside four turrets, could fire six to eight rounds per minute. The director control tower above the bridge provided fire control but the aft fire control position could take over if the main tower was knocked out.[6] The forward 'A' and 'B' turrets and the aft 'X' and 'Y' turrets could also operate manually. The *Kormoran*'s six 5.9-inch guns lacked the firepower of the *Sydney*'s guns but could nevertheless fire five to seven rounds per minute.[7] However, the raider's guns could only achieve accurate fire at 10,000 metres (10,936 yards) compared with the *Sydney*'s 18,200 metres (19,903 yards).[8] Furthermore, the raider's broadsides could only fire four guns at a single target compared with the cruiser's eight.

The *Sydney*'s four 4-inch guns located on the aft gun deck could fire twenty rounds per minute at surface targets but, as no shields had been fitted, their crews lacked protection.[9] The cruiser also had three Lewis guns in quadruple mountings.[10] In contrast, the *Kormoran*'s two 37-mm guns could fire 80 rounds per minute and her 20-mm guns could fire 100 rounds per minute.

The *Sydney*'s eight torpedoes in two quadruple tube mountings on the upper deck had a range of 12,350 metres (13,506 yards), but they could not be reloaded at sea.[11] The *Kormoran*'s torpedoes could reach 14,000 metres (15,310 yards), but could only be fired in a spread of two compared with the *Sydney*'s four.

Despite the *Sydney*'s overwhelming superiority, Detmers had one critical advantage; he knew he faced an enemy warship, as *Oberleutnant* Ahl articulated: 'Our great advantage was that we were conscious of the *Sydney* as an enemy. Therefore we were from the beginning fully prepared for battle.'[12] In contrast Burnett had seemingly encountered an unknown freighter; therefore, Detmers held the initiative.

THE *KORMORAN*'S BRIDGE

The *Kormoran*'s crew faced the horror of an enemy cruiser, and as Ahl reflected, 'I think at this moment all of us scarcely saw a chance to survive.'[13] Detmers ordered full speed and the raider turned 250 degrees into the sun, hoping to escape without being seen, while the crew ran to their action stations. The gunnery officer *Oberleutnant* Fritz Skeries, *Oberleutnant* Heinz Messerschmidt and Petty Officer Ludwig Ernst arrived in the fire control station above the bridge. Skeries directed the 5.9-inch guns, Messerschmidt manned the telephone link and Ernst calculated the gun elevation angles. *Oberleutnant* Wilhelm Brinkmann, in charge of the smaller guns, arrived at the aft director control stand on the poop deck along with Ahl who would observe the fall of shot.

The *Kormoran* reached full speed and began emitting thick smoke. At 1604 h Chief Engineer Rudolf Lensch reported that the No. 4 engine had been shut down as its piston was running hot, and the raider could only manage 14 knots.

The *Sydney* increased speed and changed course towards the *Kormoran* as the Australians had spotted the raider from a distance of 15,000 metres (16,404 yards).[14] As the raider could only manage 14 knots compared with the cruiser's 32½, she could not outrun the cruiser before nightfall.

Detmers had no intention of scuttling the *Kormoran* without a fight, but his orders prevented him from seeking battle with a warship if he could evade the enemy. Therefore, he would attempt to trick the Australians into believing his raider was the *Straat Malakka*. If this ruse failed, he would fight:

> We were, of course, strictly forbidden to seek any action with enemy naval units. . . . Naturally, if we found action with hostile naval units forced on us then we had to accept and do the best we could; but so long as we could take evasive action it was our duty to do so.[15]

As the cruiser would have to approach closer to establish the mystery freighter's identity, at the very least Detmers would be in a better position to fight since the closer the *Sydney* approached, the more her advantage of superior armaments would diminish: 'If I could get him near enough my battery of six 15 cm. guns would not be so very inferior to his eight 6-inch guns.'[16] Detmers had a plan but how events would unfold entirely depended upon Burnett's actions.

THE *SYDNEY'S* BRIDGE

Burnett and his bridge officers initially had little cause for suspicion as the lookout had simply spotted a freighter that had turned into the sun attempting to flee, as any Allied merchant ship would do after sighting a warship.[17]

Burnett probably expected nothing more than a routine identification. The first step in the process was consulting the list of expected vessels, which gave the position and course of every merchant ship in the Australia Station.[18] As the only vessel expected nearby was the tug *Uco*, 100 nautical miles away, the freighter was not expected; this was the first indication that something might be wrong.[19]

Burnett had become very familiar with how the Mercantile Movements Section generated the list from his time as Deputy Chief of Naval Staff. He frequently visited the team, making enquiries into its efficiency and knew that around 3 per cent of vessels from the Dutch East Indies and Japan arrived unannounced.[20] Burnett also knew the list sometimes contained errors and, as such, an unexpected freighter would be grounds for suspicion but not alarm.[21]

Burnett had not been hunting a raider, putting him at a great disadvantage compared with Captain Manwaring on the *Cornwall*, who had been participating in a counter-raider operation when he sighted the *Pinguin*. Although the Allies believed 'Raider G' (*Kormoran*) had been operating in the Pacific from late September, recent intelligence reports suggested she might be in the Indian Ocean. Burnett certainly would have read the weekly intelligence summary dated 3 November:

> The Dutch 'OLIVIA' which made an unspecified raider distress message on 20/10 from a position approx 250 miles north of the Seychelles is possibly a victim of the same raider which could now be on the western portion of the Australia Station.[22]

Before departing Fremantle Burnett may have read the next summary, which warned of a possible raider operating near Geraldton, Western Australia.[23] However, he understood the unreliable nature of intelligence reports as the Australian mines had been attributed to the *Orion* and then to the *Kulmerland* before being correctly attributed to the *Pinguin*. He also knew that intelligence failed to identify the *Pinguin* until after she had been sunk, as all her actions had been incorrectly attributed to the *Atlantis* and *Thor*. Therefore, Burnett could not assume a raider was in the Indian Ocean simply because an intelligence report indicated this possibility, nor could he rule it out. Ultimately, these reports could not help Burnett identify the unknown ship.[24]

Burnett certainly suspected the presence of a raider in the Indian Ocean. On 5 October he addressed the *Sydney*'s crew, saying, 'I must tell you that there is an enemy raider out there and I intend to get it.'[25] He likely hoped the raider would become known through a QQQQ warning, which would give him an opportunity to hunt her in a deliberate manner like the hunt for the *Pinguin*. He would not have expected to randomly encounter the raider on a voyage home given the extreme odds of such an equation.

In Burnett's mind the unidentified ship could be a genuine freighter or a disguised enemy supply ship, blockade runner, minelayer or raider. Burnett likely dismissed the possibility of a blockade runner or a supply ship because, with his excellent understanding of raider operations, he knew these vessels never approached enemy coastlines as they would be exposing themselves to danger for no advantage. Blockade runners and supply ships would also immediately scuttle themselves if being chased by an Allied warship without hope of evasion. The fleeing vessel clearly was not undertaking scuttling procedures as she had not stopped.

Burnett probably considered the possibility the vessel might be a raider or minelayer. He understood that raiders usually avoided focal areas and enemy coastlines except during mining operations. Therefore, the ship might be a raider or a minelayer, but he would have wondered why an enemy vessel would want to mine the waters near Shark Bay, given the area's remoteness. Burnett would have expected a mining operation near Fremantle, a major trade artery, but he lacked two critical pieces of information. First, Detmers had indeed intended to mine the approaches to Fremantle until the *Seekriegsleitung* warned him about an enemy cruiser in the area. Second, Detmers' alternative plan to approach Shark Bay had grown out of frustration and had been less about sinking worthwhile ships and more about making his presence felt. Burnett did not know about the *Seekriegsleitung* signal or Detmers' frustrations, the two factors leading to the *Kormoran*'s seemingly illogical presence near Shark Bay. To Burnett the probability of an error in the list of expected vessels would have seemed far greater than encountering a raider near Shark Bay. Although his exact reasons can never be known one thing is clear, Burnett did not consider the unknown vessel to be suspicious.

Allied warship captains had detailed orders for approaching unidentified

The Kormoran-Sydney Battle ✠ 275

merchant vessels, giving two options: 'Case A' for vessels believed to be innocent and 'Case B' for suspicious vessels.[26] Under 'Case A' the unknown ship would be approached at cruising stations before her identity would be requested. Under 'Case B' the suspicious vessel would be approached at action stations until 7 to 8 miles before being ordered to stop, followed by a boarding party inspection, or she would be ordered to adopt a given course at a slow speed. If the merchant ship failed to comply the warship would fire warning shots and if these were ignored a salvo would follow.

The *Sydney* approached the *Kormoran* to exchange signals at cruising stations under 'Case A', as Burnett believed she was a genuine merchant vessel. The absence of the ship from the list of expected vessels alone should have prompted him to adopt 'Case B'. Under Burnett's command the *Sydney* had investigated eleven unidentified freighters but had only gone to action stations three times.[27] At action stations all of the *Sydney*'s guns would have been manned and aimed at the target, including the 6-inch guns, the 4-inch guns, the machine guns and the torpedo tubes. At cruising stations only two of the 6-inch gun turrets and two of her 4-inch anti-aircraft guns would normally be manned. With the *Sydney* approaching at cruising stations, Detmers' odds improved.

THE APPROACH

The *Sydney* approached the *Kormoran* on a slight converging course about 10 degrees off the raider's starboard quarter to make a visual inspection and start the challenge procedure. Detmers' turn made identification difficult since it forced the *Sydney*'s lookout to face the sun. Burnett also adopted a narrow approach when he could have adopted a much wider approach to keep his vessel further away.

At this time Burnett and his bridge officers had no clues about the mystery freighter's identity. All warships carried the Talbot-Booth, an international register of merchant vessels, containing information on tonnage, size and other features, but this reference could not yet be used as the *Kormoran*'s distinguishing features could only been seen from about 2 miles.[28] As the distance closed the lookout would have eventually observed a modern cargo liner with a split superstructure, raked bow and cruiser stern, suggesting a vessel constructed in the late 1930s, most likely German, Dutch or Norwegian.[29] The unknown ship matched the profile of an auxiliary cruiser but she could equally be a genuine Dutchman.

Detmers observed the *Sydney*'s approach as did his gunners who peeked through small holes in the screens hiding their weapons. *Leutnant* Wilhelm Bunjes recalled the tense atmosphere: 'Behind the camouflage flap shutters everyone stands in feverish excitement and holds his breath. The camouflaged guns are loaded and kept trained on the cruiser.'[30] Detmers soon had cause for increased optimism when he realized the *Sydney* was not at action stations.[31] Ernst and Ahl could see nobody behind the 4-inch guns, and Detmers observed:

> The enemy cruiser was now coming within the range that I considered suitable for my guns, and she was already so close that through our glasses we could see every detail clearly. In particular we could see that her four double turrets with their 6-inch guns and also the port torpedo tube battery were all directed at us. As far as I could make out her eight 4-inch anti-aircraft guns were not manned.[32]

Burnett could have used his Walrus seaplane to make the identification and exchange signals without bringing the *Sydney* closer. He had sufficient time and ideal weather for a flight.[33] Burnett did consider using his seaplane as the Germans saw the Walrus being readied. Messerschmidt observed:

> As the *Sydney* approached we could see that they had prepared to send up their spotter plane, which would have given us away because we had a deck cargo of mines. But then the plane was suddenly put back into its normal position.[34]

The preparation of the Walrus suggests some suspicion in Burnett's mind, but this must have diminished because his men turned the plane's engine off and retracted its catapult.

THE SIGNALS

Under the identification procedures an Allied warship would signal the letters 'NNJ'. A friendly freighter would turn away at full speed before replying with her international signal letters. The warship would then signal the middle two letters of the freighter's secret four-letter call sign and the freighter would respond with the first and last letters. However, if the warship captain became suspicious he would order the vessel to stop.[35]

Although the *Kormoran* had turned before the *Sydney* commenced the identification procedure, Allied merchantmen often acted in this manner. At 1605 h the cruiser began signalling 'NNJ' using flags and later with her searchlight.[36] Burnett, still not suspicious, continued to approach at cruising stations.[37] Detmers ignored the signals but eventually ordered the *Straat Malakka*'s four-letter signal 'PKQI' to be hoisted, but instructed Chief Signalman Erich Ahlbach to act in an awkward manner. Ahlbach raised the flags but made sure the funnel obstructed them. As the *Sydney*'s lookout still had to look directly into the sun, the flags could not be understood and would only have been readable from around 1 to 2 miles.[38]

Detmers wanted to prevent the *Sydney*'s lookout from being able to read the 'PKQI' flags for as long as plausibly possible because, as soon as the cruiser's bridge realized the raider was identifying herself as the *Straat Malakka*, they would have information that might help them determine she was a raider. To help maintain the impression of an innocent freighter, Ahlbach and Signalman Lins wore civilian clothing, and on the bridge only Detmers and his watch officer *Oberleutnant* Gosseln, also dressed in civilian attire, allowed themselves to be seen. A few sailors dressed as civilians appeared on the deck at times and the cook, wearing a white hat, glanced out of the galley window.

At 1635 h Lensch reported to Detmers that the fault in No. 4 engine had been fixed, but Detmers maintained 14 knots to avoid suspicion. The *Kormoran*'s flags still could not be read as the fourth flag became twisted and the *Sydney* signalled 'hoist your signal letters clear' while continuing to approach closer, still on a course 10 degrees off the stern.[39] Detmers calculated that he could no longer plausibly fumble his signals and ordered Ahlbach to angle the flags so they could be read.[40]

When the *Sydney*'s officers read 'PKQI' they would have consulted their reference books and realized the vessel was claiming to be the *Straat Malakka*, but they had no information on her whereabouts; she had actually just departed the African port of Beira in Mozambique.[41] To Burnett it would have seemed possible for the Dutchman to be off Western Australia and, due to an error, had not been included on the list of expected vessels.

The *Sydney* signalled 'where bound?' and Detmers replied 'Batavia', and another signal asked about the cargo and Detmers replied 'piece-goods'.[42] As these questions were not part of the identification procedure, the *Sydney*'s bridge officers must still have been searching for the *Straat Malakka*'s secret call sign and reference material, such as the Talbot-Booth, to compare descriptions of her with the visible features in front of their eyes.

At 1703 h Detmers initiated the next phase of his deception plan when his wireless room broadcast a raider warning: 'QQQ Straat Malakka 111 E 26 S.'[43] The tug *Uco* heard it as a faint 'QQ' followed by 'QQ' and the Geraldton wireless station only heard a distorted and faint signal without realizing it was a raider warning.[44] The *Sydney*'s wireless room also likely heard the signal.[45]

To the astonishment of the Germans, at 1715 h the *Sydney* came alongside the *Kormoran*'s starboard side at 900 metres (984 yards).[46] Detmers had been trying to draw the cruiser in closer, but nobody expected her to come that close and she presented a perfect target and her anti-aircraft guns still had not been manned. The wireless room reported that the cruiser had not broadcast any signals, a further indication that Burnett had not become suspicious because he had not asked the mainland for the *Straat Malakka*'s whereabouts.

Burnett could have continued the challenge procedure from further away, ideally behind the vessel to avoid possible broadsides or torpedo attacks. In coming so close it has been suggested that Burnett had been influenced by the criticism levelled against Captain Farncomb after his encounter with the *Ketty Brovig*. HMAS *Canberra* engaged the enemy from 17,400 metres (19,028 yards), as Farncomb believed she was a disguised raider and Admiral Leatham accused him of wasting ammunition:

> It was correct that *Canberra* should have taken precautions against the possibility of the supposed raider firing torpedoes, but I think it was being over cautious to avoid approaching nearer than 19,000

yards on this account. Had a more effective range been attained quickly the enemy might have been identified sooner and much ammunition saved.[47]

However, there is a difference between maintaining a distance of 17,400 metres (19,028 yards) and coming within 900 metres (984 yards) and Burnett could have found a suitable distance in between. Burnett had also criticized Farncomb but for all the wrong reasons: 'Fancy wasting all those bricks [shells] on two harmless freighters.'[48] He failed to understand the situation faced by Farncomb, who opened fire at great range at a suspected raider to remain beyond the range of her guns. Burnett did not understand Farncomb's caution, which demonstrates a reckless streak and helps explain why he treated the *Kormoran* like a 'harmless freighter'.

The Germans observed a strange sense of normalcy on the *Sydney*. Detmers noted: 'We could see the cruiser's pantrymen in their white coats lining the rails to have a look at the supposed Dutchmen.'[49] Messerschmidt saw men on the *Sydney* walking along the deck and watching from the rails: 'You could see the ship's cook with his hat on at that distance. We saw that no-one ran around on deck and that they were not alarmed.'[50] *Oberleutnant* Greter also witnessed the strange scene:

There were that many white caps on the bridge that I would almost assume officers from other battle posts had assembled there. To all appearances, it looked as though our camouflage was effective and they believed our information.[51]

Eventually the *Sydney*'s bridge officers located the *Straat Malakka*'s secret call sign 'IIKP' and the cruiser hoisted its middle two letters 'IK'. The *Straat Malakka* would be expected to respond with the two outer letters 'IP'. Detmers and his officers did not understand the 'IK' signal as they did not know the *Straat Malakka*'s secret call sign. Under the International Code of Signals, 'IK' meant 'you should prepare for a cyclone, hurricane or typhoon', which presently made no sense. Detmers doubled checked the signals book and ignored the signal. Gosseln, still wearing civilian clothing, stepped outside and waved his hat as a farewell gesture.[52]

At 1725 h the *Sydney* signalled 'Hoist your secret call sign', an indication that Burnett still had doubts in his mind as the *Straat Malakka*'s failure to hoist 'IP' should have immediately resulted in him ordering the vessel to stop followed by a warning shot.[53] Detmers asked his signals officer *Kapitänleutnant* Malapert if he had the secret call sign but after receiving a negative response, Detmers said to his watch officer, 'Well, Gosseln, there is nothing left to do.'[54] Detmers then declared, 'We don't have the secret signal and now we will have to fight.'[55] The *Kormoran*'s crew had been at action stations for an hour. In the fire control position above the bridge Skeries made his final preparations, and Ahl recalled the targeting opportunities: 'The extremely close range gave us a chance to choose special aims for each of the four guns: the front turrets, the bridge, the aircraft because of its explosives and fire-causing petrol, the rear turrets.'[56] Skeries' 5.9-inch guns would aim at the *Sydney*'s gun turrets and bridge. Brinkmann's 37-mm guns would also target the bridge while his smaller 20-mm guns and machine guns would sweep the decks to prevent the Australians from manning their anti-aircraft guns and torpedo tubes.

At 1730 h the *Sydney* and *Kormoran* continued on parallel courses at 900 metres (984 yards) with excellent opportunities to fire broadside salvos at each other. The cruiser's bridge officers would by now have been puzzled as to why the Dutchman had not responded with the secret signal. They would have eventually finished comparing her with the descriptions of the *Straat Malakka* in the Talbot-Booth and this would have indicated that she had given a false identity as her superstructure and samson posts were different.[57] Messerschmidt noticed a sudden surge of activity in the *Sydney*'s bridge as men began rushing around and a number of officers started climbing up the director control tower and others started running along the decks. It seems that Burnett had finally ordered action stations, but it took three to five minutes to secure the cruiser at action stations. Burnett did not have this much time.

THE BATTLE

Detmers ordered 'decamouflage' and Ahlbach raised the *Kriegsmarine* flag. The gunners dropped the screens hiding their armaments, swung out the

5.9-inch guns and raised the anti-aircraft cannons. It only took between twelve and eighteen seconds for the 5.9-inch guns to be ready to fire.[58] After Detmers confirmed that the war ensign was flying at the main mast, he ordered his guns to open fire. Skeries gave his orders to Ernst who relayed them to the gunners through the telephone.

The *Kormoran*'s first salvo, a single ranging shot, fell short and the *Sydney* immediately returned fire, but her salvo went over the raider. Ahsbaas, Kobelt and Saalfrank, in control of the No. 1, 3 and 5 guns respectively, made their final adjustments and the second salvo hit the *Sydney*'s bridge and control tower. Meanwhile the secondary armaments directed by Brinkmann opened fire. Fend and Koblitz, manning the starboard 37-mm gun, aimed at the bridge and superstructure. According to Messerschmidt, 'I could see shells from the 37 mm cannon with a covering arc of fire hitting and wiping out . . . many of the men on the bridge. It was a gruesome sight.'[59] The 20-mm anti-aircraft guns and machine guns strafed the *Sydney*'s upper deck, anti-aircraft guns and torpedo batteries, which caused massive casualties among the exposed men, preventing them from returning fire. Messerschmidt recalled the slaughter: 'I saw men running to *Sydney*'s torpedo tubes being shot down.'[60] Detmers also remembered the carnage: 'Not a man could show his face on the upper deck, because of the fire of our 2 cm. anti-aircraft guns and our heavy machine guns was so intense.'[61]

The *Kormoran*'s torpedo men had raised their flaps and swung out their above water tubes; it took about thirty-two seconds for the torpedoes to be ready.[62] The torpedo officer Greter watched the *Sydney* from his station behind the bridge and the raider slowly turned to 260 degrees to allow the tubes to be angled to their correct firing position, as they could not be moved manually. Greter ordered 'fire' and his men launched two torpedoes that headed directly towards the *Sydney*.

The *Kormoran*'s third salvo hit the *Sydney*'s bridge and the forward control tower, and by this time Burnett and most of the bridge officers would most likely have been killed. The cruiser no longer had functioning fire control and her wireless aerials and masts had been destroyed. Her six-inch guns fired another salvo but missed. The raider fired salvos every five seconds and shells struck the forward 'A' and 'B' turrets, knocking them out of action. The 'A' turret had received a direct hit and the 'B' turret had been struck by a shell between the barrels without fully penetrating its armour, but it stopped functioning.[63] A shell struck the Walrus seaplane, causing an explosion that poured burning aviation fuel across the cruiser's mid-section, starting a large fire and forcing thick smoke into the ventilation shafts.

By this time damage to the *Sydney* concentrated around the forward part of the ship, the superstructure and the upper and lower decks. The fires would have been creating huge smoke problems, affecting the crew's ability both to see and breathe. The German gunners had accomplished all of their objectives, except for the destruction of the rear 'X' and 'Y' turrets, the cruiser's only means of fighting back.

After the *Kormoran*'s fifth salvo the 'X' turret began to fire rapid and accurate shots under manual control. A shell hit the raider's funnel and exploded, causing splinters to penetrate the wireless room, killings two sailors. Shells also destroyed the boiler room, an oil bunker and the transformers of the main engine. Another shell landed near the No. 3 gun without exploding, although its impact injured several crewmen, some of whom later died, but the gun still operated. The 'Y' turret also fired two or three shots, but these fell wide and missed.

The damage inflicted by the *Sydney*'s 'X' turret caused a large fire in the *Kormoran*'s engine room, but the fire extinguisher pipe had been hit and the foam extinguisher system failed to work. The engine room men abandoned their station as the fires quickly spread beyond control, killing *Kapitänleutnant* Stehr and Leutnant Gaza. The electrical system broke down, causing the propulsion motors to stop.

Around the time of the *Kormoran*'s eighth salvo, one torpedo struck the S*ydney*'s bow just in front of 'A' turret and exploded, while the second narrowly missed.[64] A large column of water hurled into the air, the roof of 'B' turret flew overboard and for a time the bow became almost entirely submerged and the propellers could be seen. The torpedo explosion caused extensive flooding in the forward areas, including the 6-inch magazines, and Greter remembered: 'Tensely we watched the torpedo tracks, the first passed the bow, the second hit *Sydney* under the two forward turrets and threw a column of water up that then washed over the cruiser.'[65]

The *Sydney*'s torpedo men had fired two torpedoes from her port mount despite the *Kormoran*'s intense fire sweeping the decks. Both missed the raider.[66]

Captain J. Burnett, RAN, on the bridge of HMAS *Sydney*. Burnett was lost in the sinking of the *Sydney* in its action with the *Kormoran* on 19 November 1941. (AWM)

At 1735 h the *Sydney* turned to port and headed south.[67] If this action was intentional she may have been trying to ram the raider or been attempting to bring her starboard torpedo tubes to bear.[68] After she passed the raider's stern her starboard side became exposed to German fire. Smoke from the engine fire prevented Skeries seeing his target so Brinkmann directed the action. The *Sydney*'s guns no longer fired and her anti-aircraft guns had never been manned. On board, damage control teams would have been frantically trying to extinguish the fires, stop the flooding and maintain buoyancy.

Detmers, fearing the *Sydney*'s starboard torpedoes, presented the *Kormoran*'s stern to provide the narrowest possible target. The raider emitted dense smoke from the engine room fires while her guns pounded the cruiser, mostly striking the mid-section of the upper and lower decks. 'A' turret received more hits as did the bridge and the fire control tower. At 1745 h Detmers wanted to turn to bring his broadsides to bear, but the engines went dead. Lensch appeared on the bridge and informed Detmers that the engines had stopped. Detmers ordered him to get at least one engine working, but all attempts to reach the engine room failed. Petty Officer Hahnert, who managed to escape, witnessed the deaths of the control position watch from a sudden burst of flame.

At 1750 h the *Kormoran*'s gunners resumed co-ordinated broadsides after proper fire control had been re-established. The *Sydney* limped south engulfed in flames and the raider continued to fire until 1825 h.[69] The cruiser headed south-east at about 5 knots with propulsion most likely being supplied by the aft boiler and engine rooms.[70] Fire had engulfed the bridge, forecastle deck and midships.[71] The damage control teams would have been overwhelmed and would have struggled just to keep basic systems working, and by this time around 70 per cent of the crew would have been dead, wounded or trapped by the fires.[72]

Burnett should have gone to action stations and never should have approached so close to an unknown vessel, but his actions were no different from many other Allied warship commanders who recklessly did the same.[73] Experienced commanders like Burnett make mistakes, which a sympathetic Detmers understood:

> Just imagine yourself a cruiser captain. You have treated every one of hundreds of ships encountered with the same precautions, and each one of them had turned out to be a harmless steamer. One moment of relaxation or carelessness, and then it's happened. That's war.[74]

At around 1900 h the *Sydney* disappeared from German view and that night her bow, severely damaged by the torpedo hit, suddenly broke off in rough seas. The cruiser lost buoyancy and rapidly submerged.[75] The *Kormoran* had sunk the pride of the Royal Australian Navy.[76]

CHAPTER 25
THE FLEET
OF LIFEBOATS

We got on quite well with the Australian sailors. We were also told
that we had sunk the 'SYDNEY'. Generally speaking they showed
quite a lot of respect for us. To another boat load of our survivors the
commander of the Australian ship said that he would have been very
proud if he had been able to take as crew such tough, tenacious men.[1]
Seaman Gustav Heinz
Sailor on the Kormoran

THE DEATH OF A RAIDER

Following the battle with HMAS *Sydney*, the *Kormoran*'s engine room fires
burned beyond control and would eventually reach the mine storage area,
so Detmers ordered the raider to be scuttled but needed time to organize
lifeboats and rafts.[2] Although about twenty men had been killed in the battle,
around 370 survivors reminded on board. The crew began the evacuation
and by 2100 h some 120 men remained on board, but tragedy struck after
a raft carrying wounded sailors capsized and around sixty men drowned.

Oberleutnant Greter went below to fire the underwater torpedoes to ensure they did not prematurely explode:

> With my heart beating, I went back down below deck to the underwater torpedo room. An oppressive silence reigned below deck. The ship lived no more, there was no longer the usual noise of the motors. The clammy coolness of the rooms reminded shockingly of a tomb.[3]

After thick smoke filled the mine deck, Detmers and his watch officer *Oberleutnant* Gosseln prepared the demolition charges in the port forward oil tank. Detmers removed his commander's pendant before boarding the last lifeboat and ten minutes later the charges exploded, although the raider stayed afloat. At 0035 h the 320 mines detonated, resulting in an enormous explosion launching debris hundreds of feet into the night sky. The rear section of the *Kormoran*'s hull had been obliterated and she rapidly sank, stern first.[4]

The *Kormoran* had claimed twelve ships, totalling 75,111 tons, an impressive tally. Detmers, a young informal officer, had a brilliant grasp of the strategic role that auxiliary cruisers played, but neglected reconnaissance by rarely using his Arado seaplanes. He could also have used the whale catcher *Adjutant* as a scout ship, which might have saved the *Kormoran*. The *Seekriegsleitung* later expressed great pride as 'the auxiliary cruiser sold her life dearly and crowned the unfortunate end of her successful career with a last success which is especially gratifying and valuable'.[5] The *Seekriegsleitung* also noted: 'The sinking of an Australian cruiser deserves special mention as this deed is probably unique in the history of the war.'[6]

The *Sydney*'s destruction had not been in vain because the *Kormoran* no longer terrorized the high seas, as Ahl explained:

> And was not *Sydney* successful indeed? She prevented *Kormoran* from laying mines on the Australian coast and by this most probably saved ships and men from perishing; furthermore she stopped the raider from threatening any longer Allied merchant ships.[7]

The survivors included 316 Germans and three Chinese sailors, while eighty-one crewmen and one Chinese laundryman had died.[8] In the darkness the lifeboats and rafts scattered.

THE SEARCH

The *Sydney* had been expected in Fremantle on 20 November and after she became overdue the Naval Board did not express concern as the *Zealandia*, which the *Sydney* escorted, had arrived late in Singapore, so the RAN assumed the cruiser had been delayed. On 23 November the Naval Board signalled the *Sydney* and received no reply. An air search commenced in the morning, primarily involving the three RAAF squadrons based in Western Australia.[9]

On 23 November the liner *Aquitania* spotted a raft containing twenty-six Germans. The survivors, suffering from sunburn and exposure, had fought off sharks with oars. After boarding the liner they received medical care, water and breakfast. The Germans mentioned a battle with a cruiser, but Captain Gibbons assumed she had signalled the mainland, so he maintained radio silence as it never occurred to him that the cruiser might have sunk.[10]

In the afternoon of 24 November the British tanker *Trocas* spotted a raft containing twenty-five Germans west-north-west of Carnarvon. After being rescued, Rudolf Lensch told Captain Bryant that he had been on a raider. The *Trocas* signalled the RAN requesting an armed guard, the first news of the battle to reach the mainland. Ten armed guards from HMAS *Wyrallah* later boarded the *Trocas* and the ship arrived at Fremantle on 27 November.

The search intensified and the auxiliary vessels HMAS *Yandra*, *Heros*, *Olive Cam* and *Wyrallah* joined the effort. The Naval Board also asked the Dutch Navy for help and two Catalinas from Surabaya in Java flew patrols and the Dutch cruiser *Tromp* left the Sunda Strait to follow the *Sydney*'s route.

On 24 November a lifeboat containing forty-six Germans landed on the Western Australian coast near Quobba Sheep Station, north of Cape Cuvier. The men, almost out of food and water, found themselves on a beach but found a sheep, which they slaughtered for food. Another lifeboat containing fifty-seven Germans also approached the coast. *Kapitänleutnant* Malapert had rigged a sail and steered by using an oar as a rudder and *Oberleutnant* Ahl navigated using the Arado's compass. The next day the men landed at Red Bluff on an inhospitable strip of coastline. An RAAF Hudson flown by

Flight-Lieutenant Cook later spotted the survivors and dropped a carton of cigarettes.[11] He reported sighting both lifeboats and, in Carnarvon, Wing Commander Lightfoot organized a truck convoy, which found the Germans and transported them to town where the Voluntary Defence Corps guarded them in the gaol.

Detmers' lifeboat contained sixty-one Germans and one Chinese laundryman. On 23 November the men celebrated the birthday of a sailor and passed around two bottles of beer. The next day, however, as supplies dwindled, Detmers worried about his men drinking seawater. At night the men caught the laundryman drinking bottles of Japanese milk and they tried to throw him overboard, but Detmers drew his pistol and the men backed down.[12] The following day they spotted the liner *Aquitania*. Detmers decided against firing signal rockets, hoping to be rescued by a neutral ship. On 26 November the men spotted the *Centaur* and, as Detmers had given up hope of being rescued by a neutral vessel, he signalled the ship. Captain Dark refused to let the Germans on board and instead towed their lifeboat but gave them food and tea, and later allowed the sick and wounded to board. The next morning the lifeboat started breaking up so Captain Dark gave the Germans two new lifeboats, and the *Centaur* with the two lifeboats in tow arrived at Carnarvon on 27 November.

Lieutenant-Commander James Rycroft, an intelligence officer, interrogated Detmers, who claimed to have sighted a Perth class cruiser that came close during signalling.[13] Detmers gave the correct location of the battle because he wanted the search to rescue any of his men still adrift.[14]

The RAN ordered the coastal steamer *Koolinda* to find a lifeboat that had been spotted by a plane. Master John Airey accordingly rescued thirty-one Germans from the lifeboat on 26 November. After the *Koolinda* arrived in Fremantle three days later, the prisoners landed and were escorted to an internment camp at Harvey, where Commander Victor Ramage, Senior Naval Intelligence Officer in Western Australia, interrogated them.

The *Aquitania* continued towards Sydney and maintained radio silence until Captain Gibbons overheard the *Trocas* signals, giving him a better understanding of the situation. He tried to broadcast a report but his wireless failed. He signalled Wilson's Promontory as the liner passed before arriving in Sydney on 28 November.[15]

One of the lifeboats from the British merchant ship *Centaur*, coming alongside full of German sailors from the *Kormoran* recovered after their lifeboat was swamped. (AWM)

One lifeboat containing seventy-one Germans and two Chinese laundrymen remained adrift. Rudolf Max, a crewman from the engine room, had been suffering from burns and died quietly on the second day. Gosseln said a prayer and the men gave his body to the sea. On 22 November a liner, probably the *Aquitania*, passed at night without noticing them. A plane appeared overhead two days later, but no rescue followed and some men drank seawater. On 27 November an Anson spotted the lifeboat and the Germans displayed a white flag with the words 'help no water'. HMAS *Yandra* soon rescued the survivors, who had been suffering from sunburn and dermatitis, and Petty Officer Otto Jürgensen expressed gratitude: 'They treated us more as ship-wrecked sailors than as prisoners of war who had destroyed a ship of their Navy.'[16] The next day the vessel arrived at Carnarvon.

On 29 November the Central War Room ended the search for the *Sydney*.[17] After the battle the men still alive on the *Sydney* had little chance of survival. When her bow suddenly broke off many men would have been inside the ship and those on the decks would have been swept off. There would have been no opportunity to launch lifeboats as the cruiser sank so rapidly. Any sailors alive in the water wearing lifebelts would have been able to survive for a few hours, and anyone in a Carley float could have lasted for three to five days.[18] Furthermore, any survivors would likely be suffering from injuries, shock, burns and smoke inhalation, greatly reducing their chances of survival as would the presence of sharks.[19] Since the search did not commence until 24 November, it is not surprising that all of the 645 crew members perished at sea.

Commander Ramage questioned the prisoners in Fremantle and his report contained an accurate summary of the *Kormoran*'s cruise.[20] On 30 November Rear-Admiral John Crace arrived and oversaw more formal interrogations, which also sought general information on raiders.[21] After the interrogations, the Australians prepared to transfer the prisoners to camps in Victoria. Erich Meyer, a *Kormoran* sailor with lung cancer, died in a Perth hospital on 24 March 1942. The Australians buried him with full naval honours, and a family who had lost a relative on the *Sydney* cared for his grave.

DHURRINGILE AND MURCHISON

The first German military prisoners in Australia were a group of fifty officers and 900 soldiers captured in North Africa and Greece. The Australians accommodated German officers at Dhurringile, a country mansion in rural Victoria near Shepparton, which had been turned into a POW camp. The remaining prisoners had been sent to Murchison POW camp, 10 miles from Dhurringile, officially called 'Number 13'. Murchison had been divided into four compounds; 13A and 13B held Italians while 13C and 13D held Germans.

The first *Kormoran* prisoners to arrive in Victoria had disembarked from the *Aquitania* in Sydney and a group of 133 sailors later arrived from Western Australia by train.[22] By January 1942 Detmers and all the officers had arrived at Dhurringile. Detmers, as the highest ranking prisoner, took over as camp leader from the *Luftwaffe* officer Hellmut Bertram. The Australians had found Bertram to be cold and arrogant and preferred dealing with Detmers. The remaining *Kormoran* prisoners soon arrived at Murchison.

All the *Kriegsmarine* prisoners in Murchison moved into compound 13C. Chief Petty Officer Paul Kohn from the *Kormoran* was in charge of all Germans in Murchison, although Detmers had ultimate responsibility. When visiting Murchison, Detmers reminded his countrymen that he would deal with any breaches in discipline.

The YMCA gave the Murchison prisoners books, sports equipment, a gramophone and plant seeds while the German Red Cross later provided more books. The officers at Dhurringile established a school, but Detmers would only approve lessons if fully qualified instructors were available or if teaching materials had been sent from Germany. The officers also made furniture, organized a sports field and started a vegetable garden.

Under the Geneva Convention enlisted men could be forced to work and NCOs could be made to supervise work. Italian prisoners harvested potatoes, but the War Cabinet would not allow German prisoners to work on farms, fearing sabotage and a union backlash. Ultimately German prisoners rarely worked, outside of camp duties.

In June 1942 the prisoners completed a tunnel that linked the two German compounds until the Australians discovered it. Shortly afterwards the prisoners in 13C found they would swap compounds with the Italians in 13A, bitter news for them as they would be leaving behind their tunnels, caches, gardens and border with the other Germans in 13D.

German Red Cross Christmas parcels arrived from home containing cigarettes, tobacco, razors and food, but 1942 ended on a note of general depression among the prisoners. The Allied victories at Stalingrad and El Alamein made them aware that the tide of war had turned against the Axis. News also reached them about the bombing of German cities, instilling fears about their families and guilt about their relative safety.

In early 1943 the Australian Government slightly relaxed its labour policy, creating some new opportunities for German prisoners to work. A new camp opened near Graytown in Victoria, where Germans could work as lumberjacks. The guards asked the prisoners in 13A for volunteers and most of the 253 men who transferred to Graytown were *Kormoran* prisoners, including camp leader Kohn.

German morale further deteriorated as Allied air raids on German cities became more devastating and some prisoners lost relatives, including Otto

Jürgensen's wife, who died in Hamburg. After D-Day the prisoners held their breath waiting for news from the front, while radio parties eagerly followed the emerging details.

On 10 January 1945 Detmers and nineteen prisoners escaped from Dhurringile through a tunnel. They had no overall plan apart from gaining a few days of freedom and the opportunity to cause some chaos. The police and military searched for the fugitives on trains, boats and at airfields. Over the next few days the Australians rounded up the prisoners. A *Kormoran* sailor Walter Rodszies and *Obergefreiter* (Private) Rudolf Kock from the *Afrika Korps* had travelled by day but were spotted at Mooroopna and recaptured. *Leutnant* Jansen from the *Kormoran* and a soldier, Paul Kissel, were apprehended near Colbinabbin. Detmers and Bertram had been hiding by day and walking at night. On 18 January Bertram twisted his ankle, slowing them down, and as they had run low on food they decided to risk going inside a shop. Bertram entered a general store at Tallygaroopna, but the shopkeeper recognized him from newspaper photographs and phoned the police who found the fugitives in a paddock.[23] After Detmers returned to Dhurringile, he suffered a stroke and recovered in the Heidelberg Military Hospital but could no longer serve as camp leader.

On 8 May 1945 Germany surrendered and de-Nazification began. The *Kormoran*'s crew faced the true nature of the regime they had served after the guards made them watch US Army films of Belsen Concentration Camp. On 25 July 1945 the Dhurringile Camp closed and all prisoners moved to a nearby camp at Tatura. The Germans hoped for more freedom and the opportunity to work on farms, but no change in policy eventuated, although some prisoners could leave the camp on parole for up to ten hours a day. Some of these men formed local friendships and worked in the black market.

On 21 January 1947, 1469 German prisoners embarked on the liner *Orontes* in Melbourne for their voyage home. Across the pier from the liner the men could see the Dutch freighter *Straat Malakka*. On 27 February the prisoners arrived at Cuxhaven and a train took them to a camp at Münster. The men began to be released individually, and some officers sent to the Soviet zone were arrested. The British released Detmers in May 1947, the last *Kormoran* prisoner in Germany to be freed.

Detmers retired on a pension due to declining health, which had resulted

German officer prisoners of war in No. 13 POW Group at Dhurringile near Murchison, Victoria, survivors of the *Kormoran*'s engagement in November 1941 with HMAS *Sydney*. **Back row, left to right:** *Oberleutnant* Joachim Greter; *Oberleutnant* Edmond Schafer; *Oberleutnant* Reinhold von Malapert; *Oberleutnant* Fritz Skeries; *Oberleutnant* Joachim von Gosseln; *Oberleutnant* Wilhelm Brinkmann. **Front row:** *Kapitänleutnant* Henry Meyer; *Kapitänleutnant* Kurt Foerster; *Fregattenkäpitan* Theodor Detmers (Commanding Officer); *Oberleutnant* Heinz Messerschmidt.
(AWM)

from a series of strokes. He then lived in the Rahlstedt district of Hamburg with his wife Ursula and wrote an account of his wartime experiences, entitled *The Raider Kormoran*, and many former crewmen and young *Bundesmarine* officers frequently visited him. Detmers died on 4 November 1976.

EPILOGUE

CAPTIVITY IN GERMANY

The voyages of the *Orion*, *Pinguin*, *Komet* and *Kormoran* ended in 1941, but Allied sailors captured by these raiders and transported to Germany faced a long wait for the war to end. These prisoners mostly arrived in France on supply ships, blockade runners and prize vessels, and after disembarking they waited in French transit camps for transportation to *Stalag XB*, the prison camp for Allied sailors, near Hamburg. James Mason from the *Port Brisbane* recalled arriving at *Stalag XB*:

> When I got off the truck in the darkness I fell in the snow. A German guard dragged me to my feet, but when I told him I could not walk because I was frozen he pushed me over again. A German doctor came to my assistance and gave me a drink out of a flask.[1]

Stalag XB was located inside the Sandbostel concentration camp, which held civilian internees from Eastern Europe. The prisoners lived off a poor diet and performed long hours of labour in the fields, but the Germans mostly treated them correctly. The Eastern Europeans endured much worse conditions and the British prisoners threw food over the wire.[2]

In February 1942 the prisoners from *Stalag XB* transferred to a new camp, *Marlag und Milag Nord*, at Westertimke near Bremen. The camp was within a

Allied prisoners on board the Norwegian tanker *Storstad*, now a German prize ship after she was captured by the *Pinguin*, being transported to Bordeaux, France. Their ultimate destination would be POW camps in Germany.
(AWM)

pine forest and had two distinct compounds: *Marlag* for naval prisoners and *Milag* for merchant sailors. Approximately 4500 sailors became prisoners at *Marlag und Milag Nord*. Initially all the guards, mostly middle-aged men, came from *Kriegsmarine* artillery units but later included army guards.

The prisoners experienced greatly improved conditions compared with *Stalag XB* and their health was generally quite good despite some malnutrition and a few cases of tuberculosis and dysentery. The usual daily ration consisted of two slices of bread and half a cup of ersatz coffee for breakfast, followed by turnip and potato soup for dinner with three potatoes. The prisoners supplemented their diet with Red Cross parcels that contained luxuries like chocolate and tobacco.[3]

Under the Geneva Convention merchant sailor prisoners in Germany could not be forced to work, but in reality they had little choice but to labour in the fields. Chinese sailors even worked in Hamburg and, on one occasion, the Germans tried to force Lascars to perform agricultural work, but they staged a sit down and dared the Germans to shoot them.[4]

Education in the camp included Merchant Marine Board of Trade examinations and promotion courses.[5] Teachers also provided general education classes involving twenty-five separate courses. The Red Cross sent textbooks and papers from London and the British Seafarers Education Service sent books to the camp via Switzerland.

Sport included football, cricket, boxing and even ice skating and American prisoners later introduced baseball. Seventeen cricket teams formed and the Australian team won the Ashes in 1942 and 1943, but the 1944 game was cancelled after the English team won the first four games. After the war Vic Marks, an Australian sailor captured by the *Orion*, took the Ashes trophy home to South Australia.[6]

A group of enterprising prisoners in *Milag* built a winery that produced a yellow raisin wine and a brewery producing a dark brown prune beer. A distillery built in 1942 just before Christmas produced a drink named 'alki'.[7] Gambling was also a pastime and a casino operated from a classroom offering poker and roulette among other games.[8] Kenji Takaki, a Japanese sailor from the *Domingo de Larrinaga*, amassed a small fortune in the camp currency *campgeld*. He cashed this in after the war through the POW Exchange Commission for £30, which he distributed among the prisoners.[9]

The prisoners also built a radio to listen to the BBC and they tracked the progress of the war, maintaining a map of the front lines hidden behind a door. At times the prisoners saw vivid glimpses of conflict, such as the bombing of Hamburg and the firestorms that appeared as a distant red glow.

In 1943 some prisoners returned home under Red Cross exchanges for prisoners with 'protective status', including doctors, medical staff and prisoners with heath problems.[10] King, a deck boy from the *Afric Star*, returned to Britain after an Italian Red Cross ship took him from Naples to Turkey.[11] Two stewards from the *Turakina*, Hurley and Owen, returned home with ten prisoners from the *Rangitane*. Head Steward Anker, a member of this group, later tragically died with his wife when a V1 flying bomb hit their home in London.[12] Able Seaman Appleby, an RAN gunner from the *Port Brisbane*, arrived in Alexandria where he gave an account of his experiences on the *Pinguin* at the Naval Intelligence Centre.[13] William Jones from the *Mareeba* arrived home in Australia after being exchanged.

After D-Day the prisoners followed the developments with great interest as the end of the war seemed one step closer. In April 1945, as the British Army advanced, the commandant and his aide arrived at the Headquarters of the Guards Armoured Division holding a white flag to arrange the surrender the camp.[14] On 27 April the commandant accompanied the convoy of ten trucks and an armoured car to *Marlag und Milag Nord* and the British Army liberated the camp. The British concluded that the prisoners had received good treatment and former prisoners spoke highly of the commandant. He was *Korvettenkapitän* Walter Rogge, the older brother of Bernhard Rogge. The Nuremberg Trials later praised Walter Rogge's conduct: 'Without exception all the prisoners of war in that camp have reported that he treated them with fairness and consideration.'[15]

One prisoner had a very different experience. The RAN gunner McStavic from the *Australind* had been imprisoned in *Marlag und Milag Nord* but transferred to a work camp near Poland.[16] In December 1944, when the prisoners could hear Soviet artillery, the guards marched them west and during this journey the group came across Jewish prisoners being forced marched. The *SS* guards ruthlessly shot stragglers and left others to die at the roadside.[17] The Americans eventually liberated McStavic, who arrived in England and stayed at a resort on the channel coast.

After the war the Allies initially sent the liberated RAN gunners to London. Hardy Enscoe from the *Triadic*, after being flown to London, reported to the RAN Office. He stayed in London for two months and attended a garden party with other freed prisoners at Buckingham Palace.[18] He caught up with some of the other RAN gunners, including Allingham, Broad and Jones from the *Port Wellington* as well as Williamson from the *Port Brisbane*, and the sailors soon commenced their voyage home to Australia.

THE CONDUCT OF RAIDER WARFARE

The raider captains acted with strong humanitarian considerations in the finest seafaring traditions, often risking their ships to rescue survivors. At first they attempted to fight a bloodless war based on the World War I 'gentleman' raider captains, such as Count Felix von Luckner, but the duty of merchant captains to broadcast raider warnings resulted in a surge of violence as Allied sailors courageously broadcast distress signals despite incoming shells.

The vast majority of prisoners on the raiders spoke of good treatment and the dedication of the German doctors. Many prisoners initially expected harsh treatment due to wartime propaganda, such as accounts of the 'hell ship' *Altmark*, but found the considerate treatment they received surprising. The auxiliary cruisers fought a war without hate.[19]

The conduct of the auxiliary cruisers is paradoxical. The raider crews fought for the tyrannical Third Reich but treated all prisoners with respect regardless of nationality; however, this paradox is easily explained. The *Kriegsmarine* inherited its culture from the *Kaiserliche Marine*, founded upon the best elements of the progressive German liberalism. Hitler himself understood this and lamented, 'I have a reactionary Army, a Christian Navy, and a National Socialist Air Force.'[20]

SUCCESSFUL OPERATIONS

The voyages of the *Orion*, *Pinguin*, *Komet* and *Kormoran* lasted longer and achieved more success than the *Kriegsmarine* anticipated, a sentiment echoed by *Generaladmiral* Otto Schniewind and *Admiral* Karlgeorg Schuster:

> The raiders' operations by the end of 1941 were considerably luckier and more successful than had been hoped for by the naval war staff. It was foreseen that this kind of mercantile warfare would in the course of time come to grief and that the raiders would probably fall victims to the enemy defense.[21]

As the war progressed, the Allies minimized losses through re-routing, as the New Zealand *Official History* explained:

> The *Turakina* and the *Rangitane* were the only refrigerated cargo ships lost to the raiders at a time when such vessels were leaving New Zealand at the rate of eight or nine a month and a similar number were arriving to load. Another refrigerated cargo steamer, outward-bound, the *Devon*, was sunk by the *Komet* a day's steam from Balboa. In view of the fact that the raiders systematically patrolled the Panama route, the loss of only three such vessels (one of them in the Tasman

Sea) is a remarkable proof of the protective value of the evasive routeing of merchant shipping.[22]

However, this view completely misses the point. The auxiliary cruiser's primary purpose was to disrupt shipping in distant waters by forcing vessels to convoy and take longer routes. The fact that shipping from New Zealand had been re-routed is testimony to the effectiveness of raider operations. Detmers made this point perfectly clear:

> Germany's auxiliary cruisers did their job very well, and their effectiveness was proved again and again from the courses their prizes were found to be sailing . . . the *Mareeba*, which put out from Batavia, did not pass through the Sunda Strait as she would have done in the ordinary way to reach her destination, Colombo in Ceylon, nor did she take the East Asia route to the north of Sumatra round Sabang Wai, but much farther north through the Ten Degree Channel between the Andaman Islands and the Nicobar Islands. In other words, enemy shipping was forced to sail circuitous, time-wasting and fuel-wasting courses, which was exactly what we wanted.[23]

The *Orion*, *Pinguin*, *Komet* and *Kormoran* won a strategic victory by forcing the Allies to create new convoys and re-route shipping through the longer Panama Canal route to avoid the raider-infested Indian Ocean. Ultimately, these actions reduced the amount of cargo reaching Britain, as Captain Stephen Roskill understood: 'The cumulative effect of the frequent and widespread appearances of these elusive enemies was far greater than the actual tonnage sunk by them.'[24] To counter the raiders, the Australian and New Zealand governments recalled cruisers from overseas stations to strengthen local defence, weakening the Allied war effort in more important theatres. In the end, the raider captains triumphed in their war fought in waters far from Germany.

GLOSSARY

AA	anti-aircraft
ABC	Australian Broadcasting Corporation
Afrika Korps	Africa Corps
AMC	armed merchant cruiser
B-Dienst	B Service (German Signals Decryption Unit)
BBC	British Broadcasting Corporation
BP	Bletchley Park (British Signals Decryption Unit)
BPC	British Phosphate Company
Bundesmarine	Federal Navy
C/S	call sign
C-in-C	Commander-in-Chief
CO	Commanding Officer
CPO	Chief Petty Officer
D/F	direction-finding
Dithmarschen	class of German naval supply vessels
EMC	moored contact mine
Etappen	Naval Supply Organization
Geier	Vulture (German Raider)
Gestapo	*Geheime Staatspolizei* (Secret State Police)
Grief	Griffin (German Raider)
HA	high angle
HE	high explosive
Hilfskreuzer	auxiliary cruiser
HMAS	His Majesty's Australian Ship
HMCS	His Majesty's Canadian Ship
HMNZS	His Majesty's New Zealand Ship
HMS	His Majesty's Ship
HSK	*Hilfskreuzer* (auxiliary cruiser)
Kaiserliche Marine	Imperial Navy
Komet	Comet (German Raider)
Kormoran	Cormorant (German Raider)
Kreuzer	Cruiser
Kreuzerkrieg	Cruiser War
Krieg	War
Kriegsmarine	German Navy
Kriegstagebuch	War Diary
Leichte Schnellboot	light speedboat
Luftwaffe	German Air Force

Marlag	Prisoner of War Camp (Naval)
Milag	Prisoner of War Camp (Merchant Marine)
Möwe	Seagull (German Raider)
MS	merchant ship
MTB	motor torpedo boat
MV	merchant vessel
NCO	non-commissioned officer
NEI	Netherlands East Indies
NID	Naval Intelligence Division
NM	nautical mile
OIC	Operational Intelligence Centre
Panzerschiff	armoured ship (pocket battleship)
Passat	Trade Wind (German Minelayer)
Pinguin	Penguin (German Raider)
PO	petty officer
POW	prisoner of war
R/T	radio
R/T	radio telephony
RAAF	Royal Australian Air Force
RAF	Royal Air Force
RAN	Royal Australian Navy
RANR	Royal Australian Navy Reserve
Reichsmarine	Imperial Navy
RN	Royal Navy
RNZAF	Royal New Zealand Air Force
RNZN	Royal New Zealand Navy
S/M	submarine
Schiff	ship
Schwere Kreuzer	heavy cruisers
Seeadler	Sea Eagle (German Raider)
Seekriegsleitung	Naval War Staff (Operational Naval Command)
Seeteufel	Sea Devil
SKL	*Seekriegsleitung* (Naval War Staff)
Sperrbrecher	Pathfinder (Mine Clearance Vessel)
SS	*Schutzstaffel* (Nazi Paramilitary)
SS	steam ship
Stalag	prisoner of war camp
Stier	Bull (German Raider)
TMB	magnetic mine
USN	United States Navy
USS	United States Ship

W/T	wireless telegraphy
Wehrmacht	German Armed Forces
Widder	Ram (German Raider)
WIR	Weekly Intelligence Report
Wölfchen	Wolf Cub (Seaplane)
XO	Executive Officer
YMCA	Young Men's Christian Association

DISTRESS SIGNAL PREFIXES

QQQQ	auxiliary cruiser warning
RRRR	raider warning
SSSS	submarine warning

CONVOY PREFIXES

HG	Gibraltar to Great Britain
HX	Halifax (Canada) to Great Britain
KJ	Kingston (Jamaica) to Great Britain
OB	Outward from Liverpool
OG	Great Britain to Gibraltar
OS	Great Britain to Freetown (Sierra Leone)
SL	Freetown (Sierra Leone) to Great Britain
US	Australia and New Zealand to Middle East
VK	Trans-Tasman
WS	Winton's Specials (Troop Convoys)
ZK	Australia to New Guinea and Pacific

RANKS OF THE *KRIEGSMARINE*

Offiziere	**Officers**
Grossadmiral	Grand Admiral
Generaladmiral	Admiral (Senior)
Admiral	Admiral (Junior)
Vizeadmiral	Vice-Admiral
Konteradmiral	Rear-Admiral
Kommodore	Commodore
Kapitän	Captain (Senior)
Fregattenkapitän	Captain (Junior)
Korvettenkapitän	Commander
Kapitänleutnant	Lieutenant-Commander
Oberleutnant	Lieutenant
Leutnant	Sub-Lieutenant
Fähnrich	Midshipman

Unteroffiziere mit Portepee	**Senior NCOs**
Stabsoberbootsmann	Senior Chief Boatswain
Oberbootsmann	Chief Boatswain
Stabsbootsmann	Senior Boatswain
Bootsmann	Boatswain

Unteroffiziere ohne Portepee	**Junior NCOs**
Obermaat	Chief Petty Officer
Maat	Petty Officer

Seemann	**Seamen**
Matrosen-Stabsobergefreiter	Senior Leading Seaman
Matrosen-Stabsgefreiter	Senior Leading Seaman
Matrosen-Hauptgefreiter	Leading Seaman (Senior)
Matrosen-Obergefreiter	Leading Seaman (Junior)
Matrosen-Gefreiter	Able Seaman
Matrose	Ordinary Seaman

A NOTE ON REFERENCES

The complete reference notes for this book are available on the Exisle Publishing website at: https://exislepublishing.com/false-flags-notes/

ACKNOWLEDGMENTS

This book resulted from many years of work and only came together because of the assistance and encouragement of a wide range of people who deserve special praise.

Firstly, I would like to thank Professor Peter Stanley from the Australian Defence Force Academy for mentoring me and providing invaluable advice on style, structure and editing. I would also equally like to thank Doctor Russell Parkin from the Australian Defence College for painstakingly proofreading my manuscript and providing a solid rock of positive encouragement.

Throughout this book many voices from the past speak for the first time in over seventy years and this was only made possible due to the preservation of historical records. Therefore, I must fundamentally thank all the diligent staff at the National Archives of Australia, the Australian War Memorial and the National Library of Australia. Without their dedication and professionalism, the eyewitness accounts found in this book would simply have been forever lost.

I would also like to thank the helpful staff at the Australian Capital Territory Writers Centre for their invaluable assistance and resources.

Without the help and encouragement of my family and friends this book never would have been completed. Therefore, I specifically wish to thank Helen, the first person to believe in this story, who taught me how to be a better writer and always inspired me to finish this project throughout the long years. I must always thank Alison, Amanda, David, James, Phillip, Roderick and Spiro who provided invaluable assistance reviewing my drafts and encouraging me to continue the work.

Finally, I would like to thank the entire team at my publisher Exisle, in particular Gareth and Anouska, for sharing my enthusiasm, believing in the project and realizing the final vision.

INDEX